THE HEALTH CARE
POLICY PROCESS

THE HEALTH CARE POLICY PROCESS

Carol Barker

SAGE Publications
London • Thousand Oaks • New Delhi

SAGE Publications Ltd
6 Bonhill Street
London EC2A 4PU

SAGE Publications Inc
2455 Teller Road
Thousand Oaks, California 91320

SAGE Publications India Pvt Ltd
32, M-Block Market
Greater Kailash – I
New Delhi 110 048

British Library Cataloguing in Publication data

A catalogue record for this book is available from the
British Library.

ISBN 0 8039 7627 5
ISBN 0 8039 7628 3 (pbk)

Library of Congress catalog card number 96–068056

Typeset by Photoprint, Torquay, Devon
Printed in Great Britain by The Cromwell Press Ltd,
Broughton Gifford, Melksham, Wiltshire

To Shubi, Kiza and my mother

Contents

List of Figures

List of Boxes

List of Tables

Acknowledgements

I should like to thank the Nuffield Institute for Health at the University of Leeds for allowing study leave for the completion of this writing. Thanks also go to colleagues there for their support in covering for my leave, and for many fruitful discussions over the years. Particular thanks go to David Hunter and to Charles Collins for some useful exchanges. Colin Thunhurst read the whole book in draft, and made invaluable comments. Gill Walt of the London School of Hygiene and Tropical Medicine also read the whole draft, and led me to improve on it in a number of ways. Shubi Ishemo has provided me with many useful references and ideas, and great support. At early stages in this work, I shared formative discussions with Meredeth Turshen.

Of course, many insights have been gained from the health care professionals from all over the world who frequent the courses at the Nuffield Institute, along with their colleagues who provide counterparts for work undertaken overseas. All these people have shown me not only what are the important issues facing health care today, but also what are the crucial aspects of the various debates. Thanks to Julie Cliff, a supportive ex-colleague who was kind enough to allow me to summarise material from her article for Box 12.1. Last, thanks to Shubi and Kiza, who provided domestic support beyond that which anyone should hope for, and kept me going.

PART I

WHAT ARE HEALTH POLICIES AND HOW ARE THEY MADE?

Introduction

This book focuses on policy making. It asks how policies are made, and how we can study the process of health care policy making in order to improve upon it for ourselves. The term 'policy' is a vague one, used in many different ways. Some of these will be explored within the book. Let us start however by saying that policy is important because it is what gives content to the practices of the health sector. Policies are expressed in a whole series of practices, statements, regulations and even laws which are the result of decisions about how we will do things. If we worked in a world without policies, then every time we wanted to do anything at all, be it establishing new fees for service or just deciding how many patients a clinic will see tomorrow afternoon, we would have to establish criteria and perhaps go through a complex procedure of consultation to make a decision. We would have no way of knowing whether that decision was consistent with any other decisions in the health service. So when members of the public came to complain that the fees were high, or in the case of the second example, that other clinics saw a lot more patients, we would have to work hard to defend our decision. Indeed, soon we would realise that to reduce the number of times we had to deal with such complaints, a policy regarding these matters was necessary.

This book is intended for health professionals and in particular those who have come to hold some kind of management responsibility in relation to health care. I hope that it will also be of relevance to those who observe the health sector with interest, even if their individual stake in it is no more than that of consumer. I have chosen, however, to keep in mind through-out the book the thought that many readers will be in a position to influence the health policy process in some way. I would argue that anyone involved in the policy process, be it at the level of policy making or at the level of implementation, needs to understand policy if they are to get things right. Also, many managers are in a position to develop policy, though some are initially reluctant to recognise their role in this respect. Discussion of these issues forms part of an ongoing debate I have conducted over a number of years with students of health management, planning and policy.

It is intended that this book should be of value not only to the student of health care policy, but also to those involved in the policy process, whether as policy makers, researchers, managers, or health care professionals with a role in policy making or implementation. To this end, an important focus will be the analysis of the extent to which policies can be changed or influenced by those involved in the different stages of the policy process, and it is hoped that the reader will learn how to assess, in real-life situations, the need for change and the scope for change.

The aim, then, is to enable the reader to develop an understanding of the scope and objectives of policy studies. It is written with an international audience in mind, and uses some examples and case studies from the developing world. This is not intended to suggest that the way we study health policy is country or region specific – nor indeed to suggest that there is any simple or clear division between the countries of the world. Throughout this book I refer to 'developing countries' for reasons of simplicity. Other authors would perhaps use alternative terms such as the 'third world' or 'less developed countries' or 'underdeveloped countries'; still more terminologies refer to the South (as opposed to the North). All of these terms have been used to describe the poorer countries of the world, and this is not the place to discuss the difference in approach which each term implies. What is important is to recognise that the policy agenda may have different emphases in the majority of countries today which count as low or middle income, than in the select few nations which are relatively rich in resources for health care. The underlying issues are not necessarily different, and I hope the discussion can get below surface appearances.

A starting point for this will be the analysis of the health care system, and the dynamics of the policy process. The relationship between planning and policy will be considered. In the first part of the book the aim is to provide readers with a working knowledge of the different ways in which they might set about analysing policy issues; a critical awareness of the problems involved in attempting to assess the views of different interest groups; and an understanding of the importance of supporting an active process of policy development.

The second part is intended to provide a basis for critical reading of policy studies, and also to help the reader in making decisions about the kinds of policy studies which may help their own policy making. It looks at the different types of policy study which can be conducted. It asks how studies come to be defined in particular ways, and identifies problems that can arise in the definition of issues for study. It then surveys briefly the kinds of evidence which might be used in a policy study, and finally looks at the range of approaches and methods which the health manager may wish to use in conducting policy studies.

Part III sets out to provide another set of tools for the health policy analyst, alongside the methodological tools of Part II. Health policy also requires tools in the sense of concepts, ideas and criteria in order to create a framework for thinking about policies. Part III examines a number of areas which are of key importance in analysing health policy today, and shows something of the range of ways of looking at these areas which exists. Each concept explored helps us to see the ways in which policies are influenced, and how different people and groups in society can exert that influence.

Part IV sets out some of the challenges and debates which are at the fore of health policy today. In this section I make a bid to influence your own agenda of policy concerns, for these are a selection of the issues which I see as dominating health policy making globally today. These major debates run through the way in which we can look at all health issues.

The book ends with a discussion of the applications of policy studies. How should the policy analyst relate to the policy making process? How wide an awareness of the policy issues is required by those involved in implementation? Above all, does study of health care policies lead to an improvement in the way in which policies are made? Do policy studies have the capacity to improve the policy making process?

At some level, of course, my own answer to this question is bound to be yes, or I should never have embarked upon this book. However, the relationship between knowledge and practice is a crucial one, and deserves to be explored; I hope the whole of this book is a contribution to that exploration.

1

Why Study Health Policy?

As we saw in the introduction, policies give content and consistency to health care. We also noted that the title of the book suggests a positive, activist approach: not just observing but developing – changing – health policy. This choice was deliberate, and it forms part of an ongoing dialogue I have conducted with students of health management, planning and policy, over a number of years.

The dialogue starts from a suspicion held by many health managers that health policy is something which is formed at the highest of levels, and which they themselves cannot influence, but only follow. The not infrequent comment is 'There's no point in *me* studying policy. The Minister makes policy. I don't. I follow orders and implement decisions.' This is odd, because the same managers frequently want to master the art of planning, a process which involves setting priorities and developing strategy – yet which somehow is perceived as technically led, and therefore within the remit of the manager. Logically, planning follows policy and policy may be seen as a higher-order activity. Yet the way in which planning is done can make or break a policy, can follow it through as intended, or render it completely unrecognisable. It is all too easy to write plans which unintentionally embody whole new policies, if the planner is not aware of the policy implications likely to follow from planning decisions. As President Julius Nyerere of Tanzania once said, 'To plan is to choose'. Planning decisions involve important choices about who benefits, and how much, from the health care system. For every winner, there is also a loser. The planner who fails to see this is unlikely to survive very long in the real world.

So it is important that the manager recognise the policy making process when he or she sees it. In many ways policy making is the stuff of good management, and characterises the manager, a proactive, strategic thinker, over and above the administrator, a servant of the policies elaborated by others. But the days of the passive administrator seem to be numbered. All over the world there are trends towards decentralised decision making; concomitantly more and more people are being drawn into management positions.

I would personally go further, and argue that even administrative practices involve dealing with policy. Even if the highest ambition of a manager is to implement the policies laid down by the Ministry of Health, it is the contention of this book that s/he must develop an understanding of how policies are made – and how they can be destroyed through distortions which occur at the stage of implementation. Equally, policies may be implemented in a manner which looks impeccable on paper, but somehow in practice has allowed vested interests to creep in, so that the powerful, rather than the needy, benefit.

Health policy studies have perhaps not been popular, because the health field has been overshadowed by those who believe in management science. At the heart of health sector reform is the notion that 'better management' is the recipe – and if we follow the recipe carefully, we can all win prizes. I want to argue here that management strengthening is a most powerful tool in improving health care, but that the skills involved cannot be transmitted in a simple recipe. Furthermore, given that the local conditions and ingredients vary to a bewildering degree, following recipes is an entirely inadequate approach. Rather, we need to be equipped with the capacity to improvise, to maximise results in poor conditions and against the odds; to see the way round problems. Policies exist in a complex reality, and even *infinitely* better management technique will not compensate for a failure to analyse what is going on.

If we seriously wish to optimise the management process, then above all, we need to appreciate that policy decisions are not always – perhaps not even often – the result of a rational process of discussion and evaluation of how a particular objective should be met. The whole approach of management science insists that objectives can be rationally defined and efficiently achieved. In the messy world of real life, objectives are not rationally defined, and are not obvious or given. They themselves are the products of the interaction of key stakeholders in that particular decision-making process. If we plan to build a new hospital, we will not start from the position that this is an agreed objective for everyone. It may well be that this objective is shared as a good one by the patients in the neighbourhood likely to benefit, the medical staff likely to work there, and the construction firms who hope to build it. It may be that others would emphatically not see this decision as a good one – rural inhabitants who feel the money would have been better spent on smaller facilities nearer their homes; the politician who would have liked the hospital had it been sited in his/her constituency.

Policies are slippery things; it is sometimes extremely difficult to pin-point a particular decision to operate things in a particular style, because an overt decision may never have been made. Sometimes things are done a certain way for historical reasons or by virtue of inertia, rather than because anyone has made a decision about them. Sometimes those with power actually use it to prevent the instigation of an overt decision-making process, because they have no good reason to want to share their decisions with, or to have to justify them to, others. Often decisions are not single identifiable entities but the result of an incremental process. This complexity in the nature of decisions makes it difficult to say that a decision is ever purely technical, or lacking in political content. The two examples given in Box 1.1 illustrate this point well. At first sight, it would seem that a decision about the introduction of breast screening ought to be a simple technical decision. Yet the context in which this decision must be made is contingent upon high-level and highly political decisions – concerning the extent of public provision of health care and who pays for it; as well as upon value judgements, which in any society will be implicit, about the value placed on women and their health. Likewise with respect to the second example in Box 1.1, one may first think that transport is a fairly technical issue, to be settled by those who know their Fords from their Mercedes. However, a moment's thought brings the realisation that, in many countries, transport is effectively organised via the processes of negotiating foreign aid; a rational approach to fleet renewal and maintenance can only be developed when those dealing with external affairs can work through the web of conditionalities to exert some kind of systematic approach from the start.

Health care policy can be seen as the networks of interrelated decisions which together form an approach or strategy in relation to practical issues concerning health care delivery. A particular health care action at any one point in time results from the combination of many current and past decisions. Some of these may be technical in the medical or nursing sense; others may be decisions which are about how things will be done in the health sector as a whole, and still others may be decisions which have been made way beyond the health sector. The tables given in Box 1.1 illustrate this point. In each of the two policy areas given in Box 1.1, a number of decisions are necessary; some of these are health service decisions and some are broader social decisions. Decisions are frequently made, or altered, not because someone has found the best way to do things, but because certain people have a lot of say in the matter. Sometimes decisions are made for stated reasons, and sometimes they are made because the decision maker has another private agenda. Decisions are the product of those people who get to have a say in making them, of the process by which the decision is made, and of the distribution of power between the different parties involved. We can see immediately that policy studies address a complex reality.

Walt (1994) differentiates those policies she denotes as *macro policies*, or *high politics issues*, which matter to everyone and which involve the long-term objectives of the state or of those in power, and those she calls *micro policies*, or *low politics issues*, which involve more localised, that is, sectoral, interests. This is a useful analytical starting point, provided one remembers that, as Walt says, a low politics issue can shift and become a high politics issue over time. It is important to remember that even apparently mundane sectoral policies are usually based on networks of decisions which themselves involve high politics issues. The policy maker has to be aware of these constraints, and has to develop a sense of what is possible. Each policy decision is made within a web of decisions, some of which are contingent upon the highest level political decisions within a society, and upon the whole approach of that society to the way in which wealth and power are distributed. By working to improve our ability to analyse these issues, we can hope to improve our capacity to make policies that work for us, in the way that we intended; if we can see what is behind a policy then we can begin to judge how best it might be implemented.

It is this interrelatedness of a wide range of policy issues which means that the manager cannot section off local issues as being unaffected by the wider political scene. It may help some readers to further illustrate this by noting the suggestion of Frenk (1994) that it is helpful to view health policy as operating at four levels. The *systemic level* deals with main features that shape the health system overall, such as the nature of public institutions involved in health care, the public/private mix, and the relationship

---

Box 1.1   Networks of Interrelated Decisions

In both of the examples given below, policy making depends upon decisions in a number of areas, not all of which can be made at once. The resulting policy in each case will depend on the particular combinations of decisions made. For each example, some of the needed decisions are listed, and the table shows how these might be classified along the lines discussed in the text. The classification given here is illustrative. It could vary in real-life contexts, and you are invited to consider whether you would classify things in the same way.

Introduction of a cervical screening programme

If cervical cancer rates are high, it may be that a decision will be made to screen women in certain age groups on a periodic basis. The possibility of doing so will depend upon a number of prior decisions, which may or may not have been taken with regard to health care. These might include, for example, the decisions listed in the table below. Those decisions might be classified according to policy level.

Decision	High/low politics	Policy level
Decisions about the priority to be given to provision of preventive health care	Low	Programmatic
Decisions about the extent of public (versus privately provided) health services	High	Systemic
Decisions about whether to charge for screening	High	Systemic
Decisions about charge tariffs	Low	Organisational
The priority given to female adult health	Low	Programmatic

Box 1.1 *continued*

Health transport policy

Most health services have some sort of transport fleet. A transport policy might cover the definition of legitimate uses for the fleet, who controls it, how maintenance is conducted and what the practice is for purchase of new vehicles. However this policy can be elaborated only in the context of decisions/assumptions about:

Decision	High/low politics	Policy level
Health services coverage	High	Systemic
Structure of the referral system	Low	Organisational
Foreign aid policy with regard to acceptance of differing vehicle brands with different bilateral projects	High	Systemic
Nature of privilege for senior staff who are accustomed to availability of vehicles for personal/family use	Low	Instrumental

---

between health and other sectors. The *programmatic level* decides about the priorities for health care, the actual nature of health care programmes, and the way in which resources should be allocated. The *organisational level* addresses the way in which resources can be used productively and to provide a high quality service. The *instrumental level* is the level at which the various instruments of good organisation, such as the human resource development system and the information system, are themselves managed. To paraphrase what was said earlier, the types of policy which are possible at the programmatic, organisational and instrumental levels will depend upon the systemic context, and so on.

That is why this book, while dealing with concepts some of which are normally associated with the analysis of high politics issues or systemic issues, uses examples of policy areas some of which would be classed as low politics. Low politics issues, or those which fall at the programmatic or lower policy levels, are contingent upon higher-level issues.

In summary

- Policies are expressed in a whole series of practices, statements, regulations and even laws which are the result of decisions about how we will do things.
- Policy making is the stuff of good management, and characterises the manager, a proactive, strategic thinker, over and above the administrator, a servant of the policies elaborated by others.
- Management strengthening is a most powerful tool in improving health

care. However, policies exist in a complex reality, and even *infinitely* better management technique will not compensate for a failure to analyse what is going on.

- Any one policy decision is made within a web of decisions, some of which are contingent upon the highest level political decisions within a society, and upon the whole approach of that society to the way in which wealth and power are distributed.
- Health care policy may be seen as the networks of interrelated decisions which together form an approach or strategy in relation to practical issues concerning health care delivery.

2

What Does Health Care Do for Society?

Debates in health care today

Health policy is an important, and fast-growing, area of debate. Over the past twenty years or so, there has been a huge expansion in the academic literature concerned with health policy and with the broad field of health and medicine in a social science context. The issues are actively discussed not only by academics and health and medical professionals, but also by politicians, community groups, the media and the public. This is so both because health care is growing in importance in human societies, and because with recent growth and development have come a range of new uncertainties; the basis for important policy debates.

In 1990, spending on health globally was estimated at around $1,700 billion, or about 8 per cent of all income. In industrialised countries, expenditure on health care has risen to levels in some cases greater than 10 per cent of gross domestic product; in other words, health care accounts for about 10 per cent of all economic activity (see Figure 2.1). Other countries can be expected to follow. While governments struggle to find means of cost containment, the amount spent on health continues to rise, as populations tend to include more and more old people. At the same time, technological advance opens up ever more clinical and diagnostic alternatives, ever more ways for us to spend money on health care and for the drug companies and medical equipment merchants to profit.

The health sector has become a major employer, which means both that it is important to society, and that many individuals in society are personally acquainted with its employees. In the USA for example, in 1910 there were doctors, pharmacists, nurses and dentists, and 1.3 per cent of all employed people were in the health sector. Today there are over 700 job categories in health care, and over 5 per cent of all employed people are in the health sector, making the health sector the largest single industrial employer there;[1] likewise in Europe the UK National Health Service (if it can still be considered as a single organisational entity) is the largest single employer.

Technical advance opens up new possibilities for care and new potential for health service activity. At the same time, technical advance stimulates new debates. Organ transplant, genetic manipulation and other high-technology activities introduce ethical dilemmas which only a few years ago

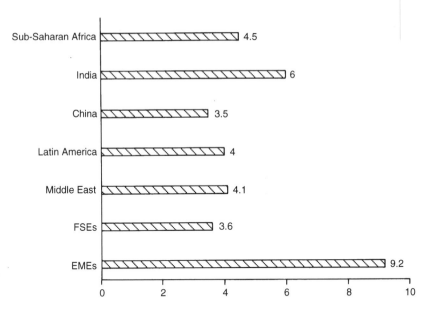

Note: FSE = Formerly socialist economies of Europe
EME = Established market economies

Figure 2.1 *Health expenditures as a percentage of GDP, 1990 (World Bank, 1993)*

would have made a good read in a science fiction novel. Perhaps the greatest of ethical dilemmas is that arising from the sheer explosion of medical possibilities. Today the rich have unprecedented opportunities for treatment for even the most cosmetic of defects; yet millions of people have no or little access to medical care. The inequalities between countries can be observed in estimates of regional health expenditure: around 87 per cent of all health expenditure is within the developed market economies, where about 15 per cent of people live. Only 13 per cent of health expenditure takes place in the rest of the world, with its 85 per cent of the total population. In 1990 the world's lowest income countries had only one physician for 11,730 people; the high-income OECD countries had one physician for every 440 inhabitants.[2] The inequalities are also within countries; the United States spends more on health care, taken as an average amount per person, than any other country in the world, and yet between 13 and 15 per cent of its inhabitants, by being uninsured, are unable to receive medical care when it is needed.[3] In real terms, for most of the world's people, medical advance has opened up not so much the promise of medical care as the frustration of unanswered need.

How much does this matter? Some would say that medical care has very little to do with improvements in health status. A rather wider lobby would say that basic public health and preventive health care *does* have an effect on health status. Clearly, those who lack access to care at present would say that they would rather not sit around to resolve these arguments, but rather have the benefit of a nice hospital bed and plenty of antibiotics and surgery next time they are ill. As the next section discusses, health care cannot only be valued in terms of its impact on health. Yet the efficacy of medical systems is today being questioned as never before, and many of the certainties which existed perhaps twenty years ago, as to the value of medicine, are now showing cracks.

The middle of the twentieth century was a period of triumphalism for medicine, and the health sector is in some ways still living off the great medical advances which enabled us, at that time, to be seduced into looking to the day when there would be a pill for every ill. In the 1950s and 1960s medicine went from strength to strength, and it seemed that a mechanistic approach to the human body would open the door to miracles.[4] The latter part of the century has been a sobering period. It has seemed as though the limits to medicine have been encountered, if not absolutely, then at least in a way that reminds us that we have only human powers. The antibiotics which seemed to offer an end to infectious disease are beginning to fail to respond to newly resistant strains of bacteria – super-bugs which threaten the return of many illnesses no longer considered medically very important. The HIV/AIDs epidemic has reminded us that medicine does not always have cures. The health threats which increasingly we see looming as a result of global environmental change cannot be combated by medicine and arguably cannot be combated at all. Within societies, we see lower mortality rates,[5] but the inequalities in health status between rich and poor which existed at the start of this century have in no way been eliminated by improvements in medical care (see Chapter 11). In many societies, most notably in the richest countries of the world, people are turning away from biomedicine and looking at traditional and complementary systems of medicine for a more holistic approach.

All this signals an end to confidence in the technical fix. Yet the global debates about health care continue to see medical care as desirable; after all, to possess a nice motor car is not essential to life, but that does not stop me thinking that my life would be all the better for owning a Mercedes Benz! The international health care scene tends to go on pinning its hopes for world health on the identification of a superior technical solution. Forty years ago, more and better medical care for all was seen as the panacea. Then the rather more sophisticated notion of primary health care was identified; not, in the first instance, as a 'technical fix' but rapidly turned into one by Walsh and Warren (1979) and their followers. Today, we are invited to pin our faith in 'essential health packages' and highly specific bits of social engineering; ensure all women have education and their children will all be healthy, we are told. The proponents of such views exhibit a propensity to believe that there is a one best way forward for health care. If we can find the best 'essential packages',[6] the way to deliver these will be self-evident. We shall merely need to apply rational techniques of cost-effectiveness analysis and decision analysis to our health systems, and the way to do things will be known.

If this book can be said to have a single unifying theme, it is that there is not, and cannot be, a single 'one best way' for health policy. This book is written in the belief that technocratic determinants of health care may condition the way in which we do things at a detailed level, but that the overall shape of health care, the general approach used in different countries, and the broad policies, have much more to do with political, social, economic and historical determinants than with technology. For this reason, the following section looks at some of the range of ways in which people value health care, and the multiplicity of factors which affect what people want from it.

The value of health care

It might be said that medicine is just one way in which human beings have attempted to improve the material conditions of their existence in communities, cure and care thus being integral features of any human society. At the most basic level, human beings have probably always shown compassion and attempted to care for the sick, even long before there was technically any hope of being able to effect cures. The development of cures, mediated through herbs or through magic, can be traced back through the history of mankind. Although this book will focus on health sector policies, it is worth remembering from the start that health care never has been solely the prerogative of the health sector, and indeed the activities of the health sector very often form a continuum with other sectoral activities. Community care crosses the boundaries of health care and social work. Nutrition is related to health status, but even more crucially to agricultural production and to employment levels in the community. An historical tour through the ages would throw up extremely imprecise boundaries between medical care and the Church, legal and penal institutions and those institutions which care for the poor.

It is perhaps in the context of Western medicine that health care has become equated first and foremost with a narrow concern for the physical health of individuals. This concern is realised through the application of medical technology by health care professionals in an institutional setting. It should be recognised that this view of health care becomes taken for granted to the extent that it serves to blinker us from recognition of all health care activity. To illustrate this point, one might imagine the different perceptions of a malnourished peasant and a Western-trained doctor, concerning the health of that peasant. The doctor might wish to offer the peasant vitamins, or more comprehensive nutritional rehabilitation. Were we to ask the peasant, he might argue that because his health and that of his whole family are dependent on the ox who draws the tractor, he would prefer to give priority medical treatment to the ox. In broader terms, Feierman has pointed out the problem that Western scholars have had in understanding the role, in pre-colonial African societies, of the organisations called 'cults of affliction'.[7] The stated purpose of these cults was the maintenance of health, and the means of achieving this was through the maintenance of a good balance in the environment. The cult practices regulated the ecosystem by ritual and the activity of mediums. For Western observers reared on the medical model of health care, understanding concern for the ecosystem as concern for health was just too great a leap. To be sure, in Western society the social role of the doctor is not fixed, and many practitioners worry about the extent to which they are expected to fulfil the roles of priest and social worker, for example. The role of medical practitioner as the person one consults when ill does, however, remain one focused on concern for the individual rather than for the community or environment. Yet in other societies, health of individuals, communities, and of the environment which gives them life and health, are seen as integral parts of the whole. Western observers may fail to understand the role of traditional medical practitioners in different societies, because Western observers fail to see that a doctor may in practice be functioning as meteorologist, marriage guidance counsellor, financial adviser and military strategist, all towards the end of improving health.

Thus, in the context of Western medicine today, only some activities which produce health are seen as health care. Nor is health care always valued, first and foremost, for the production of health. A recent issue of the UK journal *Health Services Management* (June 1993) carried an article headlined MANAGING FOR HEALTH GAIN, which went on to say

> The concept of health gain is growing in the NHS. The *Health of the Nation* is the first national strategy to set targets for health gain. The initiative holds implications for change for NHS managers in the way in which they perceive their task and the way in which they manage. The definition and methodology of 'health gain' are at an early stage of evolution in Britain. There is a lot of 'fuzziness' at the edges and discussion of how to turn the idea into reality. Evolution of the idea is currently active, however, and fuelled by strong social forces.

Had the same words been written in a newspaper or magazine widely accessible to lay readers, it might well have occasioned the question: 'Isn't the health service all about health gain?' Yet the answer of many health care professionals would be qualified. Yes, they may well say, health gain is a vision we have, but it is somewhat removed from our everyday practice. We have to be concerned with curing people who are sick, even if their cure will have no effect on future population health patterns; we have to care for those who cannot care for themselves, and alleviate suffering. If we look beyond these medical goals, it is to see a management system to be maintained. Today, the health care manager must be concerned with efficient treatments, with satisfactory patient throughput in hospitals, with keeping the accounts in credit, or in some situations making a profit, managing change in response to the political environment, and earning their own promotion.

Within society today, health care cannot be viewed simplistically, for it satisfies a range of demands and is valued in a variety of different ways. For some people, health care is a right, a human requirement which any decent society will make available for all its members. For others, it is the subject of political struggle; health care is sought after and may be used to capture votes. Some governments, perhaps an increasing number today, see health care as an expenditure, to be viewed reluctantly as an unproductive use of money which should at all times be minimised. Some may recognise that while health care is costly, it may provide a way of reducing dissatisfaction, for example among the unemployed. The position a government takes on these issues will of course depend on its overall political position, for attitudes concerning the provision of health care are a function of broader attitudes concerning the way in which goods and benefits are shared in society.

If we start from the position that health care is to be seen as an expenditure, we can view the health sector as producing health care – a resource for which people compete in society. Control over health care brings with it power; those who are most influential decide who will get large shares of health care. This is powerfully illustrated when we look at the distribution of health care in colonial societies. Health care was available for the colonial master but often only made available to others if those people were considered a health risk.[8] Individual firms placed a premium on the maintenance of good health, at least among those of their workforce who possessed special skills; such workers were often favoured by employers with the benefits of occupational health schemes. Health care was frequently made available for groups of skilled workers while there was none for workers who were regarded as easily replaceable.[9]

The apartheid legacy of health care in South Africa was the creation of a two-tiered system with only minimal care for those whose access to power in society was minimal. In other health systems the division between those who receive adequate health care and those who do not, is much more subtle, but nevertheless persists. The power to claim a fair share of the available health care is a function not only of race but also of class and of wealth. Other features such as age may also be important; in the UK today there have been recent instances of refusal of health care treatment for old people, considered not to be worth the cost. Many health planning systems seem to have an inbuilt bias in favour of the health of children, although it is less clear that the communities concerned see things the same way – or that they have ever been asked.

Some governments have seen health care not as an inconvenient expense, but as a great investment in people. Development planners have often argued that health care should be viewed as an investment in society, because it produces improved health status, and a healthier society is a more productive one. Such arguments are attractive to those who wish to see more resources coming towards health care. Yet the evidence is at best only circumstantial. Furthermore, we should acknowledge the questionable assumptions on which these arguments are based. However health care may be valued for the relief it brings to the sick, it is hard to know to what extent it can bring about long-term population health improvements. These may have more to do with improvements in general living standards than with medicine. Even if it were possible to demonstrate that health care improves health, do we actually know that a healthier society will be a more productive one? No society has jobs for all individuals. If there are still enough healthy people to fill existing posts, the fact that some people are incapacitated by illness will not affect the economy at all. In addition, many jobs can probably be done quite well by people operating at something less than their personal top capacity, and many illnesses do not directly affect people's ability to work.

Of course, it is quite possible – though rather less frequently acknowledged – that the existence of a strong health sector will play a positive role in the economy not because it improves workers' performance, but because it operates as an industry like any other. Often today there is reference to the 'health care industry'. Within this framework, health care is seen as a commodity which is to be bought and sold. To the private practitioner and the big health insurance company alike, health care is seen as a source of profit. More broadly, the view of health as a commodity helps remind us that this industry, like any other, needs inputs of goods and services; a vigorous health sector may stimulate business in other sectors of the economy. For the pharmaceuticals and medical equipment industries, the health sector is the major purchaser of their products; for a wide range of other industries and services, the health sector is an important customer. These range from the construction industry, to suppliers of foods, to computer manufacturers; from those offering management consultancy to those offering laundry services. In some countries, much of the insurance industry may be structured around medical care insurance. We saw above that the health sector is a major employer, and must count as one of the most labour intensive of all economic sectors. Of course, all these attributes of health care are of material importance; the activities of the health sector contribute to the gross national product, and stimulate economic growth. The importance of health care as an industry is often under-emphasised.

Health care, then, can be seen in relation both to political power and to the whole economy. It is also important to consider health care as a force within society. While it is those with political power who may determine the distribution of health care resources in society, it is those who control the actual provision of medical care who wield power over individual patients. In that people who submit to health care often put themselves in a vulnerable position, health care is closely related to control. The function of medicine as an institution of social control has been well documented.[10]

Medicine may be used to determine who receives sickness benefits and who must return to work; it may rule who is to be imprisoned for crime and who counts as criminally insane; it may decide who is a health risk to be segregated from healthy society and who may go free. Armstrong (1993) has considered health care as surveillance, viewing eighteenth-century medicine in terms of surveillance of the body, in contrast to twentieth-century, medicine which deals with surveillance of the space between bodies, and thus aspires to the control of bodies and their relationships, and to scrutiny of social networks. Interestingly, though, Armstrong argues that this tendency has also opened up within health care the potential for greater community and patient control because the new public health approaches have gained the insight that public health strategies are capable of being effective only when there is active community support and participation.

So within society as a whole, people benefit to differing extents and in quite different ways from health care, and have a wide range of views about what they value in health care. When the National Health Service was established in the UK, it was believed that people would most appreciate the new availability of medical help for acute illness; against expectations, what really made the public enthusiastic about the new service was the provision of free spectacles and dentures! We might also consider the value placed on psychiatric care. While in any society there will be those who care about the ability of mental health services to improve the condition of people with psychiatric ailments, there will also be those whose appreciation of such services rests with the power to shut potentially dangerously insane patients away. In yet other cases, for example in the Brazilian social system, certification as mentally sick may be the only hope for the long-term unemployed, given that the state provides sickness benefit but not unemployment benefit. To appreciate the way in which decisions are made about health care, we need to understand this diversity of views and to be able to evaluate who is likely to have the power to sway the course of events.

In summary

Debates in health care today

- Health policy is an important, and fast-growing, area of debate.
- In industrialised countries, expenditure on health care has risen to levels such that health care accounts for about 10 per cent of all economic activity. Other countries can be expected to follow.
- The health sector has become a major employer.
- Today the rich have unprecedented opportunities for treatment for even the most cosmetic of defects; at the same time, millions of people have no or little access to medical care.
- The middle of the twentieth century was a period of triumphalism for

medicine, but there are now signs of an end to confidence in the technical fix.

• Technocratic determinants of health care may condition the way in which we do things at a detailed level, but the overall shape of health care has much more to do with political, social, economic and historical determinants than with technology.

The value of health care

• Health care is an activity which is not limited to the health sector.
• In the context of Western medicine, health care is focused on the organised medical care of individuals.
• Health care is not always clearly distinguished from other activities to improve human life.
• Health care is not always valued first and foremost for the production of health.
• Health care professionals may see their goals not in terms of improving health, but in terms of managing an organisation.
• Health care may be viewed as a right for all.
• Health care is often the object of political struggle – a commodity or resource for which people compete.
• Health care may be seen as an investment in a more productive society.
• An alternative view sees organised health care as a large industry.
• Health care may be distributed unequally in society, with favoured groups, defined by class, ethnicity, age or other attributes such as skills, receiving more.
• Control over health care carries power; submission to health care creates control.
• In recent years, patients have gained a more positive role in health care and this creates the potential for greater community control.
• To analyse how particular health care policies have developed, it is necessary to analyse how health care is viewed by the various parties involved in shaping a particular policy.

Notes

1. See Kronenfeld (1993: 82).
2. The foregoing statistics in this paragraph are all quoted from the World Development Report (World Bank, 1993).
3. This is an estimate based on data quoted in Kronenfeld (1993: 2).
4. Turshen (1989) gives a useful account of the positivist approach to medicine, and in particular the influence of engineering on the biomedical model of health.
5. A useful critical account of the current state of knowledge about the extent to which mortality rates are improving, and a discussion of why they are improving, is given in Murray and Chen (1993).
6. The concept of essential national packages of health services is presented clearly, and persuasively advocated, by Bobadilla et al. (1994).
7. See Feierman (1984).

8. In colonial Mozambique, for example, there was great preoccupation with preventing the transmission of disease from Africans to Europeans, involving quarantining in response to epidemics, and attempts to create segregated housing.

9. Examples of this include studies of colonial Mozambique (Barker, 1983) where health care was virtually only available for indigenous Mozambicans through employers, and the quality of care related to seniority and status.

10. See Zola (1972) for the original statement of this idea.

3

The Policy Process

What constitutes a policy?

There are as many ways of thinking about the policy process as there are about the concept of policy itself, and as a former British civil servant once remarked, 'Policy is rather like the elephant – you recognise it when you see it, but cannot easily define it' (Cunningham, 1963). This apparently rather vacuous statement might help us to start in thinking about policy, first by asking if we *do* recognise it when we see it, and second by considering why defining policy should be problematic.

What do people normally recognise as a policy? Many, asked to produce an example of a policy, would look for a piece of paper. Policies are often viewed as statements. These might be statements about attitudes, or criteria for selecting a course of action. The policy may take the form of a plan or a more generalised statement of approach. It is regarded as having an official existence when formally agreed by the appropriate legislative or other bodies. Yet is a policy at this point of any significance, if nothing has been done to implement it? Box 3.1 asks you to consider the hypothetical stages of development of a policy concerning community participation. Can the country concerned be said to have a policy when a statement about community participation has been produced? Alternatively, we might argue that a policy only exists when effective action has been taken. Community participation is an example of a policy area in which government and health sector statements are frequent, and inaction almost as frequent. Often in real life, this area is an example of one where to have a policy looks good, because it is felt that a policy *should* be there, but no one in power has any interest in implementing it.

A policy statement acquires real significance if it is implemented – put into action. Thus the Mozambican pharmaceuticals policy, the development of which is described in Box 3.2, is a good example of a policy which was developed and implemented in post-colonial Mozambique. This is a policy which was implemented with considerable political will behind it and with the approval of all those involved. Had key workers wished to sabotage the way in which the policy was to be implemented, this would have changed the whole story. Looking at the way in which, and with what success, a policy is implemented, is an important part of studying that policy.

What would one think, though, if asked to define the pre-colonial Mozambique pharmaceuticals policy? In pre-colonial Mozambique, no

Box 3.1   Stages in the Development of a Policy

1. In country X, various aid agencies and the World Health Organization have been asking what is the policy concerning *community participation*. The Minister of Health decides a policy is needed in this area.
2. A policy is drafted and written down.
3. The policy statement is discussed by various bodies, amended and agreed by all relevant government committees.
4. A glossy pamphlet is produced about community participation policy.
5. Information is received that WHO are impressed with the new policy.
6. The Ministry of Health decides that something must be done about implementation of the policy, and a letter is issued to regional level stating that all health workers should hold meetings to start to explain the policy.
7. After some delay, it is realised that nothing is happening because the health workers don't know how to set about this task. Workers are trained, and meetings now take place.
8. The Minister is informed that his instructions have been followed, and he is pleased.
9. One such meeting comes up with some ideas for ways in which the local community can participate, but some small budgetary implications impede anything more from happening.
10. At this point, the Ministry has become very excited about a large amount of external project aid. The project aid is accepted, along with conditions about centralised control and budget monitoring, as well as requirements about the exact type of family planning and MCH programmes to be adopted. These conditions make it hard for the communities to have any impact on plans. Nothing more happens.
11. Miraculously, the project mid-term evaluation comments on the lack of local community participation in health care, and the earlier community suggestions are revived; a process of community consultation planning and running of health services is established.
12. The policy results in improved services and better results for activities such as vaccinations.
13. The results of this local activity are fed into Ministry thinking and new guidelines are issued concerning community participation.

Box 3.1 *continued*

The stages outlined here describe the formulation of a policy. Depending on one's view of policy, there is room for arguing that a policy has been created at a number of different points in the sequence above. At what stage do you consider a policy to exist, and why?

**Box 3.2   Pharmaceuticals Policy Development
in Post-Colonial Mozambique**

As a Portuguese colony, Mozambique had a largely private health service, and patients had to purchase medicines when they were needed, often at great expense. Most pharmaceuticals were imported from Portugal, or from neighbouring friendly South Africa. Almost any products could be imported and sold, and what control existed over profit margins was structured in such a way as to encourage importers to go for the most expensive brand name products.

Following independence in 1975, a Technical Committee for Therapeutics and Pharmacy was established and given responsibility for developing a policy for the Ministry of Health and for the whole of the newly nationalised health care system. Importation was centralised, and a national formulary produced to considerably restrict the range of drugs which could be bought. Procurement by an international tendering system ensured that the most appropriate products were obtained at the cheapest possible price from whichever country made a good offer. Now, drugs might come from India, from Romania, from Sweden; any tender could win, and the result was procurement prices often a tiny fraction of those achieved before. When possible, the drugs were free to users of the health service, but since many people still would in practice go to private pharmacies, the owners and employees of these pharmacies were given guidelines concerning responsible sales practice. Prescribing drugs was now by generic name (not brand name) only, and clinicians worked to therapeutic guidelines to ensure that expensive treatments were reserved for special cases. This policy was put in place within a period of about three years, and resulted in vastly improved availability of medicines.

Pharmaceuticals reform proved to be extremely difficult in other countries. What factors were significant in the Mozambican situation insofar as it was conducive to change? First, there was political will. Second, there was a tiny medical establishment,

---

Box 3.2 *continued*

many doctors having left the country for Portugal at independence. It was therefore relatively easy to negotiate and agree on technical issues. Third, there was a large influx of expatriate doctors at the time, all from different countries with different medical cultures and therapeutic practices; this in itself created a new imperative to create some kind of standard practice. Fourth, there was no pharmaceuticals production established in the country; all pharmaceuticals were imported. This was important because it meant that no single manufacturer had any particularly strong bargaining power in Mozambique at that time and none was in a position to create effective opposition to the new policies. Last, the context of independence created the opportunity and wish for change, and the wish to do something for ordinary Mozambicans.

(A full account of this process is documented in Barker, 1983.)

---

statement of such a policy existed – and this is the point at which we might in fact have trouble in recognising a policy if we saw it. Yet if we ask about how pharmaceuticals were handled at this time, a picture does start to emerge: there was no policy for ensuring the availability of medicines for those of limited means. This amounts to the existence of a policy that pharmaceuticals were only available for those who could pay. There was no policy for state procurement of medicines; this meant that in practice regulation of procurement existed only through the working of the private market. Such state regulation as existed, worked to reinforce the trend towards the import of expensive medicines. In other words, although there was no stated policy, there was certainly a process which could be defined in terms of pharmaceuticals procurement. The way in which the state responded or failed to respond to this process can be described, and analysed as the policy in this area. The issue is frequently not one of whether a policy exists, but whether the policy has been consciously developed.

In comparison now, the recognition of the elephant is beginning to look rather more straightforward than that of the policy! Which is the easier to define? This rather odd question may in fact be rather helpful. What would we mean by 'defining' an elephant? A large beast of burden? A large animal characterised by a trunk which allows it to suck up water and handle food? A moment's thought shows that what we tend to do is to think about the elephant in terms of function and use. Yet such a narrow view of this complex creature would not help us to study the elephant; on the contrary it creates a false impression that the elephant is designer made, and that we know why it was made.[1] An analogous problem arises when attempting to define policies. Policies tend to be defined by those who are involved in a debate about them, or by those who wish to study them. Those defining the problems do so because they have a particular concern. It is all too easy to start thinking about policies in terms of that one concern, and forgetting that policies, like elephants, are not often designer made.

Health care policies as systems

At this point, it may be useful to introduce the notion of health care policies as systems. Figure 3.1 gives a simplified model of the health care system, adapted from Easton (1972). It is important to recognise, before examining this figure in detail, that 'the health care system' is an abstract notion defined for the purpose of thinking about health care and analysing policies and relationships. Indeed, there is not only one 'health care system'; there is the one I might elaborate and the one which each reader might elaborate, and each is a little different. Figure 3.1 is produced, and can be further elaborated, according to the following rules. First, a decision must be made about what constitutes 'the health care system'. This may be done by defining those organisations which are involved in health care; however as Checkland (1989: 89) points out, it is important, in studying any system of this kind, not to rush too quickly to see the system in terms of organisational structure; rather we should seek to analyse what is happening in terms of process. Thus to study the example of the Mozambique pharmaceuticals policy, we would not start by defining the pharmaceuticals system in terms of government organisations but in terms of the process by which pharmaceuticals are acquired by those who need them. Likewise the health care system might not be defined overall in terms of the health service, but more usefully in terms of the broad system

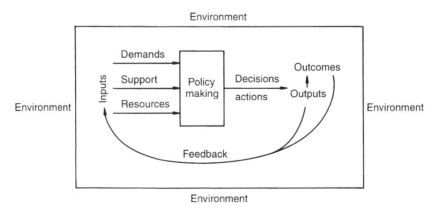

Figure 3.1 *A systems diagram of the policy-making process (adapted from Easton, 1972)*

of activities and processes by which people in a country or region seek to improve their health. In this way we establish some kind of root definition from which to elaborate a model system. Of course, the discussion in Chapter 2 helps to show that quite different root definitions are possible. We might, for example, decide to analyse the health system as a system for legitimation of illness in the workforce. Alternatively we might choose to treat it as a system for providing medical care, rather than health. The way in which we look at the health system will lead us to elaborate quite different diagrams.

Having stated the nature of the system we wish to analyse, the next step is to decide what are the *components* of the system, which undoubtedly interact, and what might be described as the *environment*, which provides the *context* in which interactions take place. What would be the components of the broad system of activities and processes by which people seek to improve their health? First, there would be a range of such activities and processes, described in whatever way seems helpful to the analysis at hand, such as scientific medicine, complementary medical practices, and family and self-care; these processes could in turn, each be analysed as a system. Staying at this level for the moment however, we might begin to analyse the interactions of these types of care, the demand which each receives and the support which each enjoys, from either the public or the state. Likewise we might begin to analyse the *outputs* of these different activities, in terms of either services or actions.

How do we decide where to draw the boundary around the system, to separate it from the environment? The environment is the context in which the system operates. The system is not isolated from its environment; there can be flows across the boundary between system and environment, and the environment affects and limits the way in which the system operates. The system does not itself, however, produce flows great or significant enough to affect the environment. Thus the health care system exists within an environment which includes all kinds of major social, political, economic, historical and biological influences. The nature of the government of the day will determine the kinds of relationship which will obtain within the health care system, and the kind of care which results. The social dynamics within local communities will determine the extent to which community self-help features in the health care system. The conditions prevailing in the global environment will affect the needs to which the health care system must react. At the same time, we can reasonably argue that the activities of the health care system alone will not have an effect significant enough to actually change the political stance of the government of the day, nor will they alone change the dynamics of local communities – if we thought they might, then we would need to rethink whether the local communities form part of the environment, or part of the health care system itself, for the purpose of this particular model.

Deciding what goes into the environment and what is part of the system itself is crucial in producing a systems model, and indeed working this out is an important stage in the analysis. In systems terms, when we consider a high politics issue, then decisions concerning the long-term objectives of the state are made within the system under study. This would unequivocally be the case if, say, the issue was whether to move to an insurance-based financing system. In a low politics issue, issues of central concern to the state or to those holding power would belong to the environment in which the issue under study is located, and although the issue under study cannot affect high politics, high politics can affect it. For the health care manager working out the system in which s/he must operate, this stage of the analysis helps to define the area within which action is possible, and clarifies the sources of influences, inputs and interference which must be avoided or tolerated, but which s/he has no power either to increase or to eliminate. It also will serve as a helpful (or at times painful!) reminder that one lives and works in an open and dynamic system; a constant stream of events and influences shape and alter the conditions within which the system components interact.

This book is not intended to be a text on systems theory, so the reader might well at this point ask, what is the value of a brief introduction to systems models? One reason for including the foregoing discussion is that the ability to sort out what might be conceptualised as a system provides a useful way of clarifying a particular area for further analysis. Thinking through what is the environment in which the system operates refines this model further. Once one system has been modelled, the systems that represent its component parts can then in turn be modelled, taking the analysis to a more detailed level but providing a means for thinking carefully about the levels at which interactions and actions occur. Used carefully, this approach also serves to ensure that we do not inject a false sense of purpose into the systems studied; systems may have *functions* without having developed for a *purpose*. Thinking carefully about a system, we can hopefully keep in mind that systems react to environmental influences in a whole range of ways, sometimes changing their behaviour, transforming their own internal structure, or even completely remodelling themselves. Lastly, we can note the way in which the results of a policy process, the outputs and outcomes, themselves have an effect on events which follow, and thus a feedback effect on the process itself.

Policy and planning

Who should study health policy? There are those who feel that policy studies are the domain only of academics or of those at the top of the health care hierarchy, in obvious positions of power. It was, however, suggested earlier in this book that the study of health policy is of vital importance for all health professionals who wish to take a strategic look at their own work, to assess critically their own effectiveness, and ensure that the policies being implemented are the policies intended. Whether the professionals concerned see their management role as operational or as strategic, this still obtains, for two reasons.

First, in today's world of decentralised management, more and more people play an active and crucial role in the policy process. In many of the world's health systems, gone are the days when all decisions were top-down. Now, much is left to those running health care at more localised levels, and each management decision, no matter how localised, has a policy content. This point leads on to the second consideration; this concerns the nature of activities which require an understanding of policy issues. If we subscribe to a view of policy in which those in charge are content to worry only about the policy statement or the appropriate legislation, then we need have only a few people who can do this, and the rest can follow the lead thus produced. On the other hand, the view of a dynamic policy system discussed above leads us to realise that policy is never made once and for all. A policy may change in the process of implementation; the intended outputs and outcomes may not at all be those which result, and those who were intended to benefit from a particular policy are not always the people who do benefit. Those involved with the policy process at all stages have a role to play in ensuring that the policies concerned have the wanted effects.

Can we talk about the stages in the policy process just as we would refer to the stages in the planning process? In Chapter 1 we referred to the relationship between policy making and planning. We noted that policy is often seen by managers as a higher-order activity than planning, even though planning may inevitably have a policy content, and planning decisions involve choices about resource allocation. It would at this stage be helpful to try to clarify the relationship between policy and planning. The definition offered earlier suggested that policies are the networks of interrelated decisions which together form an approach or strategy in relation to practical issues concerning health care delivery. On this basis, a particular health action results from the combination of many current and past decisions. I would suggest that planning is essentially about developing strategies to make policies happen in practice, and about considering what is needed to operationalise these strategies. In the planning process, policy preferences become expressed in terms of overt choices about the allocation of resources; ambitions to do and achieve certain things become tied to a time-frame; through the process of budgeting we count the cost. Walt puts this in a helpful way when she says: 'planning follows policy: planners help to put policies into practice, although the planning process itself may help to develop and refine health policies'.[2] Not all authors however share this conceptual framework. Another recent book talks of 'planning health policies' as though the planner were able to formulate policy unrestrained by the politics of the health sector.[3] This resembles a managerialist approach, and we should consider the characteristics of such an approach in a little more detail in order to distinguish the different approaches people have to policy making.

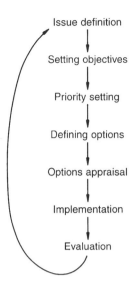

Figure 3.2   *Stages in the policy-making process*

Figure 3.2 presents a stylised version of the sequence of events which may go to make up the process of policy making. Such a representation of a sequence of policy-making activities is found in many texts, and it has an obvious resemblance to the planning spiral type of diagram found in books on planning.[4] Planning is meant to be a purposive activity, and a systematic approach can be helpful. Can we look at policy development in the same way? If we wish to focus on a broader appreciation of the way in which policies are made, Figure 3.2 should really carry a warning, for it seems to imply that policy making is always within the full control of the individual policy maker or manager, and that all these events are carried out, in order, in a conscious strategic planning process, each time a policy is made. Yet as the examples earlier in this chapter illustrated, policy making is often an evolutionary process, and our description of a policy may be a *post hoc* description of something which was not planned.[5]

The health manager cannot ever hope to fully control policy making, for certainty is not given to anyone where policy is concerned. Indeed, it is important to stress that the managerialist approach, which attempts to control all aspects of policy and policy formulation, is unworkable. Let us consider briefly the stages described in Figure 3.2 in order to make this point more adequately. To create a focus for the discussion, the example of the way in which policy might be developed in the area of HIV/AIDs is considered in Box 3.3.

The reader will observe that there are many reasons for which an issue becomes seen as one demanding attention, and that these depend heavily on how the public – and particular sections and groups within society – see the issue. The arena in which an agenda such as this one is set is highly

Box 3.3   Development of HIV/AIDs Policy

Issue definition

In different countries, different factors probably spurred governments and other organisations to start thinking of developing an
HIV/AIDs policy. Among these were (a) a sense of crisis, as
people realised that there was an epidemic; (b) the emotional
appeal of an issue which appeared to create medical demands
that science cannot yet meet; (c) the wide impact of HIV/AIDs;
(d) the relative strength of those groups in society who determined to see that HIV/AIDs was on the policy agenda. Over a
period of years, such groups achieved dominance over and
above those other groups (e.g. certain governments concerned
about public image and tourism) who wished to keep HIV/AIDs
off the agenda.

Thus HIV/AIDs was recognised as an important question. This,
however, left room for debate about the HIV/AIDs problem, a
debate that is still active today. To some people the problem
was a straightforward one of an epidemic of a killer disease; to
others it was one of mounting medical costs for incurable sick
people. Others have regarded the problem, variously, as one of
male domination or female exploitation, as one of sexual
promiscuity, of homosexuality, or of drug abuse.

Setting objectives

There may often be a difference between the objectives which
the health care manager sees as practical and those which the
public would wish to hear. Public statements of objectives in
relation to HIV/AIDs might well speak about the elimination of
the condition or control of the epidemic; the managerial objectives defined as a preliminary to working out a detailed policy
are more likely to talk about attaining a certain level of public
awareness, a certain level of resourcing for services.

Priority setting

In setting priorities to deal with HIV/AIDs, one has to think
carefully about the dimensions of choice. Priorities might be
expressed in terms of:

the population at large, or specific groups, e.g. intravenous drug
   users;
health education and preventive work or care of AIDs sufferers;
working through the Ministry of Health or through non-
   governmental organisations.

Box 3.3 *continued*

Options analysis

In examining the available options for an HIV/AIDs strategy, not all options which can be imagined will in practice be possible. For example, in many countries the option of internment of all infected persons would not be considered because of the human rights considerations. In others, a sexually explicit public education campaign might be considered too offensive to even contemplate.

Implementation

The best-considered HIV/AIDs policy could prove extremely difficult to implement. Failure at the stage of implementation might be due to:

inadequate staff briefing and education;
failure to overcome public prejudice and ignorance;
reluctance of the government to release adequate resources to
  implement the plan.

charged with emotion and with conflicting political and ethical values. Of course, this example may be regarded as relating to an issue where emotions run especially high. One could argue that this is not the case for many more mundane, routine matters with which the health service deals.

Conflict also occurs at the level of setting policy objectives, and again this can be for localised reasons or may involve debates with quite far-reaching implications. When it comes to setting objectives for the overall policy, there is possibly a difference between the objectives which a manager would regard as useful, and those which the public would like to hear. Although Box 3.3 does not illustrate the point, there may also be a conflict between the ways in which medical professionals and management would like to express the objectives – the former being more likely to focus on improving the epidemiological statistics and the latter more likely to focus on service provision. The dimensions within which priorities are expressed is a vital and highly political issue which affects both the presentation and the delivery of a policy.

When it comes to options analysis, we reach an area where a wealth of methodologies is available to those who would aspire to a managerial approach. Yet as the example of HIV/AIDs indicates, some options are often ignored before any form of appraisal has been carried out. In other cases, appraisal of the epidemiological, clinical and economic aspects of different approaches needs to be tempered with what the manager knows about public opinion. Lastly, at the implementation stage, the most perfect plans can go wrong for reasons beyond the manager's control.

This example illustrates the point that, although we can describe the policy process in terms of stages similar to those described in relation to the planning process, we must be aware that the manager is only ever at best in control of small parts of the policy process. Much of the time, the manager must try to detect the objectives and priorities that are likely to be most relevant and most likely to meet with wider approval. S/he must try to compromise with sets of objectives which can only go part-way towards meeting the policy goals, given limited resources, and must then struggle with the problems encountered in actually trying to put the policy into practice, through a specific set of plans.

If the managerialist approach is so lacking, why bother even to mention it? These issues have been considered at some length because this kind of approach is often taken as the obvious one to follow, and a surprising number of policy texts discuss policy making as though it happens in a political vacuum. To refer to the preceding section, this is to ignore the fact that the manager cannot control the environment, and it is to forget that a policy system is open and dynamic. Diagrams such as Figure 3.1 do not help us here. It is *conceptually* possible to distinguish the various stages in the policy-making process, and in thinking about how one can study policies it is useful to be able to think about these different processes and analyse each one. However it is misleading to regard these stages as ones that happen in chronological order, or to think that such a purposeful approach to policy development is, or can usually be, employed. The nearest real-life actualisation of this occurs when a strategic planning process is mounted – and this is where planning and policy development are at their closest. Although most people are accustomed to think of policy analysis as a retrospective activity which helps us understand what has already happened, policy analysis comes into its own as a prospective activity, aiding strategy development.[6]

Most of the time, the stages of policy making do not happen in linear order. It is easier to see how policy making and planning can be part of an integrated process if we think in terms not of sequential approaches, but in terms of what Rondinelli (1993) has called *adaptive administration*. This represents a *learning approach* to management which is increasingly recognised as a useful basis for dealing with uncertainty and complexity. As Korten (1980) has argued

> Its requirement is for organisations with a well developed capacity for responsive and anticipatory adaptation – organisations that: (a) embrace error; (b) plan with the people; and (c) link knowledge building with action.

In other words, public policies address complex realities, and most of the time our ignorance is far greater than our knowledge. Policy making must at any time be achieved by maximising that knowledge, but at best will be conducted in a style which emphasises flexibility, responsiveness and participation.

This section has focused on the managerialist approach to policy which sometimes results from too simply equating policy with planning. This approach allows a role for the policy maker; it is allowed that strategy can be developed. The alternatives frequently offered are approaches which totally dispense with the idea of all strategy making.[7] Pluralist and incrementalist approaches to planning see policy makers as unable to control their environment, and as having severely limited freedom of choice in policy making. The approach adopted in this book recognises the range of constraints on the policy maker. Rather than advocating that the policy-maker can then only respond by 'muddling through' or making minor incremental changes, the suggestion is that careful analysis of the policy system will allow the policy maker to distinguish what environmental constraints have to be lived with, and what are features of the health system, open to change. Strategic thinking about quite major shifts in policy may then be possible, but although perhaps radical, these changes will be made in a considered way, thought through with a degree of political realism.

In summary

What constitutes a policy?

- The policy process may involve the taking of decisions, the production of statements, the making of plans or the development of an approach.
- Implementation is an integral part of the policy process.
- Policies exist even when there has been no conscious policy making.

Health care policies as systems

- Policies are the product of a large number of determinants. To analyse policy, one must take into account the broader context of the health system, and the political context beyond that. The historical, geographical and technological contexts all have a part to play.
- It is helpful to conceptualise the policy process as a systems model of organisational relationships and influences.

Policy and planning

- Health policy is an important area of study for all health professionals, whether they see their role primarily as an operational or as a strategic one.
- Policies are the product of those involved at all stages of the policy process.

- In today's world of decentralised management, many more people play an active and crucial role in the process of formulation of policies.
- Policies are networks of interrelated decisions which provide consistency in approach in relation to practical issues concerning health care delivery.
- Planning is essentially about developing strategies to make policies happen in practice.
- Scrutiny of the various stages of the policy-making process illustrate a variety of ways in which the freedom of the policy maker is constrained.
- Although people are accustomed to think of policy analysis as a retrospective activity which helps us understand what has already happened, policy analysis comes into its own as a prospective activity, aiding strategy development.
- Policy making and planning might best be seen as part of an integrated process of adaptive administration.
- Although a managerialist approach is rejected, it is argued that development of strategies is important and possible, provided that environmental constraints are considered carefully.

Notes

1. Some readers may want to argue that elephants are indeed designer made – by God. The discussion here is not about final cause. If there is a grand design by a creator of the universe, we cannot presume to know what that is, and over-interpret our understanding of the elephant. Science has never found such an approach a profitable way forward. Rather we should understand the elephant by studying the elephant as we can observe it. Likewise with policy, we should not start out by assuming there has been a grand plan, but observe what happened and is happening in practice, and build up an understanding from that.
2. Walt (1994: 7).
3. Abel-Smith (1994).
4. See, for example, Green (1992).
5. See, for example, Gordon, Lewis and Young (1993).
6. See Walt and Gilson (1994).
7. An excellent description of the main features of these approaches is given in Walt (1994).

PART II
STUDYING HEALTH CARE POLICIES

Introduction

If a health care organisation is to be strengthened through its policy formulation, the policy maker, manager or planner must be able to develop informed views. 'Policy studies' sound abstract and academic to some, yet the process of study – fact finding and intelligence gathering – is of great practical importance. The health manager and others in leadership positions need to be able to make use of policy studies that others have undertaken. Furthermore, s/he should be competent to determine when and what new study, if any, is needed, and be able to define a commissioned piece of work.

Part II is intended as a guide to policy studies. Chapter 4 asks whether a distinction is to be made between policy studies for the health manager and those written for an academic purpose, and also sets out a framework for discussing the kinds of policy study that are possible. It then discusses the pros and cons of the alternative approaches of conducting policy studies from within the organisation, or through outside researchers.

Chapter 5 looks at the way in which people decide what to study, and the scope for arriving at quite radically different ways of asking a question about any one policy issue. Selecting and defining those studies that are a priority is a difficult and challenging task, and one which is frequently given too little attention. This chapter examines the types of evidence which may be available to answer policy questions. The emphasis here is on the diverse and multidisciplinary nature of that evidence.

Chapter 6 looks at the range of techniques and methods available for collecting the information we need. Of necessity, this is only meant to be a guide to the territory; the emphasis is on trying to see clearly what range of choice we have. Methods are considered in three broad categories: the first two are ones which enable us to gather information and opinions, and these are gathered on the one hand from the public, and on the other from experts; the third category consists of those techniques which support the analysis and interpretation of data, and, thereby, the decision-making process. It is emphasised that the methods and approaches to be used must be selected carefully, in view of the aims of the study.

4

Approaches to Policy Studies

What kinds of policy study are possible?

It is appropriate to start this discussion by commenting on the range of policy studies to be considered. A broad distinction might be made between those methods and approaches which are suitable for analytical studies of policy intended to further academic work in the health policy/ social policy area, or to add to broad public debate, as against policy studies which the health service manager might want to develop in order to strengthen the policy process from within. This is similar to the distinction made by Ham and Hill (1984) who talk about analysis *of* policy and analysis *for* policy. In other words, it is recognised that some studies are conducted from a rather academic standpoint, at one remove from the policy-making process, and that others are conducted with the direct intention of producing usable results, allowing recommendations to be made, actions to be taken, and the implementation of change to occur. However it must be remembered that the author of a study cannot control the use to which it is put. A study analysing a particular policy may be produced out of academic interest, but then in practice be influential in relation to the way in which policy makers, pressure groups or the public at large, see the issues. As Louis Pasteur said, 'There are no such things as applied sciences, only applications of science.'

Of course, some policy studies take a broad look at decision-making processes within society, perhaps going far beyond the immediate realm of action for the manager. Ham and Hill (1984) distinguish between different possible *levels* at which policies may be analysed within the whole political system. There is the *micro* level of analysis, which looks at decision making within a particular organisation; there is the *middle-range* analysis of policy formulation, and there is the *macro* analysis of political systems, including the role of the state. However, Chapter 2 discussed the complex network of interests which produce the range of different values placed upon health care, and Chapter 3 considered the need to see different organisational levels as a series of interconnected systems. In this context, policy studies at various levels can be relevant to someone who has an active role to play in the policy process. Some studies will directly inform the level at which that person is working; others will give information on the environment. For example, a study of government health care policy may be of great importance to someone working in a non-governmental organisation, not

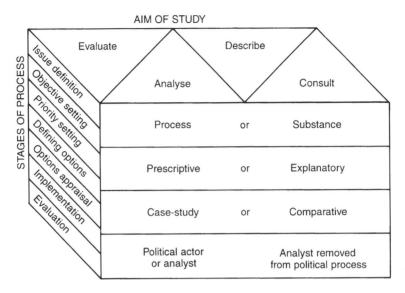

Figure 4.1   *Classification of policy studies*

because that person can directly change the government's policy, but because it may be essential to understand what government is doing in order to analyse what activities best complement those of government. A wide range of policy studies, then, is of potential interest to the manager or policy maker. Policy studies can be characterised in a variety of ways, and Figure 4.1 offers three dimensions to such a classification. First, different *stages* of the policy process can be studied, or indeed the process can be studied as a whole.

Second, the *aim* of the study can be described in various ways, and four categories are offered here. Studies aim to *describe*, in other words simply to create a record of a policy approach or its implementation or impact. As MacPherson and Midgley (1987) have pointed out, such studies may be rather barren, as they lack the use of explanatory tools to analyse what is going on. Some studies *evaluate*; they assess whether the policy is working and perhaps whether it is working well, according to specific criteria. Evaluative studies may focus on the outputs and outcomes of the policy process – these would be *impact* studies; or they may focus on an evaluation of the process itself: is decision-making effective? Is there adequate consultation? Other studies *analyse*: they use particular concepts and models in order to try to explain health policies in abstract, theoretical terms, and to ask how the observations obtained by the researcher may be interpreted. Lastly studies may allow us to *consult*. The aim of such a study may not be so much to analyse existing policy as to find out what public opinion is in relation to a particular policy area. Some consultative studies may attempt merely to record public opinion; others may combine the aim of seeking to understand public opinion with that of developing and supporting a public consultation process.

Third, a range of different approaches to the study may be adopted. A choice will be to study the *process* of policy making or to study the *substance* or policy content. The author of the study must then decide whether to adopt a *prescriptive* or an *explanatory* approach. In a prescriptive study, normative recommendations are made about what should be happening – for example, a policy concerned with supplies could be improved if the study produced clear recommendations about how to improve stock control. An explanatory study would attempt to explain what was happening without necessarily seeking a definite set of recommendations for action. A further choice is to be made in deciding whether the study should be carried out using the *case-study* approach, which focuses on the one policy case which is the object of the study, or a *comparative* approach, which sets out to compare similar policies as they are formulated or implemented, perhaps in a range of countries or states. Lastly, the authorship of the study itself involves choice, for the author may be a *political actor* – someone involved in the policy-making process – *acting as analyst* – or alternatively *the analyst may be someone who is removed from the political process.*

Box 4.1 illustrates the kinds of studies which might be contemplated in the case of a specific area, that of a community health worker scheme. If one considers the choice of focus, aims and approaches, one can see that a whole range of different studies are possible concerning this relatively simple subject. Of course, the potential complexity does not end there, as some studies may incorporate components which are descriptive combined with components which are analytical, and so on.

Who should conduct policy studies?

The question of authorship raised above relates to the question of scientific detachment. For some, the notion of a political actor becoming the analyst is quite wrong; the analyst must be detached from the decision-making process in order to view it objectively. However, we have to ask whether any observer can be truly disinterested. All of us have values which influence the way in which we analyse and evaluate what happens in society. When it comes to an area such as health service policy, it is questionable who is an outsider; the consumer – and we are all at least potential consumers of health care – may have views just as strong as those of the health care professional. Maybe no researcher should pretend neutrality, but rather we should value the work of those who seek to make explicit the values and criteria underlying their work. MacPherson and Midgley (1987) have argued that we need to distinguish between 'social policy work that clarifies causal associations between policy decisions and their consequences and that which seeks to organise knowledge to fit

**Box 4.1   Deciding What Kind of Policy Study is Needed:
A Community Health Worker Scheme**

The scheme involves the use of volunteers, paid in theory by the local community, selected by the district health officials following recommendations from each village. All nominees must be literate. Community health workers (CHWs) have a two-month training and then are expected to organise preventive work, give a few simple curative treatments, keep records and help organise assistance in emergencies.

Policy studies in relation to this scheme might:

focus on the whole policy process or on one particular stage:
For example, the focus could be on (1) the validity of the scheme's objectives on asking (2) were all the relevant options for such a scheme considered? or (3) has the scheme been adequately implemented?

involve different aims:
A descriptive study might document what happened, how many CHWs were trained and how, how many have been retained, and so on.
An evaluative study might ask, has the scheme been a success? For this study, parameters or criteria of evaluation would have to be chosen. Some people would say the scheme was a success if its inception was followed by a reduction in infant mortality rates. Others would say it was a success if a lot of CHWs were trained.
An analytical study might try to dig beneath the surface of the CHW scheme, and ask, what is going on? Such a study might start from a theoretical position – such as the assumption that community health workers provide valuable links with the community itself and increase the scope for the community's active participation in health care. The study might then select certain parameters to examine: the extent to which the scheme favours participation of all sections of the community; the extent to which participation is happening in specific cases of health care.
A consultative study might attempt to find out what various groups think about this scheme. Questions might include: Is the scheme popular with villagers? Is the scheme popular with health service staff in the areas covered by the CHWs? Do those staff perceive that it makes their own work easier?

Box 4.1 *continued*

involve different approaches:

If the approach of the study was to look at *substance*, many of the questions listed above would be appropriate, being focused on the aim of CHW provision.

The approach used in the study would be to study *process* if the objective was to examine the way in which decisions were made, the extent to which local people were consulted or the way implementation was done.

An *explanatory* study might seek to understand why the scheme was instigated at this time, or why the scheme was not working well.

A *prescriptive* study might examine the latter question, but concern itself with developing a set of changes to improve the scheme.

A *case-study* approach would focus on this one scheme, whereas a comparative approach would take a number of schemes and compare them in one or several ways, perhaps aiming to see if particular features are associated with schemes which seem to work well.

Last remains the question of *who* does the study; the schemes may have a *political actor* as analyst – for example, the district health management team might instigate or even conduct the study, or the analyst might be removed from the political process, for example, being from a university department.

preconceived ideological preferences and the attainment of practical objectives'. The former is helpful; the latter is problematic. The question of objectivity is discussed more extensively in Chapter 5.

For many today, the idea of action research has become important and positive; they might well argue that the manager or policy maker can bring to the research insights an outsider would take years to acquire, and also that the insider is more likely to be sensitive to the process of study itself.[1] This point is discussed at greater length below. Of course, many studies are carried out by authors who are neither entirely insiders nor independent. These are studies commissioned by political actors. One has to consider carefully whether such studies are written from an outsider's or an insider's point of view – the author may be writing what s/he feels the insiders want to hear. Indeed, some such studies are only commissioned on the assumption that a specific set of conclusions will be reached, and of course this can to some extent be ensured by judicious choice of researchers for the task. If one is attempting to read a policy study, it is important to ask how the work was initiated and supported.

Let us consider the potential differences when the manager or policy maker him/herself conducts a study, or when a study is done by an outsider. Although we shall consider these two extreme possibilities for the purpose of conducting a comparison, in real life there is a range of possibilities which might be seen as intermediate. The individual directly responsible for a policy area may not conduct the study, but may plan the study and organise staff to do what would remain an internal study. The policy maker may alternatively decide to commission outsiders to do the work. Commissioned research may end up looking more like an inside job or an outside job, depending on exactly how the commission is organised. At one extreme, the researchers may be identified and told how much they will be paid to conduct a study on a certain topic. At the other extreme, the organisation may seek to control the research process by defining the questions, sharing in discussions of the research design, perhaps providing the interviewers from inside the organisation, and discussing the interpretation of the results. Again however, not all research is commissioned from within the organisation under study. A policy study may be commissioned from outside that organisation, for example by those who fund the organisation or some of its activities. Alternatively the research may not be commissioned, but may be funded by an outside source such as a research body. For some evaluations and reviews, it is quite common to have insiders and outsiders working alongside one another.

The conventional assumption has been that the analyst should be an outsider, coming into the situation where study is required with the appropriate skills. An important attribute of the outsider as analyst, is that s/he can be seen as the neutral observer, able to listen equally to all views free of inbuilt prejudices. Does this model remain the ideal for which we should aim? A professional researcher may bring to the work, skills of research design which will significantly improve the validity of the findings over what might otherwise have been achieved. Against this there may, however, be problems. These include problems of the kind that exist in enlisting the services of any professional; the quality of the work produced will depend to a great extent on the quality of communication between the person who wants the study done, and the researcher. These are not just problems of language, but also relate to the ability of the study commissioner to define the study for him/herself. One crucial point is that problem definition will probably still rest with the policy maker, and as we have seen, problem definition is a crucial research stage. In the same way, the policy maker will be aware of the uses to which any study findings will be put, and will have information about the forms of dissemination which are likely to be appropriate. Of course, the researcher can be briefed on these questions, but the work of the researcher will only be as good as the initial briefing allows. It may also be that the researcher will design a study more elaborate than is strictly necessary, in order to make the work look 'scientific', and perhaps with the hope of publication in mind. If the work is being commissioned, then a clear understanding needs to be achieved concerning the intellectual ownership of the work and also the extent to which it will be confidential to a pre-defined audience. Just as when tendering for a piece of equipment, the policy maker needs to offer the researcher a clear *specification* of what is needed.

It is hard to know whether the outside researcher will actually achieve more than the insider. Ratcliffe and Gonzalez-del-Valle (1988) discuss an empirical study conducted by Ratcliffe in Bangladesh, in which the same survey data was presented to four sets of researchers. These ranged from American researchers unfamiliar with Bangladesh, its people and its culture, to American researchers who had research experience in Bangladesh and had lived there for more than two years, to Bengali researchers trained in the USA, and finally to the Bangladeshi researchers who had actually conducted the survey interviews. Major differences were found in the way the data was interpreted by the four groups, the researchers most unfamiliar with Bangladesh arriving at a context-free interpretation of what respondents were saying;[2] greater familiarity with Bangladesh increased the degree to which the findings were interpreted in a context-specific manner. The Bangladeshi researchers interpreted the responses in relation to the way in which they felt that local people saw things.

Engelkes (1990: 334) compared the use of insider and outsider re-searchers in a process evaluation conducted in relation to a Colombian primary health care programme. She comments:

> In the Colombia case, it was found that process evaluation, mainly carried out as participatory evaluation and a review with adapted WHO-designed protocols, gave the most relevant information on quality, acceptability and relevance of interventions. Costs were relatively low. External evaluations gave relevant results for policy and management levels, but because of lack of knowledge of local conditions by external evaluators, they could not say much about the process at community level. Because of the use of 'experts', their costs were (per capita) calculated to be five times as high as those of the adapted WHO review.

In listing potential worries about the use of outside researchers, in the context of less developed countries there is the concern that letting in the outsiders may perhaps lead to what Trostle (1992) has called 'scientific colonialism'. This refers to a relationship which all too easily develops in a world where Western researchers have the best access to donors and funding, and to publication outlets. Local scientists may be involved in data collection but often the data leaves the country as fodder for academic enterprise, rather than local problem solving.

What are the pros and cons of having research conducted from inside the organisation? As indicated above, perhaps the most obvious worries related to the insider's ability to be neutral; anyone who works within an organisation comes to its problems with their own assumptions and analysis, and these will be built into the research design. Even if the insider works hard to conduct a fair study, there may later be problems in that others may be cynical of their assessment of the work and its 'fairness'. There may also be times when the insider does not want to be associated too closely with what the research study might have to say. As the saying goes, 'They shoot messengers, don't they!' If the research is likely to throw light on unpalatable facts, or to reach conclusions which, while unavoidable, will have a prejudicial effect on employees' or a section of the public's affairs even in the short term, there may be good reason to let the work be associated with someone who can present the conclusions and back out fast!

Alternatively, the insider may at times see great advantages in conducting internal studies. There are large potential savings both in commission fees and in the time which can easily be spent in briefing an outsider, not to mention the time consumed by staff in ensuring that the outsider has access to the appropriate data and to those required for interviews, adequate working conditions, and even sometimes, adequate transport and living conditions. That is perhaps the minimalist approach to assessing the advantage of conducting policy studies from within the organisation. There may also be overt advantages to be gained from the 'learning process' approach, referred to above. This approach recognises that organisations are developing systems which can improve themselves; it also sees the research process not merely as having the end of producing facts, but also as a developmental process. Within an organisation, one can choose to have the outsider come and diagnose the problems in implementation of a certain programme; alternatively one can have the staff involved in the analysis of the problems defining what needs to be found out in order to have the basis for deciding between future courses of action, conducting the study and working together to think through the implications of the results. To the manager, this kind of staff involvement may be productive in developing awareness of the issues and a responsible attitude, in creating an atmosphere which nurtures the skills of problem solving, and in developing a consensus.[3]

There is no intention here to attempt to choose between these alternatives. The present objective is simply to clarify the range of considerations involved in this further aspect of choice when an appropriate policy study design is sought. As a final step in clarification, perhaps it is useful to summarise the comments which have been made in the course of this chapter, about the end-product of the research process. The importance of considering *end-use* for a study at the stage of planning it cannot be over-stressed, because one must think about the kinds of information needed and for whom it is needed. The manager may require some basic information for action, but may need to produce a more elaborate study in order to convince others that the action is on the right lines and will have the desired effects. The extent to which a study has a learning process goal as well as the goal of producing a report, will also affect the style of work to be done. Lastly, a study may validate a policy approach, and/or contribute to consensus building, in that the discussion and debate that proceeds may give participants the opportunity to develop their views. The short account of the spectrum of available research techniques which follows in Chapter

6 is to be considered in the context that *policy studies are an active contribution to the policy-making process itself.*

In summary

What kinds of studies?

- Health policy studies may be carried out as pieces of academic work or with the immediate intention of improving a particular area of health service policy.
- Health policy studies may be of value to the manager or policy maker, whether the original aim of the study was to produce academic work or change practice.
- Some studies will inform the policy maker about the system within which s/he can initiate change; some will inform the policy maker about the environment within which that system must operate.
- Health policy studies may be classified according to the stage of the policy-making process studied, the aim of the study, and the approach adopted; Figure 4.1 summarises a range of important choices that can be made.

Who should conduct studies?

- One particularly important choice to be made is that of who conducts the study – a political actor, or someone removed from the political process.
- When the manager or policy maker requires a study to be done, they may either conduct it themselves, or get an outsider to do it.
- Between these extremes a range of intermediate possibilities exists.
- The advantages and disadvantages of both research done by insiders and that done by outsiders, are discussed.

Notes

1. Of course, the insider can adopt quite different attitudes to a study. Ham and Hill (1984) quote the work of Meltsner, who identified three basic types among policy analysts working for the US federal government: the technician who might employ an academic approach, the politician interested in policy studies insofar as they might lead to personal advancement, and the entrepreneur interested in using analysis to improve policies. The outside researcher can obviously be classified in a similar way.

2. The term 'context-free' is used here because the authors themselves used it; I would have to question whether there is ever such a thing as a 'context-free' interpretation. I would expect the researchers from the USA to use American values and beliefs in interpreting the data, however hard they tried to be neutral.

3. The advantages of an approach based on action research for the health services manager is discussed in greater length in Collins and Barker (1995).

5

Designing a Policy Study

How do we decide what to study?

In this chapter, the issues involved in choosing a topic to study are discussed. It is assumed that the reader may have an interest both in being able to read critically the studies of others, and also in knowing how to set about planning a study. The second section looks in more detail at how to define the study question, stressing that there are always a range of possible ways of defining a study, and that choosing the right one is of great importance. The third section asks what kinds of evidence might be collected.

Chapter 3 has already commented on the fact that only certain issues find their way on to the agenda for conscious policy making. Box 3.3 (pp. 29–30) described the way in which HIV/AIDs found its way on to the global health care policy agenda: here was an epidemic apparently gathering pace; apparently unstoppable, its impact was being felt across wide sections of society, and some extremely vocal and well-resourced groups put their efforts into lobbying for attention. Hogwood and Gunn (1984) have developed a useful list of the factors which bring such issues to people's attention; the list includes the factors implied in this example – importance, breadth of impact, and vocality of those lobbying to get attention for the issue. In addition, they suggest that some issues may receive attention because they raise questions about power and legitimacy. This could, for example, be seen in the health sector in the conflict between doctors and managers. They also suggest that some issues arrive on the agenda simply because they are 'fashionable', though this begs the question of how fashions come into being, and who has the power in society to create or influence fashion.

Of course, many aspects of policy-making and the policy process never find their way on to the agenda at all. In Chapter 3, the case of pharmaceuticals policy in Mozambique was considered, and it was pointed out that before independence there was no overt policy making in this area. The internal conditions, which later would change, were not yet such as to trigger debate on the issues. Nor, at this stage, had the question of pharmaceuticals or essential drugs hit the international political agenda, so there was no external pressure. In the case of the HIV/AIDs issue mentioned above, some parties – in particular certain governments – *did* try to keep the epidemic off the agenda for a time, feeling that open admission of the problem might be prejudicial to their economies. In recent years a great deal of interest has been taken, within policy studies, in the question of how it is that some issues never reach the policy agenda and, indeed, demands that they should do so never even get formulated. This phenomenon is described as *non-decision making*.[1]

What factors are likely to govern the issues which become most important for the health care manager or policy maker to study? In some cases there is pressure to implement certain policies, and the manager must conduct some sort of study in order to ascertain how to set about implementation. This pressure might come from government, or may be a pressure which the manager perceives to exist in response to fashion, or to competition from other sections of the health service. In developing countries, strong pressure may often arise from the demands placed on services by aid agencies. In other cases there may be pressure to validate existing or proposed policies, to the public, to health service professionals, to political bosses or to the Treasury. Other issues may not be identified for study simply because they get squeezed out by such demands; because they are not felt to be priorities, and/or because the people whose concerns they might reflect do not wield sufficient political power.

Can the health care manager do anything to create a more systematic approach to policy studies? It is possible to develop a process of policy review over time, which might give attention both to consideration of the scope of the policy agenda as well as to specific items upon it. Such a process is set out in Box 5.1.

Box 5.1 illustrates the steps to be taken in a simple ranking exercise which can be used to establish priorities for further study.[2] It should be stressed that this list, although developed in a real-life situation, is only

---

Box 5.1 Development of a Policy Review Process

A systematic process might be established in two main steps:

A. Review areas in which policies exist or should exist

1. Invite consultation among staff, related services and among the public.
2. List areas where there is a defined policy.
3. Try to think of areas where policy development is needed, bearing in mind: areas where problems exist; areas where complaints surface, areas where there is a need for greater consistency.
4. Consider the health situational analysis if such an analysis has been conducted: it may expose areas which need a policy response.

Box 5.1 *continued*

B. Ranking exercise

The ranking pro forma is divided into three sections. The answers may be given on the ranking scale of +, ++ or +++, + implying that the issue is not important in each case, while +++ implies this is very important. In section B we suggest that you use − to designate a cost and + to designate a saving. −−− would indicate very high costs; +++ would indicate very high potential savings. The scores could then be examined visually or even added up. Please note that section D does not generate rankings to be added to the others; the results from this section must be considered alongside the ranking result.

A. How important is the issue?

1. Is change in this area feasible?
2. How urgent is the issue?
3. How large is the population group affected by this policy?
4. How much of health activity is affected by this policy?
5. How popular would resulting improvements be?

B. What is the cost of change and the cost of no change?

1. Will change cost money?
2. Will change save money?
3. Will change cost staff time?
4. Will change save staff time?
5. Will change cost effort in management and planning?
6. Will change save effort in management and planning?

C. Does this policy area have implications for:

1. accessibility
2. long-term credibility
3. efficiency
4. equity
5. quality of service

D. Does change in this policy area require the involvement of sectors other than the health sector?

If yes, tick. Then, for each column ticked, consider whether the relevant sectors beyond the health sector would be likely to cooperate. Very likely to cooperate may be given three ticks; likely to cooperate two ticks, and unlikely to cooperate one tick. These policy areas receiving only one tick in this column should be considered only with great care.

illustrative; the criteria selected should be those seen as most important by the group involved in the ranking process, in the context in which the ranking is to be done. The process enables priority-setting to be undertaken in a way which is systematic, transparent, and takes account of the views of all those who should and in practice can be consulted. More complex procedures with, for example, more sophisticated ranking techniques, exist, but sophistication is achieved at the cost of making the procedure less accessible as the basis for group discussion.

In applying the procedures outlined in Box 5.1, question D was treated as being of a different order to the rest. This question is essentially asking whether the participants see the problem under discussion as one that can be changed within the system with which they are concerned. If the problem is related to the wider environment, it is necessary to reflect on the potential for change.

Defining studies in priority areas

The reader will remember how in the example of policy development given for HIV/AIDs in Chapter 3 (Box 3.3, pp. 29–30) it was suggested that individuals may see an issue in many different ways, with diverse views as to what seems to be the 'real problem'. To some the 'real problem' is the lack of a medical cure; to others it is homosexuality; to yet others the problems in achieving widespread use of condoms. And to some, male domination in society is the basic problem. Clearly the way in which a study is defined will determine what questions are asked, and what kind of study is conducted. An in-depth study of the way in which medical research on HIV/AIDs in Africa has been based on Western stereotyped images of African sexuality has been completed by Packard and Epstein (1991). These authors argue that social scientists have attempted to explain the epidemiology of AIDs in Africa by focusing on perceived peculiarities of African behaviour to the exclusion of environmental factors, and point out that similar misconceptions figure in the history of research into tuberculosis and syphilis.

A number of problems arise in definition of the important issues. Three types will be mentioned here; (a) that of deciding which concepts and values should be used in analysing each problem; (b) relationship between correlation and causation; and (c) confusion of issues and goals with the indicators commonly used to measure them.

Deciding what concepts and values should be used in analysing a problem

We need to recognise that our analysis will depend on a whole range of values. Someone who does not accept that there is male domination of society, or who accepts male domination as a good and natural phenomenon, is unlikely to see the HIV issue as being caused in any way by male domination. Most problems will be seen differently in relation to different views of how resources are and can be shared in society, of how power is distributed in society, and of how the poor should be treated. These parameters are examined in more detail in Part III.

Considering whether the problem has been defined in terms of causal or correlational evidence

Much work in the health field these days leads towards attempting to infer causation from correlation and sometimes, one becomes confused with the other. The example of tuberculosis (TB) is a good one to take, because the difficulties in getting to the root of the problem – what environmental factors cause high incidence of TB – are well known.[3] High rates of incidence of TB are positively associated with overcrowded housing conditions; in other words, we know that there is a correlation between these two things which can be statistically measured. In many studies, in different parts of the world, it has been observed that these two things go together. Does this mean that overcrowding causes TB? The short answer is that it might do so, but that we do not know. It is possible that overcrowded living conditions directly affect people's immunity, leaving them more likely to catch TB, but the relationship could also be an indirect one. It may be that people who live in overcrowded housing tend to do so because they are poor, and that it is also because they are poor that they have inadequate nutrition, which leaves them susceptible to TB. The first relationship is a causal one – overcrowding causes TB; the second relationship is one of correlation – overcrowding and TB go together because poverty directly or indirectly causes both. All too often, this distinction becomes blurred. Another good example in the current health literature is that of the relationship between maternal literacy and child health (Mosley, 1985; World Bank, 1993). Study after study has confirmed a statistical correlation between these two variables: where mothers are educated at least to a basic level, their children are much healthier than the children of illiterate mothers. Again, we do not know if this relationship is causal. It could be that the relationship is basically an economic one – mothers who are better educated tend to be those who come from wealthier families; in these families there are more resources for food and child care, so children are healthier. Other explanations are possible, but this is not the place to embark on an evaluation of the more complex of those; the point is that reasonable doubt must still exist as to the relationship between maternal literacy and child health. Yet if one looks at the publications of international agencies such as UNICEF and the World Bank, one can see that policy directions are frequently proposed which assume a causal relationship.[4]

Confusing issues/goals with the indicators commonly used to measure them

Indicators are used to tell us how well a project or programme is working and monitoring and evaluation are essential in the improvement of health care. Yet it is vital – while quite difficult – to remember that indicators are often selected as indirect measurements of progress because they are easy or convenient to measure, or indeed, all too often, simply because they are measurable.[5] The danger is that some indicators are used so commonly in health status evaluation that people begin to think of the indicator as itself representing the problem or its solution. A good example is the infant mortality rate for a particular population. Infant mortality rate (IMR) is an indicator which correlates well with a large number of other health indicators, and is one of the most easily collected. For this reason, when it may be difficult or expensive to collect data on adult morbidity, or even adult mortality rates, it may be possible to collect infant mortality data. As numerous studies have shown that improvements in other indicators of good health or lack of disease in a population correlate well with IMR, this is justifiable practice. It is tempting, if a project is to be evaluated in terms of reduction in IMR, to gear all activities towards a direct onslaught on infant diseases and health problems. Yet the overall health of a community may be better served by tackling problems of adult health. So widespread is the practice of using IMR as an indicator to assess health project impact that one wonders if this confusion of goals and indicators is not an endemic problem in the world on international health care.

Is issue definition helped by the current emphasis that many international circles place on health systems research training?[6] There has been an emphasis on development of research geared to answering practical questions, and on recognition that health care managers may need to be involved directly in formulating and answering questions. Achieving a good definition of the right question, though essential, tends to be a neglected area in research training (Trostle, 1992). The ethos in health-related research creates considerable pressure to produce a complex and sophisticated research methodology, rather than to focus on a good formulation of the question. Yet, just as in the world of computers, people point out 'rubbish in, rubbish out', so it is with research by any method.

A number of the ways in which study questions tend to get distorted probably relate directly to the medical ethos which pervades the health sector. Foster (1987) has pointed out that health research that is successful in receiving funding is often simple quantitative testing, of the kind which comes easily to those trained in scientific disciplines. Such research routinely depends on producing a hypothesis and doing a survey, and this is fine for an epidemiological study. If, however, the question is of an investigative nature, trying to ask what is happening, open-ended, qualitative approaches may be far more appropriate. It is Foster's suggestion that the predominance of medically qualified participants in the bodies which make decisions about health research funding creates a situation where certain kinds of research are counted as 'good' and almost always are funded, perhaps to the exclusion of more interesting work. These tend to be studies which evaluate health care activity's impact on health status, leaving aside questions of policy altogether.[7]

Another problem is one that probably pervades all policy studies, but has been raised in the health context by Foster (1987). This is the tendency to define all problems in terms of 'others not ourselves'. As Foster succinctly suggests, 'To change the behaviour of others is generally considered a more attractive enterprise than to change one's own.' Thus, problems of low health service utilisation may be analysed as the result of low health motivation in the community, without stopping to consider that the problem may be low quality of care in the health services. Lack of enthusiasm for the latest family planning programme may be analysed as stemming from local ignorance of the importance of birth control, when in fact the programme has been designed badly and perhaps with disregard to a range of factors, such as local sensitivities about sexual matters, the extent to which husbands should be consulted in the programme, or simply timing of the clinic to suit the normal working day of local women.

What kinds of evidence are available for policy studies?

The earlier sections of this chapter have demonstrated the wide range of approaches which might be described as policy studies, and the wide spectrum of questions which might be the focus of such studies. This section will look briefly at what kinds of evidence can be taken into account when studying policy. What do we mean by the word 'evidence'? To some people this may sound formal, implying that policy can be analysed only in the context of large-scale funded research projects. To others, 'evidence' has connotations of the detective novel – Sherlock Holmes looked for evidence in order to solve mysteries. The *Shorter Oxford English Dictionary* offers 'Grounds for belief; that which tends to prove or disprove any conclusion'; this is a broad definition which is appropriate here. Some evidence gathered for policy studies may need to be collected through formal research processes, if it is not otherwise available; however, other evidence may be around us, waiting to be noticed, or there in the form of existing data which, if reorganised, will answer our questions.

Earlier discussion has shown that the range of concerns involved in policy decisions is large, and a policy might be studied from a range of different angles. To illustrate this point, Boxes 5.2 and 5.3 give examples of two possible policy studies.

Box 5.2 is derived from an actual study which was done in France, in an effort to make real-life decisions about the approach to be adopted to a medical problem – that of policy in relation to significant prevalence of sickle cell disease and thalassaemia. This study was important because all

---

Box 5.2   Evidence for a haemoglobinopathy screening control

Sickle-cell disease and thalassaemia are inherited disorders of
haemoglobin which occur in many ethnic groups around the
world. There is no cure for these problems but they cause great
individual suffering and a drain on health care resources.
Strategies to control the prevalance of thalassaemias are based
on a combination of genetic screening to protect carriers of the
genetic traits (who would be at risk of having children with the
disorders if their partner is also a carrier); education and genetic
counselling and foetal diagnosis (combined with further counselling if the parents must choose between having an affected
child and terminating the pregnancy). Screening can be carried
out on schoolchildren, on couples before marriage and/or before
or after conception. Within specific countries, thalassaemias may
only be found in certain ethnic groups, so there is a question
about whether any screening should be targeted. What kinds of
question must be asked to work out a policy for screening, and
what kinds of evidence would be implied by these?

Number	Question	Evidence
1	What is the prevalence of the traits?	Epidemiological
2	What is the possible range of control strategies?	Genetic and medical
3	Is screening feasible in terms of total cost?	Economic
4	Would targeting at-risk groups increase feasibility?	Economic to consider cost; ethical and sociological studies for ethnic factors
5	Can screening be made mandatory?	Legal
6	Should screening be made mandatory?	Ethical
7	Would communities be receptive to voluntary screening programmes?	Sociological
8	In which laboratories could the tests be done to adequate standards?	Genetic (in relation to test standards), management information on laboratory standards
9	Is screening best done to schoolchildren, to couples to be married, or during early pregnancy?	Given the complexity of this question and the implications for counselling, numbers of tests to be done and cost, this question requires information related to almost all the above-mentioned categories of evidence

Ideas for the questions to be posed in this example were taken from Le Gales
and Moatti (1990).

possible policies – including 'no policy' (retention of the status quo) – have implications for the health service and for the public. In the box, a list of some of the major types of question which were addressed in this study is given, and for each there is an attempt to categorise the kinds of study which would provide the relevant information. Of course, this is not to say that someone conducting such a study would necessarily have to go and collect new information in each of these categories. The first step would be to see what evidence already exists, and if this step leaves some gaps, to see who might help to provide more. Examination of the types of evidence required here shows that a wide range of disciplines and studies are potentially involved. Some technical information is required, in the sense of the requirement for baseline epidemiological information to give us a feel for the size of the problem, and also some genetic expertise to provide a judgement about the possible range of control strategies which could be considered. This policy decision is not simply a technical one; advice or information will be needed on ethical, legal, sociological, economic and management questions.

Box 5.3 gives an imaginary example of a study which might well be considered necessary at some stage in many developing countries where pharmaceutical regulation is weak or nonexistent. Here only a selection of the questions which might be asked has been given, to demonstrate again the range of types of question. In this study the need for specifically medical expertise is somewhat less, although advice about the scale of medical risk of leaving things as they are would probably be crucial in moving towards a decision to study policy alternatives. Here we can see the need to gather evidence not only on the implications of change, but also on the likely *reactions* to change, both among the public and in the health service.

These two examples show us that policy questions are multidimensional, and that the evidence needed is multidisciplinary in nature. How can the policy analyst ever hope to complete studies of such a wide-ranging nature? One approach would be to involve a multidisciplinary team in the work. An academic researcher would be likely to favour this approach for first preference, but funds will not always allow for the most desirable approach. Another possibility is to limit the scope of the study to one or two of the potential areas defined, choosing whichever seem to be the most important for decision making, on the grounds that research design must not be over-ambitious if high quality work is to be achieved. The manager struggling with a real-life problem may be able to decide which aspects of the policy area in question are most crucial to study. In the case of the haemoglobinopathy study in Box 5.2, for example, the manager might decide that the availability of adequately equipped and staffed laboratories is likely to be a major question and may be a factor which limits the range of choice of possible strategies, whatever might be said about all the other questions. If so, then s/he may decide that the priority is to deal with the laboratory question first, and then think again. On the other hand, the

Box 5.3 Policy for over-the-counter drug sales

In many countries, the range of pharmaceuticals which can be bought over the counter is virtually unrestricted. This raises problems in that many pharmaceutical products should not be taken lightly and can be dangerous if used without medical supervision. In addition to actual risk to health, patients stand to waste money on ineffective treatments. If patients have no other guidance, they may be lured into buying a fancy, well-packaged, patented product at great expense when a simple generic product would have served just as well and cost them a lot less. Without some kind of regulation, there is a high risk that many patients will take incomplete courses of antibiotics; this increases the probability of resistance developing and of antibiotics being ineffective when really needed. It may be considered useful to study the possibility of restricting over-the-counter sales to a defined list of off-prescription medicines. What kinds of questions would need to be asked in such a study, and what kinds of evidence would be needed?

Number	Question	Evidence
1	Would the proposed changes involve legislation?	Legal
2	Does the public have adequate access to the health service in order to get prescriptions?	Management information; sociological and geographical studies
3	Would the public be given the impression that medicines were less easily available?	Sociological study or less formal approaches
4	What would be the economic implications for the health service?	Economic
5	What would be the economic implications for the public?	Economic
6	How much extra work would be created for physicians?	Management
7	Has any form of regulation of medicines been tried before, and if so, are there lessons to be learned from the experience?	Historical
8	What has been the experience in other countries where pharmaceuticals regulation has been introduced?	Comparative
9	What would be the public health implications of the move?	Medical
10	Would the move be popular, and if so, with whom?	Political

manager frequently does have to deal with multidimensional choices. In this case, the important thing may be to look to see what evidence already exists.

Although studying a policy question is a form of research, not all research demands that we collect new or *primary* data. Often, the first effort is to see what existing or *secondary* data there is. For example, in the study described in Box 5.3, we might reasonably expect to find existing data on the degree of access which the public currently has to health services; this may not be quite in the form we would have wanted, but use of what there is might be a more realistic option than trying to set up a new study. Historical and comparative data may well be available from secondary sources. On the other hand, if we wanted to assess the economic effects of increased regulation of over-the-counter sales, we might have to collect new data.

It is worthwhile, therefore, to look around when embarking on a policy study, and to ask what kinds of evidence may have a bearing on the questions which have been asked. The 'Sherlock Holmes' stance, which searches for the smallest shreds of evidence and for unexpected clues, may be a more helpful starting point than the parody of academicism which insists that we start with large-scale surveys. For example, in the haemo-globinopathy example (Box 5.2), there is a question mark as to whether we need to study racism. The first step may be to consider what we know about the degree to which racism is an overt local problem, by making use of press cuttings and by asking community leaders. In the same example, there is a question about the levels of awareness of thalassaemia and sickle cell disease in local communities. Here it may be possible to get some clues again by talking to community leaders, and by asking what health service workers know about the frequency with which community members come to them with questions or anxieties about these conditions.

Even these simple examples raise questions about what constitutes allowable evidence. First, should all evidence be *quantitative*, or is *qualitative* evidence allowable? The way in which quantitative studies seem to pre-dominate in the health sector has already been touched on in this chapter. For those trained in the medical and natural sciences, quantitative studies come naturally; one develops a hypothesis, produces numerical data which can then be compared with the data one would expect to find on the basis of the hypothesis, and then proves or disproves the hypothesis itself. Sometimes, however, it is important to start with open-ended exploration. We could take the example of the racism issue referred to above. Let us suppose that preliminary evidence indicated that racism is a major issue in the community, and that if the health service were to target all schoolchil-dren in particular ethnic groups for genetic testing, this would be seen as offensive. It is considered necessary to attempt to confirm these findings. It would be possible to conduct a community survey, working out a relatively simple questionnaire and seeking responses to this from a large sample of local people; the results could then be analysed and a view established as to whether the results provide evidence of widespread racism. This would be a quantitative approach. In this case the interviewer formulates the questions and the respondents have no chance to say 'Well, I wouldn't quite put it like that; as I see it, the problem is. . . .' In developing a survey, the researcher is in control, and limits what people can tell him or her.

Alternatively, one could set up open-ended, in-depth interviews with a small number of people or groups of people. The number of interviews would be limited by the time needed for each one, and there would be no hope of acquiring enough data to process statistically. In any case, one would not want to process such data statistically, as for each interview the responses would come in a different form, expressed as the respondent wanted to make the point, not as the interviewer wanted them to. The respondents would be less limited by the views and preconceptions of the researcher. Each would have the time to try to say what they really wanted about a difficult and sensitive subject, putting things from their own point of view. Of course, it is not easy to create an environment in which people say what they really think. A great deal depends on the ability of the researcher to listen well, and to create the opportunity for discussion, rather than over-structuring the discussion. Thought and planning are necessary in creating a suitable environment for the interview, in selecting respondents, and indeed in deciding who should do the interviews, for the ethnicity and class of the interviewer could be very important determinants of the extent to which the respondents will talk openly. Such a qualitative approach to research would be, in its own way, as demanding as the survey. It would produce information which would be more limited in that fewer respondents would have been consulted, but which might have much greater depth than the survey could ever produce.

The intention here is not to argue that either qualitative or quantitative methods have innate superiority. The intention is to stress that one must select the right tool for the job, and that in health services studies there is a particular need to bear in mind the possibility of qualitative approaches, because all too often the research ethos, dominated by those who control funding for formal research studies, is biased towards the norms and expectations of biomedical research; that it will produce statistical answers, that it will aim for conclusions which can be generalised. A policy study may seek to understand one situation, even if that explanation is strictly of local significance.[8]

This same research ethos, which leads us to value quantitative evidence also leads us to value *official* as opposed to *lay* evidence. Official evidence is that produced by governments or by those in authority; it is likely to rely both on scientific data, and on the world-view of those who have the most power in society. Lay evidence is that which might be offered to us by ordinary people with no special status in society, and no claim to represent anyone beyond themselves. The following quotations concerning sickle-cell disease exemplify an official and a lay account of this subject. The official account is quoted from the source of the questions used in Box 5.2 above (Le Gales and Moatti, 1990: 431):

> Although the prevalence of major haemoglobinopathies in southeastern France . . . is lower . . . epidemiological data suggest that, in this region, the frequency of the beta thalassaemia trait and HbS trait are 0.79 per cent and 0.22 per cent, respectively, in the general population, but can be much higher (from 2.5–8 per cent) in populations of certain ethnic origins. However, because of the complex history of migrations around the Mediterranean border, it is not so easy to identify clearly these at-risk communities. Although beta-thalassaemias are the most prevalent of the haemoglobinopathies in the region's populations, there are a number of individuals with a significant abnormal haemoglobin trait (HbS, HbE, HbC). However, incidence of alpha-thalassaemia is extremely low and has not been a public health concern.

The lay account is quoted from an article by Anionwu (1989: 77–78) and is based on a taped interview with a mother visiting the Brent Sickle Cell Counselling Centre, the only centre of its kind in Britain at that time:

> It started just over a year ago, when Julie was about two years of age. She had a temperature and I took her to the doctor. He said, 'It's natural for a child of her age to have a temperature.' But I insisted that she should have a blood or urine test. So he sent me down [for the blood test] and he diagnosed sickle-cell anaemia. He said, 'It's sickle cell, which the majority of coloured people, black people have, and there is no cure.' He just told me that. He said, 'They can't do anything about it, but if she gets any funny symptoms I should try giving her Junior Disprin or aspirin and try to keep her warm; and that's about it.' But she keeps on going in [to hospital] very often, with swollen legs and hands and pain in her tummy, which I couldn't understand, which they didn't really explain. . . .
>
> [Before that] I have never heard anything about sickle-cell anaemia. It was only after the diagnosis that I was reading in the *West Indian World* paper about your Sickle Cell Centre in London. So my sister here in London advised me to come and get more advice about it and I put it off. I said, I can't do anything because here is Dr G telling me one thing and different people tell me another. Finally they persuaded me; if I didn't come to London my child would probably die on me and I would probably be blamed by the Welfare for not taking care of her. They should explain better how you can deal with it and where you can go to get advice. . . . I have had to come sixty miles to hear more about it [from the Sickle Cell Centre], which I don't think is really right. I think it should be the GP that you turn to really.
>
> Now I'm going to see my doctor and have a word with him. I know you don't really think about these things until your child is ill but it's really terrible. You say 'It couldn't be me because I'm never ill' and my husband says it couldn't be him: and we're just blaming each other, but there is none of us to blame really, it's just traits; we can't help it.

These two quotations stand in sharp contrast. The first is informative if the reader knows enough about medical science to understand it; it succinctly gives factual information about the prevalence of the inherited disorders of haemoglobin in one area. It relies on scientific studies and data. The second quotation is from a lay person, who knows little about the medical complexities of such a disorder but who is living through the experience of having a child who suffers one. This account tells us nothing in medical terms. However it tells us a great deal about the quality of service which was available to this woman and her daughter. Her GP did not even know enough to realise that she should be referred to a genetic counselling service. The lack of such help has left the family suffering in ignorance, husband blaming wife and wife blaming husband, in a way that need not happen with improved services and policies.

Lay accounts may give us insights which can never be acquired from official evidence, because they allow us to see things as people – the consumers and the final arbiters regarding the quality of the health service – see them. They also may be of great value in allowing us to see particular views, those of individuals or groups in society. Official evidence is often based on generalisations about whole populations, and this has the disadvantage that the interests and problems of minorities get lost. In this regard, it is of interest to look at another quotation presented by the author of the above study, who refers to a different official account, a 1976 UK textbook on genetic counselling: 'Sickle-cell anaemia is not of great consequence to us in the context of genetic counselling in the United Kingdom. The sickling trait and sickle-cell anaemia appear to be confined to people of African and Eastern origin.'[9] Here is a case of official evidence which may be entirely accurate for many UK citizens, but completely obscures the needs of a significant group within the community.[10]

Suggestions that lay accounts and other informal sources of evidence such as newspaper reports should be taken seriously in the study of health policy, raises yet another important question concerning the nature of acceptable evidence: *subjectivity* versus *objectivity*. We tend to assume that scientific studies and official accounts are objective, that is, that such studies are in some way less biased and more fair, that the views of the researcher are cancelled out by the inbuilt safety precautions of experimental design, and that the quest for objectivity will reward us with 'the truth'. The corollary is that qualitative studies and informal sources of evidence produce 'subjective' or 'biased' accounts which are then regarded as unreliable. There are three problems with such assumptions. The first is that 'objectivity' is a doubtful concept; as Patton (1990: 482) points out, 'scholarly philosophers of science now typically doubt the possibility of anyone or any method being totally "objective".' Quantitative studies may seem objective because the values which underlie the definition of the problem, the approach to the study, and the selection of evaluation criteria, all become lost within the study itself, and the reader of the final account of the study has to work very hard to know or guess what these were.[11] As Patton (1990) suggests, it is probably better for the researcher to cease to worry about objectivity at all, and to replace this concern with a concern to be fair; to try to be scrupulous in recognising that there are likely to be many different perspectives from which an issue can be seen, and to attempt to treat each perspective with equal respect and seriousness. The researcher does need to be worried about his or her own biases; but we all have preferences and values which creep into the way we do things. The fundamental duty of the researcher is not to attempt to eliminate their own values, but to be prepared to test these biases just as stringently as s/he would test the biases of others. Equally, when the researcher must present work to others, it is the researcher's duty to state all the assumptions on which the work was based, if possible even discussing how things would look if a different set of assumptions was used.

The first problem area related to the values which creep into research. The second problem area concerns the relative nature of the results of research, or the nature of statistics which we may wish to use as secondary data. There is often an assumption that if scientific methodology has been rigorously applied, the research will somehow give us 'absolute truth'. This is to fail to understand that data and measurements may be *context-specific*; that is, they are only meaningful in relation to the context in which they were observed. Good examples of context-specific data abound in comparative studies. For a number of years, the World Health Organization refused to publish doctor/population statistics on a country-by-country comparative basis (Bridgmann, 1976). The reason for this was that it was recognised that meaningful comparisons between countries could not be made on the basis of these ratios alone, because both doctors and populations vary too much – 'doctor' needs to be defined in terms of years of training, functional role and role in relation to other health cadres, as well as taking into consideration hours of work and freedom to conduct private practice; the balance of curative and preventive work, and so on. 'Population' is assumed to express health service need, but of course in practice populations place quite different demands on health services, depending on their characteristics – proportions of young and old people, morbidity and mortality patterns, population density and so on.

It is quite common to assume that results of quantitative research studies will somehow be generalisable. For example, it is often assumed that a conclusion reached in one setting concerning the cost-effectiveness of a medical technique is somehow valid anywhere else.[12] Yet costs vary from one place to another, even within a country, and effectiveness is governed by the practical conditions within which a technique is used. It is also assumed, in measurements such as the newly proposed DALYs (disability-adjusted life years), that there is an absolute measure of ill-health, when in fact health, like disease, has no absolute value.[13]

There is one further problem with the assumption that we must aim for objectivity. It is that in dealing with policy, we are dealing with an area where opinions and values are of paramount importance. We cannot eliminate 'bias' when we are trying to construct policies which are seen differently by each party involved. If we were to return to the example given in Box 5.3 of regulation of over-the-counter drug sales, we might be able to construct a study which would establish a certain number of 'facts', such as the volume of sales of certain drugs and the extent to which these are accompanied by prescriptions. However, it would be of at least equal importance, in coming up with a policy, to establish what are *views* as opposed to facts about this issue: would it be popular with the public, with the pharmacists, with doctors? It would undoubtedly *not* be popular with the pharmaceutical industry – and they would be the first to make their views known to the government! To the policy maker, evidence about views and who holds them is often crucial in developing a workable policy, which professionals will be happy to implement and which will result in public satisfaction. For that reason, Chapter 6 takes the gathering of opinions seriously in looking at techniques available to the researcher of policy issues. Taking this line of thought one step further, it is also recognised that the very act of gathering opinions may have a formative or developmental effect on the opinions themselves. In any research, the observer has an effect on that which s/he observes. The traditional approach, especially in natural sciences, is to strive to eliminate such effects. Yet more recent work, particularly in management sciences, has led to the development of the 'learning process approach' (Korten, 1980), which not only acknowledges the importance of the research process itself but aims to maximise the potential benefits.

In summary

Deciding what to study

- Issues find their way on to the policy-making agenda because in some way they are forced to people's attention.
- Some issues never find their way on to the agenda.
- Corresponding pressures operate on the health service manager when s/he considers the study or review of policies.
- The health service manager can however consider making conscious efforts to establish a systematic policy review process.

Defining studies

- Once an issue has been picked out as important, it is necessary to define the kind of study that is needed.
- Three problems arise in the definition of issues:
  deciding what concepts and values should be used in analysing a problem;
  considering whether the problem has been defined in terms of causal or correlational evidence;
  confusing issues/goals with the indicators commonly used to measure them.
- Achieving a good definition of the question has been a neglected area in research training.
- Health research, including policy studies, suffers from a preponderance of quantitative work. This may be because quantitative approaches are best understood by those with a biomedical background.

- There is a tendency to define all problems as affecting 'others not ourselves'.

What kinds of evidence?

- Policy studies may involve evidence drawn from a range of disciplinary perspectives.
- Research may be based on primary and secondary data, in varying proportions.
- Evidence may be qualitative or quantitative.
- Evidence may be official or lay.
- It is probably misguided to aim for 'objectivity'.
- It is important to aim to be fair.
- It is also important to recognise that findings are often context-specific.
- Sometimes policy research is concerned with views rather than 'facts'.

Notes

1. The HIV/AIDs example discussed here is an example of what was first described as 'non-decision-making' by Bachrach and Baratz (1970), who coined the phrase in 1962: a process by which conflicts are suppressed. The lack of a clear policy on pharmaceuticals in Mozambique can be seen as non-decision-making if, as Lukes (1974) points out, this process can be seen in relation to institutional, not just individual, power, and if it can be taken to refer not only to actual conflicts over which no decisions are taken, but also to latent conflict. In other words, in pre-independence Mozambique, wide sections of the population had no political voice and the ruling groups in society exercised their power to keep things that way. It was very difficult for the majority, who had no access to medicines when they needed them, to make any demand for change.

2. The approach suggested here is adapted from a procedure for priority-setting developed by the author and further refined and field-tested in the four provincial health services in Pakistan, to be described in more detail in a forthcoming publication by Barker, Thunhurst, Ross and Rana. The author thanks those colleagues for their collaboration in developing this approach. Hogwood and Gunn (1984) offer a somewhat longer list of criteria: their list however focuses less on questions that generate answers which can be ranked. Zalot and Lussing (1983) offer a similar approach, tending to be even less prescriptive in terms of the categories, and focusing on the importance of the group decision-making process for selecting criteria of choice and weighting these.

3. I owe this example to the course team for the Open University course, 'Health and Well-being'; Beattie et al., (1992).

4. The World Development Report (World Bank, 1993) *Investing in Health* exemplifies this point. One of its 'three key messages' for governments making policies to improve health, is to 'foster an environment that enables households to improve health' and one of the three potential actions which governments are urged to consider in order to achieve this, is 'expand investment in schooling, particularly for girls'.

5. Rifkin, Muller and Bichmann (1988) provide an interesting example of an attempt to find indicators for things which are important but *not* measurable, such as, in their study, factors influencing community participation – leadership, organisation, needs assessment and so on.

6. The report of the Commission on Health Research for Development (1990) exemplifies recent interest in such research; the Health Systems Research Training Series published by the International Development Research Centre, Ottawa, Canada, in conjunction with the Programme on Health Systems Research and Development of the World Health Organiza-

tion (see Brownlee, 1991; Varkevisser et al., 1991; Brownlee et al., 1992; Pathmanathan, 1992; Pathmanathan and Nik-Safiah, 1991), is perhaps the most significant contribution to training in the field, though this series should not be regarded as exemplifying the problems mentioned in this text, many of which it has managed to avoid.

7. The tendency to focus on health impact in assessment of health care activity has been noted by various authors; see for recent examples Van Norren et al. (1989) and Schretten-brunner and Harpham (1993).

8. This point is argued in more detail in Barker (1995).

9. This quotation was taken from Stevenson and Davison (1976).

10. Happily today the picture is a more enlightened one. A 1989 UK report on genetic screening (Royal College of Physicians, 1989) devotes a whole chapter to the subject of ethnic minorities.

11. The way in which this applies to economic evaluations has been discussed in Green and Barker (1988).

12. A well-known work which based many arguments on such assumptions is that of Walsh and Warren (1979), who claimed that selective approaches to primary health care had been shown to be cost-effective; Unger and Killingsworth (1986) give an excellent critique of the use made by Walsh and Warren of economic data.

13. DALYs or disability-adjusted life years were proposed as a measure of the global burden of ill-health in the 1993 World Development Report (World Bank, 1993); the extent to which these values are situation-specific is discussed in Barker and Green (1996).

6

Techniques and Methods for Policy Studies

Choosing methods

The intention of this section is to consider the range of techniques which might be used across the spectrum of policy studies considered in this chapter. The intention is not to produce a 'how-to' guide, but simply to consider the applications of each group of methods, and to discuss the features of each which should be considered in making choices of approach.

Much information is to be gained from existing sources. While what follows focuses on collecting new information, it is always important to see what information is already available. To illustrate the point, one might again consider the table in Box 5.2 (p. 51). If attempting to gather the different kinds of evidence outlined here in order to consider policy in relation to haemoglobinopathy, one could expect to find quite a lot of information in written form. For instance the legal position could be well documented, as could the epidemiological picture. Genetic studies have been done, and the range of possible medical strategies could be taken from the literature. If laboratory standards are defined they will be documented. There could be published discussion on ethical questions, and even published position statements from religious groups. Some of the economic issues may have been studied. The area least likely to have been studied and documented is the question of community acceptance of possible approaches, something which could be tackled in a wide variety of ways.

The rest of this section covers a range of ways of finding out what is happening or what people think. Some of these would conventionally be called intelligence gathering rather than research. For clarity, the techniques are loosely grouped into categories – those which constitute approaches to asking public opinion; and those which involve asking the views of one category or other of experts.[1] The remaining brief discussion concerns those methodologies which go beyond the seeking of views and which actually attempt to help in clarifying the choices before the policy maker; these include options appraisal and decision analysis.

Asking the public

Simple observation and secret customer techniques

A great deal can be learned about the impact of some policies from simple observation. Clearly, this is only the case when a policy can be considered in a fairly localised context; for example, if it concerns the organisation of a clinic appointment system, one can learn a lot by going to see what is happening in the queue. If the study were, say, to examine the effects of implementing a policy of user charges, direct observation at any one time and place would not be so informative. Observation can be a good starting point from which to decide if more studies are needed. It may often be possible to involve the staff of an organisation in acting as observers, although of course one must consider the extent to which staff will be able to see the issues as others might see them. Community and consumer groups may well conduct their own observations of services.

Commercial enterprises, and in particular marketing firms, have for some time employed the technique of using 'secret customers' or 'simulated clients' in an attempt to see things as the consumer sees them. The customers are members of the public who would be in any case using the relevant services, but who have been contacted in confidence by the manager responsible for secret customer information. Each individual recruited agrees to make use of the services as they would have done, but to take special note of the quality of service, especially in relation to aspects which are considered currently important to study. Each must submit a report and must agree to keep their status as a secret customer a confidential matter. A short training session is organised for each new batch of secret customers, and a small fee is later paid to them for their work. This has been found to be a simple but most effective method of acquiring information on the implementation of specific policies. In the UK National Health Service, this approach to gaining intelligence about services has been used quite extensively. In developing countries, such methods seem to have found a special place in the family planning literature, as a tool for examining the quality and acceptability of services.[2]

Some disciplines, notably anthropology and some areas of sociology, depend on observational techniques which are far from 'simple'; these involve a range of different approaches to observation and to the role of the observer. However, the existence of sophisticated techniques should not detract from the value of reports, even from a totally untrained observer. These will often be the starting point for recognition that a policy area needs some attention.

Random sampling to collect information from the public

Within this category are methods among the best and the least known in health sector circles. The random sample survey is a familiar tool for collecting all manner of information about populations, from information about disease prevalence to information about awareness of health issues, and attitudes towards health problems. The general intention of such a survey is to find out about the characteristics of a specific population or group. A sample of the population is studied, on the basis that if this sample is selected from the larger population at random, and if it is large enough in relation to the total population size, the characteristics found will be representative of those of the whole population. A limitation to this approach was pointed out in Chapter 5. Collection of data by such means will lead to generalisations based on what the majority of a population is like, obscuring any large degrees of variability within a population and failing to identify important characteristics in minority groups. It is of course possible to learn more about specific groups by using a different definition of the population to be studied, and techniques such as cluster sampling and stratified random sampling exist to check on whether generalisations do indeed apply to specific sub-groups and areas. In relation to policy work, random sample surveys are likely to be used to provide us with baseline data which will help in defining what we believe to be the needs of the population.

While the random sample survey as defined above may provide information about population characteristics, a specific type of random sample survey – the opinion poll – may be used to tell us about the views of the population.[3] Opinion polls have been relatively little used in health services research.[4] It may be that they enjoy low levels of respect in some quarters because of the ways in which politicians have manipulated the use of opinion polls to say what the politician wants them to say. It is of course possible, by judicious selection of the population groups to be sampled and skilful wording of the questions asked, to go some way towards rigging the results of such a poll. However, it is equally possible to put effort into the construction of a fair opinion poll, and given that bias can consciously be built in to manipulate the results obtained using most research methods, if one tries hard enough, it seems unreasonable to reject the use of the opinion poll on these grounds alone. One must, however, have a full knowledge of its limitations as a method for finding out about public opinion. Being a form of random sample survey, it suffers the above-mentioned problems of dealing inadequately with the diversity of views in the population. Since relatively large numbers of people must be sampled, the questions must be relatively simple, both to limit the time it takes to complete each set of responses and, given the complexity of processing the resulting data, to analyse the poll findings. This frequently may mean that arguably *over*-simple questions are asked. Opinion polls will not come up with great new insights, or subtle ways of looking at problems. However, they may have great value in telling us whether there is overall satisfaction or dissatisfaction with a service, and telling us about the population's priorities for service improvements.

Opinion polls have been little used in any society where the views of the public have not up to now been taken seriously. However, as Al-Swailem

(1991) points out, careful construction of the protocol of questions to be used can overcome many potential weaknesses; the act of responding to an opinion poll is itself of developmental value in getting people to think about the issues, and may be instrumental in fostering a more positive and participative public attitude towards health care. With recent trends towards privatisation, the need to gain competitive edge may lead to health services taking the views of the potential consumer much more seriously, with a renewed interest in the opinion poll.

Purposeful sampling to collect information from the public

Random sampling methods are used typically when a large sample of people are being studied and the numbers falling into the different categories of interest within the study can be counted. Qualitative research methods are used when the aim is to conduct in-depth studies, perhaps interviewing people at some length over issues which do not lend themselves to quick questionnaire methods but require more open-ended discussion; in this case it may be impossible to take a large sample. In random sampling approaches there is a limit to the number of questions which can be asked, while in purposeful sampling approaches there is a limit to the number of people of whom one can ask them. It is quite possible to set up a qualitative research design which is based on a random sample, but one would only do this having chosen very carefully (i.e. purposefully) the population from which the random sample would be taken. The purpose of then taking a random sample would be to demonstrate fairness in approach, not to establish statistical generalisability.

There is a range of other ways in which a purposeful sample may be chosen. Space does not allow a comprehensive discussion of all possible approaches to purposive sampling here; Patton (1990) provides a detailed account. As will be apparent in the examples given here, it is often necessary to know something about the population or group from which the sample is to be taken, before purposeful sampling can take place. For instance, suppose that a study of community participation in health services was to be carried out, and the suggestion was that an in-depth study be conducted in two or three villages which might be taken as typical of the range of locations in the study area. One would want to establish that the villages selected were not unusually large or small for villages in that country; that they were not unusually distant from health care facilities, nor unusually well served. This would be *typical case sampling*. As against this, one might decide to sample in a way that picks out cases which are somehow defined as important. For example, a study of a surgical procedure might be based on detailed examination of all cases in which the patient died within three months of the operation. As another example, a review of waiting list procedures might be confined to study of the cases where patients waited more than a period of time which had been pre-designated as the maximum satisfactory waiting period. This would be *criterion sampling*. One might decide to sample only *critical* cases: suppose we wanted to study ways of improving the work situation for female health workers, we might decide to examine how the proposals work in a district known for its inability to retain female staff – 'if it can work here, it'll work anywhere'. One might choose to sample *extreme* cases – human resource policies in situations where prevailing staff morale is very high, along with others where it is very low. The important thing is that the sample is taken thoughtfully, in a way that is likely to provide answers to the research questions.

Focus group interviews These are a special form of interview which was first developed as a tool in market research, and has become extremely popular in health-related research. They are semi-structured group interviews, described in more detail below; they are based on a purposefully selected sample homogeneous in nature, such as a group of people who are relatively similar to one another in terms of the subject being studied. Thus a study of the local hospital's policies on maternity care might be the subject of an interview with a focus group consisting of young mothers. More informal group interviews are also possible, and indeed in some situations, such as in a village, it may be impossible to be too dogmatic about who will participate in a particular discussion; people may just wander in and out.

Group interviews Focus group interviews are a relatively formal way of interviewing a group of people together. Khan and Manderson (1992) have produced a useful description of how focus groups have been used in a health-related context, and make the point that this form of interviewing should be seen on a continuum, which goes from *totally informal discussion* with a group of people who happen to be together at one time, to *informal but focused group discussions*, to more formalised *focus group interviews*. The first of these might be the sort of discussion that one would have with a group of people on a bus, in a clinic queue, or while out shopping. The second type of discussion remains informal, and may start equally by chance, but the interviewer may seek to clarify what the group is saying and to check whether all are in agreement on important points. In a focus group, people (usually around 8–10) are invited to a meeting, and the interviewer (or 'moderator') defines the subject and steers the meeting along. The meeting is conducted for as long as it takes to exhaust the topic under discussion, either because a consensus is reached or because people agree to disagree.

Focus groups have become enormously popular in health-related studies, in investigation ranging from attitudes to disease, to health education related topics, to policy areas. So popular are they that one begins to wonder if this method is being over-used! Focus groups are just one method among many of constituting a sample to study, and one way among many of conducting an interview. Group interviews are valuable in that they provide a way for getting in-depth discussion, and not just scratching the surface of a topic; people are more likely to lose their fear of voicing an opinion when in a supportive group context. However, a group interview is only one *interview*; this is not necessarily a quick way of getting the views of a lot of people. There is a danger that focus groups have become popular just because people see them as a quick way to interview perhaps six or eight people at once. This both overvalues the results of one interview, and may lead to a rather simplistic use of the methodology.[5] Group interviews are sometimes best; sometimes individual interviews may work better; sometimes observational techniques should be used. Interviews based on purposive sampling are never substitutes for surveys based on random sampling; the two may, however, be complementary.

Undoubtedly, another reason for the popularity of focus group interviews is that they have come to be seen as more than just a research tool, indeed, as a means of facilitating a process whereby a community can discover its own commonly held views and reach decisions. Yet, as Thunhurst (1992) has pointed out, there are a whole range of group-decision support methods available which serve this end. These must be distinguished from group interviews, because normally the researcher determines the constitution of a group for interview. It cannot, then, be claimed that the group is a body developed by the community for its own decision making. In group interviews we are generally collecting information from the public, generated through the research process. Let us now move to considering how we might collect that information which the public *wants* us to have.

Receipt of information generated by the public

All the above discussion considers ways of getting information *from* the public; it is all too easy to assume that we need to be proactive in extracting information, and to forget that the public may well be trying to tell us things! Different approaches and attitudes lead to different degrees of receptivity to public statements. The policy maker or manager with a 'top-down' approach will attempt to centralise all decision making, and if s/he consults the public, will want to do so by setting the questions – working out the agenda. Indeed, one needs to be especially careful, because some of the methods which *claim* to gather community views actually place the community in a consultative rather than active role. For example, the 'community diagnosis' approach, which has enjoyed popularity in the health care field, is actually health worker-led.

The policy maker or manager with a 'bottom-up' approach may have a more open view of decision making and a more participative style. This would allow the recognition that questions from the inside may and should be aired in public debate, but that also any organisation should be open to receiving public views and criticism in the terms and concerning the issues which the public themselves choose to raise. Information may come from public meetings, where there has been no official or 'researcher' input; it may come from the simplest of devices such as a complaints box. Alternatively, information may come as demands from political parties and pressure groups. Some such information may be addressed to those running the health service; some may be gleaned from party statements or from the press. There are few rules about the way in which such information should be collected, but the wise policy maker will do well to remember that it is vital to keep one's ears open.

Of course, in any society, some people are able to shout louder than others. The better-educated are more skilful at putting forward their views and less intimidated by authorities and by professionals. The rich can bend the ears of the powerful, and even buy newspaper column inches. These are issues of power. In Chapter 7 the various ways in which power can be understood are discussed. It is of relevance here to mention some of the ways in which policy analysts set about considering what groups exist in society and how these relate to each other within the policy debate.

There is, for example, the notion of *stakeholder analysis* which is recognised by some international donor agencies these days as an important pre-project activity. The idea is to look at the chief actors in relation to a specific policy or activity, and ask for whom the success of the policy/activity is important. If a health project is to have a chance of success, then assessing who has a stake in that success helps one to speculate on how far the policy/activity will be supported and championed. Equally, the analysis may show that some stakeholders actually have an interest in the policy/activity being unsuccessful, and it is then important to take a sober assessment of how damaging this could be.

The mode of analysis, including the criteria for deciding who are the stakeholders and what are their roles, is not a singular methodology. One could do this analysis differently depending on how one views the distribution of power in society (see Chapter 7).

The underlying approach of some attempts at stakeholder analysis is *rational choice analysis*, which has received a lot of attention in the social science literature.[6] The tenets of rational choice analysis (RCA) stem from a recently increased interest in the economics behind politics – the notion that people behave so as to maximise their economic advantage comes in here. These ideas are creeping into many of today's debates about how organisations and groups in society relate, so much so that it is useful to be able to identify this underlying approach even if only to reject it. RCA and stakeholder analysis are not mutually exclusive, and some analysts would use the former to conduct the latter. RCA works on the basis of assuming that individuals (people or organisations) make choices on the basis of rational judgements about what courses of action will most favourably work in their individual self-interest. This is an interesting idea to explore. However, there are real problems about speculating on what is the self-interest of different people and groups. First, people deal in making choices with conflicting ideas about short-term self-interest and long-term self-interest. Second, 'self-interest' itself may mean quite different things in different societies and cultures, and even within different sub-groups in society. Third, people and organisations rarely have all the information they require in order to make rational choices. Fourth, there is a problem about the extent to which people make free choices (see Chapter 7). Fifth, there is a problem in assuming that organisations behave simply as an aggregate of rational individuals. Last but not least, do people really behave in a self-interested way all the time? Is it not possible to consider that some people and organisations are genuinely motivated by factors other than economic ones, and that their actions are driven by ethical, social or religious considerations? At risk of sounding contradictory after giving such an apparently damning list of objections, rational choice analysis may still have its uses; the main thing is that we remember its limitations.

Forms of analysis which stem from the rational choice approach include rent-seeking analysis and transaction cost analysis. Rent-seeking analysis attempts to study the way in which people operate, and compete with each other, to maximise their own gains from the resources of the government.[7] Transaction cost analysis has developed – and is continuing to develop – as a reflection of recent insights from microeconomics, from sociology and from organisational studies, that an important part of life is engagement in transactions of all kinds. We all buy and sell something, whether goods or our time and skills.[8] From economics has come a recognition that these transactions cost money; from the other fields the notion that transactional behaviour has to be understood in terms of people's ability to bargain, to take risks, to use their social connections and so on.

The way one sets about any of the above types of analysis will be conditioned by the way in which one views power relationships in society; the reader may like to look back at this passage after having read Chapter 7, and then consider how the different approaches might be combined with the different views of power.

Asking experts

There are many ways of asking for expert opinions about health policy issues; these have developed especially in relation to the activities of technology assessment, and also in relation to attempts to forecast 'futures' (future directions and needs). The simplest of these is *brainstorming*, which simply involves getting a group of people together and allowing them to throw out ideas, which can then be shared, discussed and evaluated. Another approach, which may involve great skill and know-ledge but is methodologically very simple, is *reconnoitre of technological advance*, in which experts are consulted as to whether knowledge of technological progress, with changing ways of doing things, may lead to a need to review policies. An example is a situation in which surgeons were so consulted, and forecast that the trend towards day surgery (where the patient is essentially an out-patient who is allowed a few hours' recovery time only) would become much greater because of new techniques such as laser surgery. This could occasion a review both of surgical admissions procedures and of the current use of hospital beds.

Slightly more developed approaches to forecasting, and thus to generating new policy options, may come from *scenario writing*. Here a group of experts from related fields, perhaps including both clinical and management specialists, come together and try to envisage the future, maybe developing different pictures of the future as seen from different initial assumptions. An area where scenario writing has been important is that of population projections. Health services need to be developed with future population structures and densities in mind, and scenario writing here may be based on most sophisticated *computer modelling techniques*. These allow future population size and structure to be determined, according to what might be expected given certain economic and political conditions. Of course, these models depend heavily on the assumptions on which they are based. One could spend much effort to achieve a sophisticated population forecast for a country which was then plunged from peacetime into war; the forecast, built on presuppositions about the peacetime state of food supplies, social stability and so on, would be worthless, as an entirely new assessment of birth and death rates as well as migration rates would be needed. For this reason, scenario writing needs to look at different possible scenarios, given different conditions.

Formal future-gazing: the Delphi technique

The Delphi technique was developed for future-gazing within the business world, specifically at the RAND Corporation in the USA, but it has been used in a wide range of circles including those concerned with health policy and with resource allocation decisions in the health sector. An issue is chosen for study, and a panel of experts are asked their views. Each expert is asked to complete a written questionnaire giving his/her judgement about a number of related questions. The same questions are given to each expert, but the experts do not meet. The written answers are taken and an attempt is made to produce a statement containing a consensus of all the views. This is then fed back to the panel individuals, who have a chance to comment on the validity of the resulting statement or forecast. If the comments are still at odds, a further attempt to modify the consensus statement is made, and the document goes between the experts and the panel convenor until a state of agreement is reached. The value of this approach is considered to lie in the fact that there is no face to face exchange of views between panel members, which reduces the chance of the most persuasive or powerful members receiving more than their fair share of attention.[9]

Towards decision making: consensus development conferences

Consensus development conferences have been widely used in the USA and Western European countries as an approach intended to make best use of expert knowledge (sometimes in combination with lay insights) in the development of detailed policy in specific areas. Consensus conferences are typically organised by academic institutions or bodies such as medical research councils. They have frequently been held on technology policy issues, but there is no reason why other policy areas should not be treated in the same way.

A topic is selected by virtue of its perceived topicality or importance, and a conference convened to discuss health policy in relation to that topic. For example, if the topic were the treatment of cardiac patients, an effort would be made to bring together surgeons and medical professionals able to comment on the best approaches to clinical treatment of such cases; nurses who are knowledgeable about the intensive care needs of acute patients, along with others who can comment on the post-operative need for nursing care; economists and health planners who can comment on the use of resources for such patients; families who have had to deal with the long-term needs of patients who have recovered from heart attacks, and patients or ex-patients themselves. A panel of speakers is selected, some lay and some expert; the panel may be chosen in an attempt to create a neutral basis for discussion, or with the intention of creating maximum disagreement in the first instance. Although there are likely to be some invited members in the audience, it is usual for the conference to be thrown open to the public – though it must be assumed that likely participants in such an event would hardly constitute a representative cross-section of the public. The conference would attempt to see the problem under discussion from a range of views, bringing in issues of efficacy and safety, issues concerning resource use, and political and ethical questions too. The panel has the task of listening to all the contributions and then, usually after a day or so of discussion, drawing up a consensus statement as the best approach to this problem, to be presented to and endorsed by a final conference session.

The consensus conference has been extensively discussed,[10] and sharp questions can be raised about the validity of the process in reaching any kind of true consensus; in particular it is often suggested that the audiences for such events should in no way be seen as 'representative' of the public at large. That said, the consensus conference may well have potential in a wider range of applications than that for which it has been used to date. Its attraction lies in the possibility of combining discussion on evidence of quite different kinds, and of being not only a tool for gathering of information but a developmental tool in seeking to build consensus.

Techniques to assist the decision-making process

All the foregoing discussion has involved consideration of ways of gathering information from or about people – individuals or groups, lay or expert. An overview of the means by which the health policy maker can gather intelligence would be incomplete without reference to the range of techniques for processing and evaluating available data, which are available to help decision makers choose between options. These include, most importantly, *operational research (OR) techniques* and *economic techniques*. Both involve a range of complex approaches which cannot be discussed at length in a short account of this kind. The more ambitious aim to provide ways of combining, and taking into account in an option appraisal, diverse considerations which may be valued in quite different terms to start with. This is done by finding ways to 'operationalise' the relevant concepts; that is, the researcher must find some sort of empirical indicator for those things which cannot be measured. For example, in *cost-benefit analysis*, every factor which is to be taken into consideration must be given a value in money terms; this seems easy when we think of the cost of treatments, but is more contentious when it comes to attempting to value human life, for example by considering the value of life insurance pay-outs or salary levels (is the life of a high earner then worth more than that of a low-paid worker?) Likewise in *multicriteria decision analysis*, some quantitative data, such as that for costs, will be included directly, while qualitative judgements will have to be turned into quantitative ones: characteristics such as 'practical feasibility', 'acceptability' and 'impact on education'[11] must be judged on a scale of 1–5.[12]

Clearly, such techniques will only be as good as the judgements fed into them. Proponents of option appraisal on the basis of economic or operational research techniques argue that these techniques merely clarify the issues, and that the debate about what variables should be included, and how, is an essential part of the process which serves to clarify perceptions among decision makers. Critics of such approaches argue that the production of complex data causes decision makers to forget the subjective judgements which have gone into the analysis, and makes the results look more objective than they really are. A more pragmatic, but significant, criticism is that the data requirements of some of the methods referred to here are considerable. Most health services managers would neither have the information needed, nor the means to collect it.

Cost-effectiveness analysis is a more limited technique than those just mentioned, as it does not attempt to value a wide range of variables – merely the cost of a particular activity or treatment, and its effectiveness. As this is much easier to do than cost-benefit analysis, cost-effectiveness analyses are more frequently conducted. Indeed, sophisticated variations on cost-effectiveness analysis, such as those involving a weighting of the effectiveness measure, such as QUALYs (quality-adjusted life years) and DALYs, are among the most frequently cited formal attempts at option appraisal today. Simple cost-effectiveness studies suffer from the problem that effectiveness is usually measured in highly specific terms; a measure of effectiveness for a renal transplant procedure would perhaps be comparable with the measure of effectiveness for a renal dialysis procedure, but would *not* be comparable with a measure of effectiveness for a family planning programme. Introduction of a method to create more generalised assessments of effectiveness, such as the QUALY runs into problems of operationalisation.[13]

In recent years, operational research practitioners have become aware of the criticisms levelled against traditional OR techniques, and serious attempts have been made to find methods which embody new approaches (Rosenhead, 1989). The resulting so-called 'soft OR' methods aim to reduce data demands, and recognise the need to combine data with social and ethical judgements; they aim to clarify rather than resolve debate, and to enable people to see more clearly what is involved in any particular decision. Such techniques, which might be classified as decision analysis rather than options appraisal, include soft systems methodology, robustness analysis, strategic options development and analysis (SODA), analysis of interconnected decision areas (AIDA), and metagame and hypergame analysis. These techniques do not so much add to our knowledge of an issue as provide another useful set of tools for exploring the dimensions of choice and developing consciousness of policy issues among groups of staff or the public. While such techniques do have a valuable role to play in the assessment of options available, some also offer a methodical approach to thinking about policy issues. 'Problem-structuring' has been a key area of development.

Choosing the technique or approach

The foregoing discussion has provided a broad overview of the range of ways in which health policy making can be aided by methods and techniques which either improve the knowledge base for decision making or studying past decisions, and/or are likely to be useful tools in the process of decision making and consensus building.

Table 6.1 summarises the range of approaches in relation to the various categories which were considered in the first part of this chapter; a number of the classifications made in this table merit debate. A technique will provide information which can be used in a variety of different ways. The same data could in principle be the basis for a descriptive or for an analytical study; some techniques might be equally well used in prescriptive or in explanatory studies.

These various techniques and approaches are by no means mutually exclusive. In research, it is well recognised that the use of multiple approaches, involving different kinds of data, different researchers, different methods and/or different approaches to data analysis, is possible. The name applied to this technique is *triangulation*. Such mixed approaches are

Table 6.1   *Applications of different approaches to finding out about policies*

	Observation/ secret customer	Random sampling – surveys	RS – opinion polls	Purposive sampling methods	Community meetings	Receipt of pressure group information	Receipt of media information	Stakeholder analysis	Brainstorming	Reconnoitre of technological advance	Scenario writing	Delphi technique	Consensus conferences	Operational research – decision analysis	CBA	CEA
Issue definition	✓	✓	✓	✓	✓	✓	✓		✓			✓				
Objective/ priority setting		✓	✓		✓	✓	✓	✓				✓				
Generating options				✓	✓	✓	✓				✓		✓			
Options appraisal			✓	✓	✓			✓	✓	✓			✓	✓	✓	✓
Implementation	✓	✓	✓	✓	✓											
Evaluation	✓	✓	✓	✓	✓											
Process (P) or substance (S)	P S	P S	P S	P S	P S	P S	P S	P	P S	S	S	P S	S	S	S	S
Prescriptive (Pr) or explanatory (E)	Pr E	E	Pr	Pr E	Pr E			E	Pr	Pr	Pr	Pr E	Pr	Pr	Pr	Pr
Case-study (CS) or comparative (Co)	CS Co	CS Co	CS Co	CS	CS	CS Co	CS Co	CS						CS	CS	CS
Descriptive	✓	✓														
Analytical	✓	✓		✓			✓									
Evaluative	✓	✓		✓				✓								
Consultative			✓		✓	✓	✓		✓	✓	✓	✓	✓	✓	✓	
Qualitative or Quantitative	*	#	#	*	*	* #	* #	*	*	*	*	*	*	#	#	#

* indicates an approach which is predominantly qualitative
# indicates an approach which is predominantly quantitative

regarded as producing more reliable data than would otherwise be possible. Quantitative methods may be mixed with qualitative methods; different interviewing techniques used at different points in a study; primary data may be combined with, and compared with, secondary data. The only limitations are time, cost, and what really makes sense in terms of the task to hand.

In selecting a combination of tools for policy study, there is also a need to consider carefully the way in which any likely policy changes will be received by those involved at different stages of the policy process, and the extent to which the emphasis of the study needs to be on the different ends which have been referred to in the course of this chapter. As we have seen, the value of some studies lies in the production of new information; the value of other studies lies in the *learning process* which the work itself engenders; some studies are seen to have a role in *validation* or in *development of consensus*. Again, a combination of these aims may be possible. Before embarking on a study, one should work out exactly what *is* intended, and which social or professional groups need to have involvement – either in the study itself or in receiving the results. Not only does one need to think about how to make such involvement a practical possibility, one needs to think about whether the end-products of a study will be accessible and comprehensible. Effort must be focused on the issues of most importance to people, on ensuring that those who will be involved in implementation of policies are likely to be in sympathy with the policies put forward, and that they have acceptability among a wider audience.

In summary

- A range of methods for both gathering information and collecting views is discussed. These are summarised in Table 6.1.
- These techniques and approaches are by no means mutually exclusive. A combination of different approaches will strengthen the resulting work.
- Policy studies may produce new information, may engender a learning process, and/or may have a role in development of consensus. Some policy studies may even achieve all three of these aims.

Notes

1. For this purpose, it may sometimes be appropriate to consider health service workers and professionals as 'public' and at other times, as 'expert', depending on the investigation.

2. Two recent examples are Huntington and Schuler (1993) and Maynard-Tucker (1994).

3. The following comment is taken from a footnote in Marsh (1982) and is too good not to repeat here: 'There is no objective basis to the distinction between polls and surveys other than the snob value of Latin-root words as opposed to Anglo-Saxon ones. Poll is to survey as cow is to beef. (I would prefer poll is to survey as beef is to cow – partial as opposed to whole and frequently cooked!)'

4. An excellent short discussion of this topic is provided by Al-Swailem (1991).

5. Kitzinger (1994) has commented on the fact that in using focus group methodology,

researchers seem frequently to ignore the interactions of focus group participants in the course of an interview, despite the fact that these interactions are in themselves a rich source of evidence.

6. For a basic description of the rational choice approach see Staniland (1985).

7. A useful assessment of the value of rent-seeking analysis in studying the allocation of public resources in developing countries is given by Moore (1990).

8. See for example Leblebici (1985). The transaction cost approach must not be confused with transactional analysis, which is the organisational psychology field which is based on analysis of human interactions as transactions, even if these two fields may one day meet somewhere.

9. Linstone and Turoff (1975) is a good source of information about the range of ways in which the Delphi technique can be used. Van Dijk (1990) compares the use of the Delphi technique with the use of interviewing techniques. While the Delphi technique is normally seen as involving the use of experts, or at least people who are literate, Oranga and Nordberg (1993) have used an adaption of the Delphi technique in a largely illiterate community by using interviewers to collect the views.

10. A useful overview of the way in which consensus conferences are organised in different countries is given by McGlynn, Kosecoff and Brook (1990). For a process evaluation of consensus conferences in the USA, see Wortman, Vinokur and Sechrest (1986).

11. These particular categories are taken from the decision analysis work on haemo-globinopathies conducted by Le Gales and Moatti (1990).

12. Such quantification is acceptable so long as it is remembered that such a scale gives a ranking; that is, indicates that a particular characteristic is present to a large extent in a particular case compared to others, but does not provide a measure of how much more. In other words, any numbers generated are ordinal, not cardinal.

13. These problems relate to the fact that the quality of life is basically conceived within a biomedical framework, and that different people have variable ideas about what constitutes a good quality of life. There is a debate about who should make decisions on these issues. A useful review is that of Fowlie and Berkeley (1987).

PART III

ANALYSING HEALTH CARE POLICIES

Introduction

The study of health policy requires the use of tools in the form of methods and approaches to study, and Part II consisted of a brief overview of the choices available to anyone conducting a study. Health policy also requires tools in the sense of ideas, concepts and criteria in order to create a framework for thinking about policies. Part III attempts to give an overview of some central concepts which are used in this way. The aim is to present an introduction to thinking in each particular area; as each of the concepts discussed is itself complex, each area of the discussion is of necessity limited, but will hopefully provide a starting point for the exploration of ideas.

In Chapter 7, the concept of power is examined; this concept is crucial to the analysis of the policy process and the extent to which different groups have any say in decision making. Some alternative approaches to understanding how power works in society are explained.

In order to see how power is used, we need to study the way in which people relate to each other, not only as individuals, but in and between different organisations. One powerful way of tackling this is to look at the roles people take on within organisational structures. To do this, Chapter 8 looks at professionalism – the characteristics which go with professional status such as that enjoyed by health professionals. It then looks at bureaucracy. Essentially this word is a collective noun for government officials, although these days it is recognised that there may be little difference between the ways in which government officials behave, and the behaviour of officials in other large organisations.

So we look at power, which provides the dynamic for the policy process, and at some of the features of organisational structure which are important in understanding how things happen in the health service. Each of the concepts introduced here has explanatory power in analysing how the health sector works as a whole and how it relates to other sectors, as well as in looking at the detailed affairs of the health sector.

7

Power

What fuels the policy-making process?

Why should a book on health policy need to discuss concepts of power? To answer that question, let us first look at some questions which might concern us in relation to policies:

'How are decisions made as to which health care activities get priority?'
'Who decides which groups will get what share of health care resources?'
'Should clinicians be allowed to dictate surgical policy without having to justify their decisions?'

These questions are important and the answers are not simple. Problems arise because each question exemplifies an area where, in all societies, some people make decisions on behalf of others, and where the will of some members of society is exerted over and above that of others. Those making decisions do not necessarily do so from a purely selfish point of view; indeed often the decision maker will strive to do what seems best for a community or group of people. The decision maker often becomes the subject of considerable pressure. The health service manager, for example, may experience pressure from a wide range of agencies in everyday decision making. These agencies might include competing health service agencies, government, health professionals, the public, aid agencies, multinational corporations and the media.

In the first part of this book we saw how people and groups within society value health care in different ways and want different things from it. This kind of discussion shows us that in looking at any health policy question, these varying individuals and groups will have their own conceptions of who will gain and who will lose from different courses of action. Policies will depend upon how the differences are resolved or how solutions are imposed. Chapter 2 provided an introduction to the people who are involved in the policy process, while Chapter 3 provided a structure for looking at this process. We thus have the beginnings of a conceptual model for analysing this process, but what is lacking up to now is any understanding of the dynamics which make the model work. By analogy, if we were to analyse the process of getting from one place to another by car, we would by now have some insight into the car drivers and into the structure of the vehicle, but no way of looking at what makes the car go. Just as cars need power, policy processes need power too – and that is what Part III is really all about.

If you were asked to consider what drives the policy process, power might not be the only reply you would give. You might come up with a list something like this:

- Power
- Resources
- Ideas
- Technology

I would argue that resources, ideas and technology are all important, but that the way in which all are used depends upon the distribution of power in society. The way resources are controlled is what many analysts would see as the most fundamental aspect of the use of power. Ah, you may say, but resources are not only problematic because of the way they are shared; there is a fundamental question about whether we have sufficient resources in the first place. At some level, undoubtedly, this is true. However, if the discussion is at the level of the health sector, the question of adequacy of resources could arguably be reframed as a question of resource distribution between the social sectors; an even broader question about the adequacy of resources for social welfare could be reframed as a question about resource distribution within society at large (an issue to be touched upon in Chapter 12).

Are ideas an independent variable? The answer to this question rather depends upon one's understanding of power, and the following sections take up this issue.

The decision maker may also feel that a particular decision can *only* be taken by experts or professionals, because technical choices are involved. The notion of technological determinism figures especially strongly in the health sector, perhaps because medical professionals have often played a major role in health policy making. At a certain level, of course, technical considerations do affect the way in which the health sector can do things. A public health strategy for tuberculosis would not get very far if it failed to recognise the technical issues connected with the lengthy antibiotic therapy needed to deal effectively with the infection. Modern surgical techniques in the Western world are transforming the way in which surgery is done, and will in time reduce the average length of stay in surgical beds. However, these are factors which play a supporting rather than a central role in the policy process. It is useful to see technical factors as constraints upon the way things can be done, and determinants of what activities may cost.

The same argument applies when we look at the technical content of management decisions. Walt and Gilson (1994) have argued cogently that a deficiency in the recent debates about health sector reform is the tendency for such debates to focus on the *content* of the reforms (the shape of the financing system, the role of the non-governmental organisations, etc) rather that on the *actors*, the *processes*, and the policy *context*.

The proposition here is that there are rarely choices where the optimum course of action can be determined solely on the basis of technical advice.

Decisions about health care are also decisions about resource allocation, about what we value in terms of health status, and about whose needs come first. Such matters go far beyond scientific and technical issues.

Why discuss concepts of power?

Power is that which enables us to do things. Yet discussion of power almost invariably focuses not on this positive aspect of power, but on the more negative insight that power held by one person or group is often over and against the power of another person or group. There is in society a whole network of relationships of power: between individual people, within and between families, between groups of all kinds. Within particular situations, people have different amounts of power depending not only on who they are, but on the part they are playing – thus the teacher is all-powerful in the classroom but a mere patient when after school she goes for medical advice. At the other end of the scale, a politician may be Prime Minister one day and face the firing squad the next. Power needs to be analysed in terms of the conduct of *all* the relevant actors in each situation; the teacher's power is relative to that of, in turn, her pupils and then her doctor, *in particular social situations*. As the politician is no doubt acutely aware, power is not only the product of complex social relationships. These are also *constantly changing* relationships; one day the Prime Minister takes decisions for and concerning the masses, and the next, the masses take decisions for and concerning the Prime Minister!

Power is a product of other personal or group attributes, and there is room for debate about which attributes are most central to the acquisition and retention of power. These include:

political power or the power to make decisions;
power based on wealth;
power based on hereditary status;
power based on professional status;
power based on ideas or knowledge;
power based on physical, military or other force.

To what use is power put? A useful typology is that of Foucault (1986: 211–212) who examined the different focal points for struggle – in other words, the applications of power or the areas where people confront power. He recognised three categories: struggle against ethnic, social and religious domination; struggle against exploitation which separates people from what they themselves have produced; and struggle against submission and subjection. This third type focuses on the status and rights of the individual to self-determination and to a place in his or her own community, against what may be determined by pressure based on knowledge or administrative expediency, to conform.

The essential thing here is to explore the kinds of power which are held by principal actors in the health sector, and what implications this has for the shape of health services. This account will only open up questions, all of which will have potential for further explanation. Now, in order to consider the way power is manifest in the health sector, we need to look at the ways in which it is manifest in society at large. Different theorists see this in quite different ways, and we shall examine some of the most important approaches in turn. These are:

pluralism
elite theory
Marxist approaches
structuralist approaches

The objective is not to attempt to say that any one approach is 'correct'. That would be quite impossible in a short section like this, as each approach is in itself complex, with a wide range of possible interpretations within each broad approach. Furthermore as Ham (1992) and Walt (1994) have pointed out, each approach can be considered to contribute to the range of overall insights available to us, for often each one focuses on different levels of organisation and decision making within society. Here we will look briefly at each one, attempting to summarise in a few words its most important features, and then comment on what that approach brings us by way of insights into health policy.

Pluralism

The pluralist approach is central to the policy literature of the Western world. The underlying conviction may be summarised as: 'S/he who shouts loudest gets heard.' To the pluralist, everyone in society has the chance to make their views known and to contribute to the decision-making process. Pluralist theory argues that power in Western industrialised societies is distributed between various groups. No group is totally lacking in power to influence decision making and no group is totally dominant. Pluralist theory might be traced back to liberal theories of democracy based on the importance of widespread political participation on the part of individuals. Later interpretations of democracy have viewed the process as a more limited institutional arrangement. However, later interpretations have also recognised that opinions are represented by pressure groups in society which on specific issues may play as crucial a role as do the political parties themselves.

Power is not equally distributed within the society as seen by pluralists. It is distributed most unequally and the least powerful lack the money, information, expertise and other resources which make it easy for voices to be heard. Power is a shifting attribute, which depends on the current combinations and coalitions of interests in different issues. This crude formulation of the pluralist position has had its adherents, but is most obviously to be criticised (by many pluralists as much as by outsiders) by the argument that, while power may well be widely distributed, it is certainly *unequally* distributed in all known human societies; to take this into account, the above summary needs an extra clause: 'S/he who shouts loudest gets heard, though some have the money to buy a microphone, a newspaper concern and/or a radio station, while others get listened to because of their hereditary/professional position.'

In pluralist approaches there is no concept of class in the sense of groups in society defined by their wealth and position (as in elitism) or by their relationship to the means of production (as in Marxism). The state is a passive institution which reacts to public policies developed as a result of group interactions; government agencies are simply one set of pressure groups in society, alongside others. There are individuals, interest groups and pressure groups, and indeed a great contribution of pluralist studies has been the level of detail with which such groups and their activities have been studied. Within a particular sector, different interests may prevail at different times; the only way in which we know about people's interests is through their expression of preferences.

The view of health policy (Ham, 1992) which follows from the pluralist position may be summarised in the following way. Views about health and medicine emerge out of the consensus in society; the medical profession plays a part in building this consensus but not a very special part; it is one interest group among many. The dominant or official view of health and medical care is the product of societal consensus and this provides its legitimation; the fact that this view has not really changed much over time confirms that consensus.

We shall not digress at this point to discuss whether or not views about medicine really are changing over time, but will note that out of just such analyses has developed the realisation that one cannot always take people's expressed preferences at face value. First, people may not say what they really think, because of a variety of pressures to conform to someone else's view. Second, is power being used to ensure that only certain items get on to the political agenda? We noted in Chapter 5 the concept of non-decision making, used to describe the process whereby some things never get discussed or taken seriously in terms of decisions and policies being made. Taken more broadly, these insights lead us to realise that it may not always be so important to ask why things happen as to ask why nothing happens; as Crenson, whose study of the politics of air pollution policy has widely been regarded as breaking new ground in this area, said, 'the proper subject of investigation is not political activity but political inactivity' (Crenson, 1971: 26).

In medical terms, one might consider in this way such questions as, 'Given that it is widely recognised that to focus on preventive medicine is often a more rational long-term approach to improving health than to focus on curative medicine, why is it that the vast majority of all health care resources in most countries still go to curative medical care?' Equally, one might ask, 'Given that in many developing countries, the rural health care infrastructure is minimal, why have resources not been diverted in that direction?'

Elite theory

The approach here might be summarised as: 'Not *what* you know but *who* you know.'

Elite theories place a central emphasis on the existence of a political elite which in any society will hold power, and which will consist of a network of those most powerful not only in political but also in business, military, aristocratic and bureaucratic circles. The world they dominate is, in decision-making terms, defined within a broader political class, including a variety of politically active people such as political leaders in opposition, trade union leaders, and whoever of the rich and influential are not in sympathy with, or feel their interests are not well represented by, the ruling elite. There is here a concept of a ruling class, and it is assumed that the state will follow the preferences of the elite. Agencies of government will fall within the elite network.

In thinking about the range of interests and sectors in society, one would on this basis expect to find a range of elites within sectors, for example an educational elite consisting of well-connected head teachers and vice-chancellors; a medical elite might consist of similarly well connected surgeons and heads of medical colleges, and so on. Such an elite would be expected to operate in the interests of the ruling class.

Such an analysis might be used to explore the ways in which health care resources are distributed; it might be posited that large hospitals are maintained in capital cities, even when a rational review of resource distribution would argue for reduction in the extent to which recurrent expenditure is skewed in this direction, because of the elite interests which demand such large hospitals. Similarly, an elite analysis might be used to consider why human resource investment in the health sector seems to go towards the training of more expensive doctors, when in many countries, considerations of cost-effectiveness argue for greater proportions of investment going into paramedical training.

Marxist approaches

For Marxists, power is to be understood by observing the position of individuals and groups in society in relation to capital – that is, to the real, productive wealth of society. Those who own the means of production in society – the factories, the plantations, the mines and the other enterprises which actually make things and create wealth – are the really powerful. By virtue of this ownership, these people are the ruling class or bourgeoisie Those who support the position of the bourgeoisie and the status quo are the petit bourgeoisie; these consist of what other people might describe as the middle classes, including for example technical and clerical workers, shopkeepers, professionals of all kinds. This group is regarded within Marxist analysis as being dependent on the ruling class for their own well-being, and their interests will often coincide with those of the bourgeoisie. Workers, termed the proletariat, have a completely different relationship to capital because they do not own capital or have a professional or similar skill, and therefore to make a living must sell their labour power by working for someone else. These notions about class are basic to Marxist thought, although much contemporary debate has focused on the extent to which societies can be analysed purely in these terms – how does one deal, for example, with peasantry or slave societies, or with developing countries where most of the means of production are owned by transnational capital, not local capitalists?[1]

In Marxist thought, the state is seen as playing a role in support of the ruling class, though with a degree of independence; essentially there is a partnership between those who own and control the state, and those who own and control the means of economic activity (Miliband, 1983). Government is an instrument of the state. Ham (1992) points out that the state's attitudes towards health care can be analysed in Marxist terms; insofar as the state supports capital's need for a healthy labour force, it will support health care; insofar as health services provide for those who are not working and help to maintain social satisfaction, they also are to be supported. However, the lack of value attached to non-productive groups such as the elderly and the mentally ill explains why their services are so often the 'Cinderella services'.

On a broader front, Marxists have looked at the reasons for ill-health and found its roots to be, at least some of the time, in capitalism itself. Thus Stock (1986) suggests that whereas some third world health problems are to be seen as the 'unwanted side-effects of development' which can be identified and systematically eliminated, these problems should properly be seen as *integral* to the kinds of capitalist development which take place in the developing (or underdeveloped) world.

There is a major difference between Marxists and pluralists regarding the way in which views are expressed in society. Whereas pluralists start from the point of people's expressed preferences – what they say they want – Marxists see the class domination of society as extending even to the realm of ideas. Gramsci, for example, has developed the view of ideology as 'a conception of the world that is implicitly manifest in art, in law, in economic activity and in all manifestations of individual and collective life',[2] through which the ruling class exercises hegemony or leadership over other classes. In this analysis, the 'official' account of health (see Chapter 5) would be seen as the view of health which supports the position of the ruling class, by for example masking the causes of illness which are rooted in capitalism. Likewise, the ruling class would in turn support the official account of health and defend it as its own. From this perspective the medical model of health has to be seen in terms of class consciousness. This is not, however, to say that non-Marxists in any sense fail to recognise the significance of 'official' accounts of health; indeed some schools of thought, such as that of the post-modernists, accord official accounts almost a political life of their own, seeing such accounts as playing a role of domination in society.

Structuralist approaches

The structuralist approach is not strictly comparable with the foregoing categories, in that while pluralism, elite theory and Marxism all attempt to provide ways of analysing the *whole* of society, structuralism works best when looking within an organisation. The basic idea is that at any one time there will be groups whose interests are well served by the way in which that sector is structured. These groups will be happy with things as they are, and will therefore defend the status quo. These groups have interests which we would term *dominant* (Alford, 1975). Other groups will be less happy, seeing that their interests would best be served by structural change; the interests of these groups are termed *challenging*. Yet other groups are unhappy or potentially so, their interests not being well served; these groups have *repressed interests*. This approach is not based on a class theory of society; it does however assume that within each sector is a dominant group, and it may be that links or affinities exist between different dominant groups; this would arrive close to the position of elite theorists. It should also be clarified that this approach does not depend on an analysis of pressure groups. In this way, it is to be distinguished from pluralist approaches. Indeed, as Ham (1992) has pointed out, the two are not mutually exclusive. Pressure group competition may well take place within groups sharing the same structural interests; for example, as the next paragraph will discuss, the medical profession may share a structural interest based on their overall professional position, yet may contain pressure groups who are in conflict over specific issues. Examples of the sorts of issue which would produce pressure group conflict might include levels of remuneration for consultants, working conditions for junior doctors, demands placed on community practitioners – issues which in their own right do not threaten the whole profession, but which are of great importance to some groups within it.

In Alford's well-known study of health care in New York City (Alford, 1975) the *dominant interests* were considered to be those of the medical profession, who were seen to be served by existing structures. These had been developed on the basis of *professional monopoly*, and in such a way as to depend upon – and in turn guarantee – professional control. Law, custom and organisational practices all worked in favour of the medical profession, who therefore needed to do nothing. This interest in pro-fessional monopoly was seen to be shared and supported by physicians in state and in private practice, by biomedical researchers, and by those in allied health professions.

The *challenging interests* were seen to be those of 'corporate rationalisers': the health planners and administrators. These were able to see that care could be reorganised in the name of providing a more comprehensive and cost-effective service for most people, and that this would imply change on a considerable scale. Alongside the health administrators in this group were the medical schools, the public health agencies, the hospitals and the insurance companies. This rich organisational mix had in common a shared interest in extending control over the work of professionals; this group was found to provide the majority of members for the various commissions of inquiry which had been constituted to look at the 'health care crisis'.

The *repressed interests* were those of the community, only minimally and occasionally organised into interest groups, and lacking both the organisational basis and resources for developing their position in a coherent way. It is obvious that the community is in most ways disadvantaged in speaking out against the more organised structural interests; the community has no organisational backing, no official account of health to which to turn. In order to speak out at all, the community must create organisational form out of truly disparate interests, and must formulate common concerns where these have never been articulated – sometimes needing to create new concepts and language in order to do so. Thus, structuralism provides an explanation for the fact that some concerns never make it to the political agenda.

Alford's analysis was made nearly twenty years ago, and Kronenfeld (1993) has recently pointed to the tremendous changes which the medical profession in the USA (and by implication elsewhere) has undergone since then. We shall return to this point in Chapter 8, but for the moment, while acknowledging that there is room for debate about trends in the position of the medical profession in society, it is still reasonable to suggest that in most countries the medical profession is of considerable importance. To conclude the discussion of power, it is worth noting in full the following quotation from Alford:

> The distinction between interest groups and structural interests is not made in the pluralist literature because of a tendency to assume that it is a societal consensus – values, rules of the game – which creates and allows the power and privileges of particular groups to continue. Thus, several writers have argued that it is the high esteem in which physicians are held by the society which provides them with the leverage they have to influence the content of legislation, the composition of administrative boards, and the actual implementation of policy. A widespread consensus in the society on the importance of health care and on the key role of physicians in performing this function provides them with the basis for the power and in effect grants them their professional monopoly.
>
> If I am correct in asserting the importance of dominant structural interests, then the causal order may be precisely the reverse. Rather than a societal consensus giving the doctors power, it is the doctors' power which generates the societal consensus. Or, in the language I am using above, the existence of a network of political, legal, and economic institutions which guarantees that

certain dominant interests will be served comes to be taken for granted as legitimate, as the only possible way in which these health services can be provided. People come to accept as inevitable that which exists and even believe that it is right. But this is quite a different argument from the one which says that because people believe in doctors, they give them power.

Thus, the formation of consensus around the provision of health services by a professional monopoly of physicians is not an independent causal force in its own right. Rather, the reinforcing and reproducing power of the institutions which guarantee the monopoly generates legitimating symbols and beliefs. (Alford, 1975: 17)

This structuralist position is very close to one recently argued by Petras (1989: 1955), a leading contemporary Marxist intellectual:

The thrust of our argument in the first instance is that power creates its own legitimacy. Those who do not have power seek it and not legitimacy. Power, in turn, revolves around class interests and control of the state. Those who do not have power nor are able to defend their class interests do not necessarily consider authority legitimate or illegitimate. They may pursue private interests, illegitimate or legitimate activity or collective political action outside the institutional framework of the political class.

In summary

- To understand how health care decisions are made, an understanding of power is needed.
- In the pluralist view, power is unequally distributed, but shifts between different individuals, interest groups and pressure groups.
- In the elite view, power in any society is in the hands of small networks of elites who are powerful because of their wealth and social position.
- Marxist approaches understand power in relationship to the ownership of the means of producing goods and wealth.
- Structuralist approaches are applicable mainly at the level of understanding power structures within organisations. Structuralists distinguish dominant interest groups, challenging interest groups, and repressed interest groups.

Notes

1. A succinct discussion of these points and others raised in this section is given in Bottomore's entries on 'Bourgeoisie', 'Working class' and related terms in Bottomore et al. (1983) and Harris's entry in the same volume, on 'Critics of Marxism'.

2. Gramsci (1971: 328).

8

Professionalism and Bureaucracy

The foregoing discussion has contained several references to the medical profession, and the section dealing with structuralism referred to the clashes that occur between medical professional interests and those of the 'corporate rationalisers' – the health planners and administrators. These groups are the main contenders for power in the health system, that is, to the extent that actors internal to that system have power. Medical power rests on professional status; administrative power is seen to be related to the existence of large bureaucracies. In much literature which makes such assumptions without analysing them, the professionals are seen as the 'good guys' and the bureaucrats as the 'bad guys'. Before sentence is passed, could there be a case for review of the evidence? This chapter looks at the role of professionals and bureaucrats, and at the extent to which each group has power to determine what happens in health services.

Professionalism

What is a 'profession'? As Jeffery (1977) points out, there are really two approaches to defining professions. The first is about values and attitudes. Taking this approach, the length of training and prestige of the profession are key features. On this basis, professions are occupations with distinguishing characteristics. These include:

- an ethic of service to individuals;
- specialised knowledge;
- training of their own new recruits, probably linked to a well-developed socialisation process;
- exclusive rights to practise in the area of their expertise;
- internal regulation of standards of practice and of admission;
- existence of a code of professional conduct.

This definition rests upon the pluralist position described in the quotation from Alford, above. Society grants a special place to the profession because of its inherent prestige, its long training and so on. This approach is quite useful in creating a descriptive picture of the professions, although it has to be said that this is somewhat to accept the professions' own description of themselves at face value.

The alternative approach starts from asking what are the central features of *professionalisation* – the process by which a profession gains its status and recognition in the first place. This brings us back to the structuralist approach to which Alford was referring. Here, the powerful position of the profession is based on *monopoly*; this is essentially a monopoly over a particular group of opportunities to provide specialist services. The internal regulation which the group can exercise helps to support its monopoly position; the professional group itself also regulates the supply of new members. The expertise which the group keeps to itself, combined with the long years of training required to enter the profession, enables the professionals to command high fees or salaries. Although the group does not enjoy total monopoly of the definition of 'good health' it is, as all but the pluralists would argue, extremely influential in this respect. As Ham and Hill point out (1984), the definition arrived at is notably set out in terms of what doctors can do to sustain good health or what they can do to restore it when it is absent – even though there are many determinants of health beyond medical practice.

Besides monopoly, the process of professionalisation results in *autonomy*; that is, the profession has the right to organise its own work and to set its own standards. This is a kind of *discretionary* power, and we shall consider this form of professional discretion below, in comparison with the discretion accorded to bureaucrats. We should, however, note the far-reaching nature of this autonomy, which extends arguably beyond the competence afforded by medical training into such areas as decisions about sanity versus insanity, normality versus criminality, life versus death.

How dominant is the medical profession?

The monopoly of medical care which the medical profession has tended to enjoy, at least in the Western world, combined with its autonomy, has tended to create a situation in which the medical profession has a great deal of say in relation to health policy. A major preoccupation of the literature concerning professions in recent years has been the subject of medical decline. Is the medical profession losing its dominance or becoming deprofessionalised? In the terms of the structuralists, is the medical profession losing its dominance in the face of the corporate rationalisers? It is certainly true that the medical profession has now become relatively less important in terms of the human resources within health care. This is not a decline in the absolute number of physicians, but, at least in the industrialised countries, the tremendous increase in the range of other health professions, which has come about largely as a result of the increased sophistication of medical technology. With new categories of technicians, therapists, records personnel and so on, there are now more than 700 different job categories in the health industry (Kronenfeld, 1993). Of course, medical dominance is not just about numbers; it is also about the kinds of health care on offer in relation to what people want, and what it all costs. In an interesting study of obstetrics in one hospital in the USA, Annandale (1989) found that medically qualified obstetricians were losing considerable ground to midwives, in terms of both where and how babies are delivered, and in terms of who attends births. These changes were seen both as an erosion of the dominant medical view of childbirth, among a public who are increasingly claiming the right to view childbirth as a natural and not a pathological process, and also as the result of a concern on the part of consumers, insurers, corporate interests, management and the state, for cost containment. For the structuralists, this would be a case of the repressed interests beginning to find a voice.

The broad debate about recent developments in the medical profession in industrialised countries has tended to work from agreement that the medical profession is in some way losing ground. There are two main schools of thought about how this is happening. One is the analysis, which might stem from either a structuralist or a Marxist position, that the profession is losing power and control relative to the big corporations and to the increasing institutionalisation of health care, a function of change both in health care financing and in the more socialised forms of medical attention which develop in a high technology setting. From this viewpoint, the medical profession is becoming *proletarianised* – more like workers than professionals.[1] The alternative approach is to argue that the medical profession as a whole still retains overall control in the medical field and of its own self-conduct; however, there has been a tendency for divergence to develop within the medical profession, with some doctors at the level of rank and file hospital practitioners losing status and autonomy, while others in senior, policy-making roles retain their status.[2] This process is described as *restratification*.

Some observers would argue that apparent threats to medical autonomy have yet to damage the status of the medical profession; Hunter (1993) for example has argued that in the UK a new breed of physician-executive is likely to play a key role, particularly at the level of purchasing of health services.

Health professionals in developing countries

What about the medical and other professions in developing countries? Here, the literature is much thinner; oddly so, given the importance which is attached to the role of professions in development (Bennell, 1982). Ugalde's early studies of the role of the medical profession in Colombia and in Honduras (Ugalde, 1979, 1980) indicated that in these countries the medical profession was indeed similar in many ways to its counterparts in the USA and Europe, and arguably comparatively *more* powerful, with doctors enjoying both a high level of personal wealth and a high degree of control over public health.

Ugalde himself suggests that medical dominance is a global phenomenon.

However, other authors (in particular Johnson, 1973) have suggested that in ex-colonial countries a different situation prevails. It is suggested that professions did not so much develop in the colonies as be exported, direct from the metropolitan context. Thus the professions in these countries were established on the basis of norms and goals derived from elsewhere, of dubious value in their new context. Professions were subordinate to the colonial state; they did not have a life of their own, and they did not develop as independent, autonomous bodies. Johnson viewed this as a consequence of the over-dependence of the new national professions on the state. Jeffery's (1977) work on the medical profession in India painted a picture of a profession losing ground, prestige and bargaining power; this was seen in terms of the dependent position of Indian scientific medicine, which had weak local professional associations and still used the British medical system as an important reference point. By contrast, Bennell's interesting study of a Ghanaian profession, that of pharmacists (1982), suggests that here, although the legacy was similar, the professions managed to defend themselves against the state, which has allowed them to maintain at least the status and patterns of remuneration which were inherited from the colonial period. Certainly there will be differences, which are to be understood in the context of differences in the detailed colonial and post-colonial history of each country, but it is probably fair to say that in the ex-colonies a significant local medical profession, with its own strong professional association and its own accreditation procedures even for the more esoteric areas of medical specialism, is a relative rarity. This is related to a situation in which medical professionals from many developing countries still, today, see European or American medical practice as a reference point, and is a vital factor to consider when attempting to analyse the continuing major problem of medical migration from the developing world to the West.[3]

Professionalism and complementary medicine

Professionalism is a developing feature of complementary medicine and traditional medicine in many countries. In developing countries, in colonial times, biomedicine was vigorously promoted, sometimes with force, while indigenous medicine was suppressed. In both India and China the ambivalent and opportunistic attitudes of the imperialist governments have been noted; indigenous practitioners were restricted in various ways and their activities controlled, but they were allowed to continue to practise because it was recognised that no other medical workers could be supplied in their place.[4] In Africa, a feature of the medical scene was the systematic restriction of indigenous medical practitioners. The authorities feared that cult leadership would threaten their rule, particularly after this happened in the Maji Maji rebellion in Tanzania.[5] Feierman (1986) has argued that a concerted effort was made on the part of the colonial authorities in African countries to restrict the activities and influence, and in essence to de-professionalise, indigenous medical practitioners, whose power they recognised as extensive, and whose influence among the local people they feared.

In the post-colonial period, however, a variety of medical systems have come to flourish in developing countries. In the African case, Last (1986: 11) sees these as 'a kind of "second generation" of traditional healers who have adapted their methods to meet the competition, and organised themselves to defend their right to practise against criticism from an expanding medical profession'.

In the UK and in other industrialised countries, the challenge of alternative medical systems has strengthened considerably in recent years. In the UK for instance, there is growing use of complementary practitioners; the Consumers' Association's 1991 survey showed that one in four of those asked had visited an alternative or complementary practitioner as against one in eight in 1986.[6] There are perhaps 18,000 complementary practitioners of various kinds in the UK as against 80,000 orthodox medical practitioners;[7] however, the number is growing. Statutory councils are being set up to provide the framework for professional self-regulation of selected complementary medical professions such as osteopathy, and within this framework training opportunities are tending to increase.

All around the world, scientific medicine is facing a growing challenge from complementary medical systems, and we can expect to witness a variety of scenarios, as in some cases the medical profession will fight a last-ditch stand to discredit the competition, in some cases will encourage the professionalisation of complementary practitioners as a subsidiary wing of orthodox medicine, and in some cases incorporate complementary medical practices into their own approaches.

Bureaucracy

Administrative power is sometimes seen to be related to the existence of large bureaucracies, and bureaucrats are seen as the 'bad guys'. The term bureaucrat today is used in common language as something approaching an insult, and that kind of perception exists on both the political left and the political right, many of whom would be horrified to realise that they have something in common with Karl Marx! Marx and Engels saw bureaucracies as a feature of the capitalist state, and failed to see that managements with bureaucratic characteristics would become prevalent in large enterprises in industry and commerce (Hegedus, 1983). It was Max Weber (1947) who first developed the proposition that bureaucracy was of great importance in analysing modern society, and attempted to develop a more objective assessment of the role of bureaucracies in modern society.

Weber's analysis is based on the notion of authority. To pluralists, authority may be an important driving force in society; Marxists and structuralists would perhaps wonder what power supports authority. Weber suggested that societies are based on three types of authority. Over historical time this has tended to be either *charismatic* authority, based on the following and the popularity of an individual, or *traditional* authority, based on a regard for the importance of traditions, and the status of those who exercise authority in the name of the traditions of that society. Weber suggested that *rational legal* authority has developed with the evolution of modern industrialised society. To Weber, the large modern industrial enterprises and the modern capitalist state demanded a new – bureaucratic – system of administration with permanent officials administering, and being themselves bound by, rules. Rational legal authority is based upon belief in the validity of such a system, and the rights of its officials. Such administrative systems were characterised by Weber as being based on administrative and/or technical rules; providing continuity, organisation, hierarchy, and the practice of recording in writing all important acts and decisions. Bureaucratic systems are run by officials who are employees and who have the following characteristics:[8]

1. They are personally free but subject to authority in respect of official functions.
2. They are organised in a clear hierarchy of officers.
3. Each office has a clearly defined sphere of competence in the legal sense.
4. There is in principle free selection for each official position.
5. Candidates are selected on the basis of technical qualifications. They are appointed, not elected.
6. They are remunerated on fixed scales.
7. The office is treated as the sole occupation of the incumbent.
8. It constitutes a career and involves a system of promotion.
9. The official has no ownership over that which s/he administers.
10. S/he is subject to systematic discipline and control in the conduct of the office.

Weber saw in such systems the potential for a tremendously progressive force within society. His vision was that bureaucracy allowed societies to dispense for ever with the irrational, even whimsical, authority of charismatic leadership, and with the innate conservatism of traditional authority. Bureaucratic systems, being based on rationality and served by officials whose position was constructed in such a way as to eliminate behaviour motivated by personal interest, would allow for a new era of human progress. Weber provided us with a model of bureaucratic behaviour which can be tested by comparison with real-life behaviour, and which can enable us to study whether such systems provide the advantages Weber foresaw – along with evaluating any disadvantages. This work has been of great importance in the development of organisational studies, and we cannot undertake a comprehensive review of all the debates which have followed from Weber's work here. Instead, the following section attempts to pick out a few areas of particular relevance to health service policies.

Do organisations today need bureaucrats?

The model presented above is an ideal model, and we shall need to ask if it normally works as it should. First though, we should ask whether the ideal model, working as it should, would be an optimal model for organisations today. The most obvious point to make is that this model is concerned with ensuring that organisations run on rational lines, and that subjective or unfair interests are where possible eliminated. What we have then, is a model for a continuing system but it is not an *output* model. In other words, there is nothing inherent in this model which provides an incentive for productivity – although of course in real life, incentives can be created. The model leads us to the question: if bureaucrats have no incentive to increase productivity, and if, unlike businessmen, they are not motivated by profit, what *will* motivate a bureaucrat's behaviour? The most likely scenario in general is that a bureaucrat will be rewarded if his/her empire expands – if the bureaucracy itself enlarges as a result of their efforts (Tullock, 1993: 112). This will not necessarily involve any activity related to the organisation's mission; indeed, Tullock suggests, the pathological case would be a businessman who 'devotes the bulk of his time to essentially leisure activities (some of which, like reading history or solving crosswords, may be located in his office), and time he devotes to work will be solely devoted to an effort to expand his office with no concern at all for its ostensible object'. This may be a caricature, but many of us will be able to think of organisations where the pen-pushers remain pen-pushers, while the real focus of the energy of those who will advance is related to a network of contacts based on the bars and life after office hours. The question, then, is whether these are people who are merely behaving at one extreme of the range possible in the bureaucratic model, or whether their behaviour has to be seen in terms of other factors entirely.

How close is the bureaucratic model to real life?

How often is the ideal model of a bureaucrat realised anyway? One might consider the example of item (4) on the above list; the principle of free and fair selection of officials. There is considerable debate about the extent to which employment selection processes in the UK and in the other industrialised countries are free of bias. In many countries, the same questions are valid; the source of bias away from selection purely on merit may be related to a tendency of appointment committees to select candidates like themselves (e.g. in terms of class, ethnic origin, gender). Sometimes the bias involves more overt prejudice, against people in specific ethnic groups, for example. Sometimes the bias is more positive and related to such features as political affiliations or family networks. Sometimes, as Wallis (1989) points out, bureaucracies must coexist with traditional forms of authority such as chieftainships. These observations point to a flawed process of selection; it is possible to raise similar questions about processes of promotion, of the functioning of hierarchies, and of the extent to which bureaucrats function free of considerations related to the interests of family and peer networks.

An interesting case study of Liberia (Brown, 1989) suggests that although the Liberian bureaucracy differs significantly from the Weberian model, one should not conclude that it is a 'failed bureaucracy'. Rather, Brown argues, it is successful in terms of local political conditions. The Liberian bureaucracy was lacking in a career structure, and positions within it depended little on technical competence. From the point of view of the small Anglo-Liberian settler elite, however, the bureaucracy was a remarkably efficient way of achieving political stabilisation. Administrative salaries were small enough to be funded out of local revenues, yet being paid in hard currency was considered attractive – the more so because the work demands were so small that they hardly affected the capacity of individuals to earn income on their farms and indeed from a portfolio of outside interests, some of which developed through their work. While conflicts of interest were nominally forbidden, they were actually tolerated and as individuals enriched themselves, the more closely they were associated with the political establishment. The resulting lack of incentive to move up the career ladder resulted in no apparent association between performance and reward. However, occasional promotion, albeit on an apparently whimsical basis, further served to cement loyalties. The ruling group achieved stability by allowing a small proportion of indigenous Liberians to better themselves.

Brown's work provides an explanation for the operation of an apparently irrational system – not, on scrutiny, irrational at all. All too often, explanations of weaknesses in management in developing countries stress cultural factors, providing a rather lame explanation for things. As Brown points out, an explanation of bureaucratic behaviour based on the political environment is much more convincing, and holds promise of seeing a way forward.

Some concerns about bureaucracies, then, are related to the notion that bureaucratic aims may be distorted by the local political situation. Other concerns tend to relate to the notion that bureaucracies may be too successful, becoming a source of power in their own right. One frequent concern – most notably voiced by the pluralists – is that bureaucracies will develop as groups within a managerial class, with their own interests, and functioning at times like a pressure group in their own right. The pluralist position matches this worry with an assumption that democracy will protect us from bureaucracy – though some authors (e.g. Tullock, 1993) have pointed to the tendency in UK society for bureaucratic decisions to be increasingly removed from the arena of democratic control (on the basis presumably that these are technocratic decisions which will be made rationally and therefore in everyone's interest). Elite theorists view bureaucracies as important sources of power in society and have devoted considerable concern to what they see as the increasing power of bureaucracies, focusing particularly on the problem that if bureaucracies are an elite, or part of one, they will seek the interests of that elite and not of citizens in general; one solution suggested is to widen the pool from which bureaucracies such as the civil service are recruited.

Marxists generally see bureaucracies as acting in support of the dominant class interests in society. A particular variant of this is seen in the work of Shivji (1978), who in considering class formation in Tanzania proposed that the growth in public bureaucracy, in the absence of a strong ruling class within the country, had led to the development of what he termed a 'bureaucratic bourgeoisie' – a privileged group who could to some extent manipulate the state and its activities in their own interest.

A wider range of left-wing critics have suggested that in developing countries, bureaucracies work in the interests of the few who are already privileged. Some authors trace this back to the origins of administrative systems in a colonial framework, where administrators from the metropolitan country were privileged over and above local people. Certainly administrative systems were shaped by colonialism. MacPherson (1982) has noted the way in which, within British colonies, bureaucracies operated much as they would if running a government department at home, patterns of work, recruitment and promotion being similarly modelled in the metropole as in the colonies. Yet, if anything, the colonial bureaucracies were encouraged to be more powerful and more centralised, since they were seen as the holders of power and the guardians of law and order in the colonies. Many developing countries today are trying to shake off the legacy of an over-centralised bureaucracy, designed more to maintain the status quo than to make policies work. Dwivedi and Nef (1982) have discussed the way in which, in post-colonial times, administrative systems in the ex-colonies have persisted, under the leadership of expatriates or of Western-trained local leaders, to be imitative of the West and unrelated to local traditions and needs; regardless of the local reality, the prescription has been scientific management. These authors suggest that this has produced administration devoid of content, reproducing the symbolism of other systems, but lacking the capacity to support implementation of appropriate policies.

Developing world bureaucracies have, however, come under just as much attack from the right, who argue that the state sector has become too big and that either the private sector must be given a chance to do more, or else bureaucracies must be forced to compete. Chapter 6 alluded to the notion of rent-seeking, a term for the way in which people operate to maximise personal gains from government resources. Supporters of rent-seeking theory argue that state bureaucrats are in an enviable position to achieve this. However, it has to be said that the same can be true of non-state employees. The state sector has no monopoly of any of the various sins it gets blamed for, from rent-seeking to corruption, to inefficiency and over-staffing.

Can doctors be bureaucrats? It is certainly the case that Weber saw bureaucracy as requiring both administrative and technical expertise appropriate to the specialist area, such as medicine. Indeed, as Ham and Hill point out (1984: 118), it may be seen as a shortcoming in Weber's thinking that he failed to foresee the inevitable conflict arising from authority based on administrative knowledge and that based on technical knowledge. Administrative knowledge fits well with hierarchical authority: the person at the top has both. Technical knowledge can be a problem for the maintenance of a hierarchical structure, because specialist technical knowledge may be possessed by subordinate staff in an organisation, hired because they can provide such specialist knowledge; or they may have acquired specialist knowledge by working in a detailed manner in one specialist area. Experts who play a dual role, such as medical professionals managing a group of clinicians, may themselves have to live with such conflict. Where medical professionals are organisationally subordinate to non-medical managers, the issue of professional autonomy can lead to major conflicts.

If, as the structuralists suggest, corporate interests in the USA and Europe are succeeding in increasing the level of bureaucratisation of health services, we need to consider the extent to which the physician-manager will become more of a bureaucrat, more of a manager. Some argue that physicians are increasingly coming under the control of lay managements; others that physicians have one way or another succeeded in retaining control. Yet if this control is retained by virtue of physicians becoming managers, some ask, does this mean that they begin to function with managerial values and interests, as opposed to clinical values and interests, uppermost?

Discretion

One of the ways in which conflict between the technical and administrative roles of medical professionals may surface is in relation to the amount of discretion which individual professionals may exercise. The concept of discretion relates to the degree of flexibility which is allowed within the context of making any particular decision, whether of a medical or an administrative nature.

Let us first consider administrative discretion. In the bureaucratic model there is an emphasis on rules, and indeed some would see the ideal situation as one in which every single decision which a bureaucrat has to take is dictated by application of the rules. In this situation the official in direct contact with members of the public is able to act even-handedly, basing his/her decisions on predetermined norms and criteria; where there is any query, the official can depersonalise the issue by reference to the rule-book. To the official at this level, public demand for services may seem like a bottomless pit; the rule-book provides a way of limiting that demand and of saying 'No' (Hudson, 1993). If an official has very little discretion to bend the rules, this may be favourable to those who are the most vulnerable in society, and who – lacking education to provide articulate arguments, family contacts to provide influence, or money to provide bribes – are otherwise unable to demand their rights. Within the health care field, administrative decisions taken on a daily basis may include those concerning who is or is not able to pay fees for health care, or whether or not to treat a patient who turns up at the wrong health care facility, either by arriving from another catchment area or by attempting to use emergency services when they are not an emergency.

While the bureaucratic model minimises discretion, professional autonomy tends to work in favour of extremely high levels of discretion; while administrative decisions need to be constrained by rules and criteria, it is considered that professional decisions will be constrained by technical considerations. Yet we noted earlier that some decisions that doctors have to make are arguably outside medical competence; certainly the extent of medical discretion raises important questions about ethics and human rights. Examples of areas where disputes may arise would include a surgeon's right to go ahead and remove an organ, having only had permission from the patient to conduct an exploratory procedure; a physician's right to decide to stop or withhold medical treatment of a patient whose life is in one way or another not thought likely to be worth living. (A recent example of this in the UK involved the decision not to give, to a mentally ill patient with no family, antibiotic treatment needed to ensure survival from pneumonia; this resulted in litigation.)

Clearly, professional decisions are not entirely distinguishable from administrative decisions, and conflict arises at the area in the middle. In the UK recently, some health authorities have become caught in conflict with the public because they have attempted to make rules about who might benefit adequately to qualify as recipients of certain surgical procedures – renal transplants only for under-sixty-year-olds; *in vitro* fertilisation procedures only for mothers under thirty-five. Directly analogous issues, concerning use of expensive medical technologies, are the focus of struggles between doctors and corporate interests, particularly within the insurance companies, in the USA today. In developing countries, it has been the medical professionals themselves who have at times reacted uneasily to attempts to limit prescribing practices to those treatments considered most cost-effective. Maybe, however, trends towards privatisation will limit bureaucratic interests within developing country health services, and medical discretion will again increase.

In summary

Professionalism

- Professions can be seen as occupations to which society grants a special place because of their inherent prestige, long training, high skill levels, etc.

- Alternatively professions can be seen as groups who have managed to establish a position of monopoly in relation to their expertise.
- As an occupational group becomes professionalised, it acquires autonomy in the sense of the right to organise its own work and to set its own standards.

How dominant is the medical profession?

- There is currently a debate about whether the medical profession is losing its dominance or becoming deprofessionalised.
- The medical profession is today only one among many professions operating in the health care field.

Health professionals in developing countries

- The extent to which the medical profession is powerful in developing countries is little studied, but would seem to be variable. Its position may be somewhat weaker in ex-colonial countries than in others.

Professionalism and complementary medicine

- In many countries, complementary medicine is becoming professionalised.

Weber and bureaucracy

- It was Max Weber who first developed the idea that bureaucracy was of great importance in analysing modern society.
- Weber saw within bureaucratic systems the potential for a tremendously progressive force within society, being based on rationality.

Do organisations today need bureaucrats?

- Although the bureaucratic model is a rational model for organisations, it may foster conservative policies rather than ones which would further progress and productivity.

How close is the bureaucratic model to real life?

- It is questionable whether real-life organisations, particularly in developing countries, resemble very closely the bureaucratic model; sometimes bureaucratic authority must coexist with traditional forms of authority.
- Different theories of power lead to different views about the role of bureaucracies, but most share a concern that bureaucracies should not hold too much power in society.
- As medicine becomes corporatised in the Western world, it is important to consider the extent to which medical professionals are becoming part of the bureaucracy – or subordinated to one.

Discretion

- Conflict may arise for medical and health professionals who effectively play a dual role as technical experts and administrators; this conflict relates to the amount of discretion which individual professionals may exercise.
- Within the bureaucratic model there is an emphasis on rules, and discretion is minimised; professional autonomy however tends to work in favour of high levels of discretion.
- These considerations may be of great importance in analysing the relationships between professionals, governments and corporate interests.

Notes

1. See, for example, McKinlay and Stoeckle (1988).
2. See for example, Friedson (1986).
3. Although this is the case, in a significant number of developing countries today the medical profession has been trained, or many of its number trained, in the ex-Soviet Union.
4. See Jeffery (1982) for discussion of the situation in British India, and Bibeau (1985) for an analysis of the evolution of present-day Chinese government attitudes towards traditional medicine.
5. See Feierman (1986).
6. Cameron-Blackie (1993).
7. The number of orthodox medical practitioners is calculated from the statistics in the *World Development Report 1993*. The number of complementary practitioners was calculated by summation of the numbers of practitioners registered as UK members of the various professional societies and associations representing the main branches of complementary medicine in the UK today (data from *Here's Health*, March 1995, London).
8. This list is a summarised version of that in Weber (1993: 105–109).

PART IV

KEY ISSUES IN HEALTH POLICY

Introduction

This part of the book looks at a number of areas of debate, chosen because these seem to be debates that run right through health policy making today. Chapters 9, 10 and 13 deal with questions of equal importance anywhere in the world. Chapters 11 and 12 are of more obvious relevance to middle- and lower-income countries, but even here some of the discussion and issues raised are generally applicable.

These issues are ones which, I believe, need to be understood by anyone with a responsibility in shaping health policies, or understanding those of others. Although the precise nature of the relationship between health and socioeconomic status is not well understood, we do know that some such relationship exists. Even defining poverty proves to be an almost impossible task, yet surely an essential one if we aspire to direct health care towards where it is most needed. Those who aim to achieve policies which will maximise health improvements should be aware of the debates in this area. The issue of poverty will not go away. Despite technical and scientific advance, despite Green revolutions and the constantly increasing ability of mankind to produce food and other essential goods, the poor increase rather than decrease.

This increase is related to, but not necessarily identical with, increased inequity in the world. Even the wealthier countries seem unable to banish the gap between rich and poor. It is not wholly clear to what extent the observable ill-health of the poor is better seen as due to poverty as such, and to what extent to disadvantage – and here we need to look at equity also (Chapter 10). The manner in which the health care cake is divided is a matter of justice, and it is also a matter of significance in the political life of any country. The concept of equity is at the heart of debates about resource allocation. Health care may be seen as an area of social welfare, and in organising any services, the question of who should benefit is fundamental. Frequently today, efficiency is given greater priority than equity as a policy goal. Yet can we afford to see either as more important? Can the two be reconciled?

Inequities on a global scale are considered in looking at issues of and approaches to socioeconomic development in Chapter 11. There are deep divisions in the world today between those who would argue that things are getting better, and those who would argue that the future of mankind is gloomy. The former see increased wealth overall, and scientific advance. The latter see the deepening divisions between haves and have-nots, and the worsening environmental prognosis – and wonder if global disaster lies ahead. Although a book on health policy cannot hope to debate these issues in depth, let alone resolve them, different views of development must be seen in this broader perspective and we must understand the implications of the development strategies pursued and pushed at any one time by the various international agencies. As this chapter shows, the emphasis has swung over time, largely between approaches which accord great importance to equity, and alternative approaches which give priority to economic growth. The health policy maker, as well as the analyst, needs to be able to distinguish one from the other.

Increasing our knowledge of all the above issues helps us to see what kinds of changes are likely to be for the better, in health as in broader development areas. Yet many efforts to improve the health situation for people, through improved availability of resources for health-related activity and through specific projects, turn out badly. All too often, investment in a certain area stimulates a flurry of short-lived activity which is not seen through in terms of enduring improvement to the quality or quantity of health services available. In order to address these issues, Chapter 12 considers the topic of sustainability.

Of course, an issue which runs through all policy debates today, and indeed currently configures debates about equity, development and sustainability, is that of market-based approaches to health care versus public sector-based approaches. Chapter 13 argues that the debate about privatisation underlies many other issues of current importance, such as the broad question of health sector reform – and is fundamental to the attempt to establish effective policies with concern for poverty and equity. No debate is currently of greater importance to health and health care.

All these issues are big issues; they are part of the fabric of national and international politics, and apparently outside the arena which the health service manager can hope to inhabit. Yet this is in line with the approach established earlier. Decisions which at first sight appear to be located at the organisational level, on closer inspection are contingent upon questions which are the stuff of high-level decision making, and what Walt (1994) has called 'high politics'. The policies adopted on such questions may be regarded by the manager as part of the environment rather than part of the decision-making system over which s/he has any control or even influence. Some will say, let us then be philosophical; if we cannot influence these things, let us be pragmatic and worry about other issues which are more directly within our control. This would, however, be ostrich-like. It is of great importance to understand what is going on in a broad sense, if we are to locate new policies sensibly. Failure to understand the environment means failure to see the likely consequences of any policy decision. This is true both in pragmatic, practical terms – is it likely to work? – and also in political terms – will it fit in with the overall approach of the day? Will it be well received by the public?

It is also in these broader debates that health care policy becomes infused with values. What broad social goals should health care serve? What if any structural obstacles stand in our way in achieving these? It is hoped that this section will help the reader to clarify the underlying values of different approaches, and establish which offer a fruitful way forward.

9

Poverty

Ill-health and deprivation

Within much of the literature on policies in the fields of health and more broadly of social welfare, there is agreement that special attention must in some way be given to the status and needs of those who are most disadvantaged in society. However the nature of this concern, and the range of views as to what should be done, span a wide spectrum of political views, and a wide spectrum of views about the nature of health and of disadvantage. It is generally agreed that those who are worst off in any society are likely to be least healthy; the same people may have few means of getting help, and their ill-health may leave them less able to help themselves.

Broadly speaking there are four approaches to the problem of ill-health which is associated with deprivation: (1) we can aim to treat the health problems of those who are deprived through special provision for that group; (2) we can regard deprivation as the root cause of ill-health and aim to improve the health of the deprived by improving their material position; (3) we can aim to provide health and welfare services which are accessible to all, while not laying on special provision or attempting to define who is deprived; (4) we can aim to eliminate inequalities in society and thus, by implication, the problem. Clearly the health sector has the capacity to implement some of these approaches better than others; the fourth solution is most unlikely to be instigated from within one social sector. However it is of great importance, in deciding what *can* be done, to distinguish different types of approach and ask which of these might be effective.

In order to provide the basis on which that judgement can be made, this section discusses the nature of disadvantage – is there an objective condition called 'poverty'? To what extent do we need to look beyond simple calculation of people's material assets in assessing deprivation, and consider social justice and the extent of inequality in society? How should we view the relationship between poverty and health?

Defining poverty

If asked to explain what poverty is, most of us would probably refer to people not having enough money, or perhaps not having enough food.

Isn't this rough definition adequate to explain something which is only too familiar to most of us, admittedly at second hand? Actually, it is not adequate, because it is almost impossible to achieve general agreement about what is 'enough'. People have different needs and priorities, and different ideas about what constitute basic needs. One does not seek to discuss the definition of poverty in order to indulge in philosophical debates; the important thing is that there are several different ways of looking at poverty and none is wrong, but each stresses different issues. The way in which we look at poverty is likely to have a major effect on the policies we develop.

Many people would feel that the *biological* approach to poverty is the common-sense way to deal with the most basic needs we have; in this approach deprivation is equated with not being able to have enough food, and poverty with malnutrition. However, it can be very hard to say whether or not people have enough food. First, there is the problem that even experts disagree as to how many calories of food intake per day constitutes an adequate amount for average people. As Townsend points out (1979) 1,000 calories might support an adult 'provided he remains inert' and is living in a favourable climate. More usual estimates for an adult male are around 3,000 calories, but absolute need will vary considerably depending upon what activity a person is called upon to do in a day. Bhattacharya et al. (1991) in their interesting study, 'How do the poor survive?' noted that in the rural West Bengal setting of their research, the adult male members of the extremely poor households studied were surviving on an average calorie deficiency of 34–37 per cent – yet these people were capable of hard physical work. Doubt about the nutritional status of a group of people is not confined to developing countries. In the 1960s, malnutrition was found to exist on a massive scale in the USA, yet while the Citizen's Board of Enquiry into Hunger and Malnutrition estimated that 10–14.5 million Americans were seriously underfed, the House Agriculture Committee reported that there was little actual hunger, just people eating a badly balanced diet (Chelf,1992).

Nor do the ambiguities end here. How would we treat the case of someone who has enough money for food provided that they only eat the same staple food *all the time*? Would we consider a peasant to be rich or poor, if s/he is growing ample food on their plot but has no cash income at all, and needs money for taxes, school bills and medicine, not to mention clothes? This last question raises the issue of essential possessions other than food. In the aforementioned West Bengal study, a notable feature of the households studied was their lack of material possessions of even the cheapest kinds, along with persistent debt. The authors concluded that observation of available shelter, clothing, bedding and household equipment was much more revealing than study of calorie intake in differentiating the very poorest households.

Consideration of extreme cases may be helpful here. To many people, famine is the ultimate starvation scenario; a situation in which people die for lack of food. Yet de Waal (1990) points out that if one analyses specific notable famines of this century, mortality has not been closely associated with starvation as such; other factors including lack of water, spread of infectious diseases, and violence have been more important, constituting, de Waal suggests, a 'health crisis' – a changed disease environment caused by social disruption. The social disruption is not just food shortage, but a major threat to people's way of life, and in response people do not merely seek the next meal. In fact they are more likely to safeguard their *assets*, giving priority to maintaining animals, buying seed, etc., than merely buying food. This rational behaviour indicates that an analysis of poverty based merely on current calorie consumption would be a superficial one.

The biological definition alone will not do, and an important part of the reason for this is the *relativity* of poverty. As Townsend eloquently explains, our ideas of what is essential in life are socially conditioned:

> Tea is nutritionally worthless, but in some countries is generally accepted as a 'necessity of life'. For many people in these countries drinking tea has been a life-long custom and is psychologically essential. And the fact that friends and neighbours expect to be offered a cup of tea (or the equivalent) when they visit helps to make it socially necessary as well; a small contribution is made towards maintaining the threads of social relationships. (Townsend, 1979: 50)

In the same way, the items considered essential in a personal wardrobe are to be viewed on a relative scale. So is shelter – to some, a house must have three bedrooms; to others, any structure offering some protection from the elements would be an asset. Items considered luxuries in some communities, such as a television, will be necessities in another.

Relativity varies depending upon the frame of reference one uses (Sen, 1981). A poor peasant may compare her lot with that of a rich peasant or her landlord. Knowledge of life beyond the village boundary may increase dissatisfaction. Chossudovsky (1991) offers some interesting comparisons; for example, in 1990 when an agricultural worker in Peru's northern provinces was receiving $7.50 per month, the domestic price of many consumer goods was higher in Peru than in New York; in 1991 a Filipino peasant had to work for two years to earn what a New York lawyer earned in an hour. As Chossudovsky goes on to point out, in World Bank estimates, only 19 per cent of the population of the Caribbean and Latin America is 'poor' – a proportion comparable with that estimated by the Bureau of the Census for the United States. Yet estimates of under-nourishment in Latin America indicate that this is the condition of more than 60 per cent of the population, a proportion hardly likely to be equalled in the USA even on the most pessimistic estimates. Whatever the shortcomings of the biological approach, such observations do lend a useful sense of perspective to the discussions.

To some authors, the relativity of poverty is seen as so important that poverty becomes, for them, an issue of inequality. One ceases to worry about the details of individual incomes and what is needed to support a family, and looks instead at the contrast between the highest and lowest incomes in society. In a society where there are substantial income differences, the frame of reference of the poorest will certainly be enlarged and they will arguably *feel* more deprived than they would do if everyone around them was poor. Again it is illustrative to consider an extreme case. As Sen (1981) points out, a society where a certain level of inequality exists could have all its members living comfortably. If external change then caused a decline in income for everyone, some people would perhaps be left in real hardship – though the degree of inequality would not have altered. It would seem unrealistic to argue that for these people the level of poverty was no worse. A concern for equality is probably more appropriately considered in relation to the notion of equity, or social justice.

We should note that for some people, the important thing is to arrive at a 'policy definition' of poverty: an official definition of the way in which poverty can be identified and assessed. 'At last,' some readers are saying, now we can get down to a *useful* way of looking at this. Unfortunately, as Sen (1981) again points out, there is a dilemma, related to the fact that a policy definition may refer to the standards which a society feels *should* obtain if all its members are to have a reasonable life, or may refer to the standards which it can realistically hope to help all its members to meet. In other words, the poverty line may be pitched at a realistic but extremely low level which is the basis for development of policies ensuring that no one will really starve, and in a generally poor society this may be the most anyone can hope for. This may well leave people feeling that the society makes harsh judgements, when it is apparently content to leave people with no shoes, no resources to cover schooling or housing and no security, yet still say that these people are not in poverty. On the other hand, the same society, creating a more 'humane' definition of the poverty line, would find itself faced with unrealistic demands. There is no technical way of resolving this dilemma; the poverty line will be set through a decision-making process which will be based not only on people's feelings about what is deprivation and what are basic needs, but also about how much wealth the richer are prepared to forgo to subsidise the poorer. One approach to making such decisions is offered in Thunhurst (1985).

Lastly, it is worth giving attention to the notion of poverty developed by Sen in his now classic *Poverty and Famines* (Sen, 1981). This author, while arguing that any consideration of poverty must in some way consider people's ability to avoid starvation, suggests that the crucial issue is not just *having* food at a particular time, but a person's *ability to command* food. This latter quality is related to what Sen calls *entitlements*. Entitlements are the means through which people have a right to food. Thus someone has an entitlement to food if she grows that food; someone else may have an entitlement because they grow food for someone else and thereby earn a wage. In some societies the unemployed may have an entitlement in the form of a right to unemployment benefit. Others have entitlements because of their position within a family, and as Sen points out, the rules and conventions about who is entitled to what are sometimes really complicated. Poverty and starvation are related to a failure to have enough entitlements. This is a powerful idea, even if some limitations have been recognised, both by Sen and by others.[1]

Wealth and poverty as determinants of health

We have now had the opportunity to look briefly at the range of views that exists concerning poverty and deprivation; in this section we shall consider how socioeconomic status relates to health. The main concern of studies in this area has been to attempt to increase our knowledge of what makes for good health. It is easy to postulate that at least a reasonable nutritional standard is basic to health, and clearly people below a certain poverty level in any society are likely to be unable to achieve such a level – even if the foregoing section has demonstrated the difficulty in defining such standards and levels. One can, however, speculate that income-dependent factors beyond food come into play and give health advantages to the better-off. One can also hypothesise that those who can afford health care will be advantaged in relation to their health status. Lastly, one can consider the possibility that too much affluence may not be good for health; could health status be prejudiced, beyond a certain material level, by the diseases of affluence?

The debate about what determines good health ought to be a wide-ranging study, for health is a complex and difficult concept and its determinants are not only biological and economic but also historical, social and political.[2] In practice the main focus in the literature on health determinants is on studies which endeavour to show statistical correlation between good health and measurable variables. Study of factors which may have a causal link to low mortality has largely been conducted on the basis of sophisticated multiple regression analysis, looking not only at correlations of mortality rates with different individual factors, but also at different combinations of factors. Good summaries of such work are to be found in Mosley (1985) and in the two conference volumes by Caldwell et al. (1990). As discussed in Chapter 5, studies demonstrating correlation do not (and cannot) prove causation; this must be borne in mind when using this literature.

The study of health determinants is further limited in practice to an overwhelming focus on mortality rates rather than on morbidity or disability. The recent work conducted in relation to the 1993 *World Development Report* is impressive in being a major effort to surveying world health in broader terms, and as more work is done in this direction, it may be that the debate on health determinants will likewise be better informed. Arguably, information about conditions of ill-health is more important to the organisation of health services than is information about mortality. However, it is reasonable to argue that mortality rates are important (if not perfect) indicators of the average health status of a population. Furthermore there are good reasons for the use of mortality data, in that morbidity data is much less often available and suffers from lower levels of reliability (it being obviously easier to know when to record a death than to be sure about a particular diagnosis). In particular, the records from which historical demographers work give mortality data, but little else. In the discussion that follows, the focus is on the determinants of mortality rates because that is the focus of the literature reviewed.

First, let us look at the links between socioeconomic status and health status as they have been studied in whole populations. The most frequent approach to studying these links is to look at the relationship across a range of countries, of mortality rates and per capita income. Per capita income is less than perfect as an indicator of socioeconomic status, partly because this measure does not express social position, which may well go with material privilege not expressed as income. Both measures, of income and of mortality rates, are averaged across the whole of a national population, and there is the disadvantage that such measures hide inequalities within that population. Nonetheless, it is of interest to ask whether there are broad correlations between them. An early study by Preston (1975) concluded that there was certainly some link between mortality and income, but that there were other factors which influence mortality rates over and above income.

What is the range of 'other factors'? There is no one answer to that question, because there exists a vigorous debate in the area of theories of mortality change. Globally, there have been surprisingly great and consistent improvements in mortality rates during the twentieth century.[3] A particularly interesting and comprehensive summary of many aspects of this debate is provided by Murray and Chen (1993).

Let us look briefly at five approaches to explanations of mortality change:

- income
- socioeconomic differentials
- modern health care
- cultural and behavioural change
- combinations of the above

Income

Public health debates have always recognised that income, and thus living standards, is important as a determinant of health. Perhaps the best-known of all researchers on this subject is McKeown,[4] whose work with colleagues studied in detail mortality declines which had taken place in England and Wales. They noted that there were major improvements in mortality rates long before modern medicine could have had any part to play in improving health. By exclusion of other possible explanations, they attributed the drop in mortality rates as being due to improvements in standard of living and food intake. These improvements, they argued, would cause improved resistance to disease and result in a drop in mortality caused by infections. It should be noted that studies by Mata (1978) suggest that infection is itself a major cause of malnutrition, especially in children. This does not contradict McKeown's work, but may suggest that these factors are synergistic and likely to cause a downward spiral of ill-health.

One does, however, need to treat income/mortality data with care. A correlation of these two variables may be explained in many ways. For example, Antonowsky (1993) has suggested that people who are self-employed or in professional positions may have less illness resulting from stress than their less skilled worker colleagues, because those who have more control find that their work has a 'sense of coherence'; they find their work meaningful and they will feel able to cope. Workers who feel undervalued, who may have to take orders they don't understand, lack a sense of coherence and thus are more likely to be stressed. Morbidity and mortality related to such stress would show up in the statistics among those with lower income.

Socioeconomic differentials

In the literature on mortality change and health improvements, it is generally accepted that within populations there are mortality differentials and differentials on other available health indicators, related to socio-economic class status of individuals. It is difficult to provide a succinct and consistent demonstration of this assertion, because it is often hard to come by relevant data. Few governments collect health statistics classified by social class or occupation, and many are unenthusiastic about confronting social inequality. Some of the clearest evidence comes from the UK, where the Black Report (Townsend et al., 1988) assessed health and mortality in the British population on the basis of six social classes, divided according to the occupation of the head of the household. Members of the lowest social class (V) experienced a mortality rate more than twice as high as members of social class (I); this inequality was mirrored in the morbidity data, and persisted even when age and race were taken into account. Feinstein (1993) has reviewed both UK and USA data on inequalities in health. In the USA there are no occupation-based statistics, so studies are based on data relating to income, to geographical area of residence and, perhaps most frequently, to ethnic origins.

In other countries even more diverse indicators have been used, including religious affiliation, educational attainment and land tenure or ownership. One useful recent study in Mexico, however, does analyse infant mortality in relation to the social sector of the persons economically responsible for support of the mother.[5] This study was able to disaggregate national infant mortality data into occupational categories, consisting of agricultural and non-agricultural workers, the latter group being broken down into working-class salaried and non-salaried workers, and middle-class manual and non-manual workers. Considerable differences were found between sectors, the lowest infant mortality rate occurring in middle-class non-manual workers (27.9 deaths per 1,000 births) and the highest rates in agricultural workers (48.6 deaths per 1,000 births). A useful review of relevant literature covering child welfare and infant mortality in a number of developing countries is provided by Cornia (1984b). So far as can be judged, social class mortality differences are higher in Britain and in developing countries – particularly Latin America – than they are in the USA (Preston and Haines, 1991).

Two observations are important in relation to socioeconomic differentials and mortality. The first is that where there have been absolute decreases in mortality rates, class differences persist. If, for example, we look at data for infant mortality in the USA, we see that from 1900 to 1980, and again up to 1990 (Wise and Pursley, 1992) the differential between the mortality rate among white infants and black infants has been constant: about twice as many black babies die, even though absolute rates have declined. The reasons for this are not known.

The second area of interest is that societies where income differences between individuals and groups are not great, enjoy lower mortality and higher life expectancies than do societies with the same income but with greater inequalities between individuals.[6] Thus Sri Lanka, China and Kerala State in India all have life expectancies of over seventy years, in line with much richer countries. Murray and Chen (1993) suggest that multiple factors may determine the relationship between income and longevity, including the effectiveness of public policies and of expenditure on health. They also point out that the relationship between personal income and mortality at the household level is non-linear. This means that for a poor country, a small increase in income will have maximal effect on life expectancy if it is equally distributed.

It is possible to speculate on reasons for this. Where a society is relatively egalitarian, prices will settle at a level which most people can afford. One would expect to find relatively few people actually going short of food or other essential goods; fewer able to afford housing with water supply and sanitation, and so on. In contrast, where a society is based on an uneven distribution of wealth, prices for some goods may be quite high, being what the market can bear. This may mean that a significant group of people are in poverty. Likewise, an egalitarian society may be equated with more people having greater control over their work situation, and thus a greater 'sense of coherence' (see p. 110).

Modern health care

A major debate in public health, and one which is of significance from a health policy viewpoint, revolves around the question: to what extent has modern health care been instrumental in mortality decline? The activity of many governments and international agencies, UNICEF being the best known example, have in recent years been based on a belief that massive application of child survival technologies, such as oral rehydration therapy and immunisation programmes, can improve children's chances even in times of economic squeeze. Murray and Chen (1993) have, however, argued that the evidence for any major impact of these activities on mortality rates is negligible. They point out that there is little correlation between the precise areas, periods of time and age groups covered with child survival technologies, with those time periods and groups which show persistent mortality declines. Furthermore, many areas with a substantial mortality decline have enjoyed no health service improvements at all. Of course, this is not to deny that good health care has benefits for those who receive it, and such an argument does not in any way suggest that we should accord low priority to health services. For one thing, health services are about much more than saving lives. For another, Murray and Chen's observation was limited to the distribution of specific technologies – oral rehydration therapy and immunisation – not about the distribution of health services. This point is significant in policy terms if we think about selective approaches to health care, not if we are concerned with an integrated approach to health service development.[7]

Cultural and behavioural change

An area to which increasing attention is being paid in the debate about health determinants is that of social, cultural and behavioural determinants of change. An increasingly significant sector of the literature in this general area focuses on such areas as educational standards, especially for women,[8] female autonomy in decision making, and levels of knowledge about health as determinants of health-related behaviour and thereby health. Even the work of McKeown (see p. 109 above) has been challenged on the basis that McKeown failed to recognise the importance of the role played by public health campaigns and changing personal hygiene in the mortality decline in Britain (Szreter, 1988).

There is a range of approaches to the way in which people see cultural and behavioural determinants fitting into the health picture. In order to discuss these, it is useful to refer to Table 9.1, which is reproduced from Feinstein (1993). Feinstein makes a useful distinction between factors which directly affect people's health (his 'life span' factors) and those which affect their health indirectly by affecting their ability to access and use health services. Second, he recognises that factors in both of these categories may be classified according to whether they are of a 'material' nature or a 'behavioural' nature. Let us first focus on the latter division. Clearly, there are observers who strongly believe that good health hinges largely on behaviour, and that to improve health we must persuade people to change their behaviour. Others believe that good health is determined far more by social and material circumstances, and that to improve health, we must focus on these, and stop 'blaming the victim'. This debate has

Table 9.1 *Source of inequality*

Type of explanation	Life span	Access to and utilisation of health care system
Materalistic (access to resources)	Housing, overcrowding, sanitation, transit mode, occupational hazards, environmental hazards	Ability to purchase health care, ability to purchase pharmaceuticals, regular physicians
Behavioural (psychological, genetic, cultural)	Diet, smoking, exercise regime, leisure activities, risk taking, alcohol and substance abuse	Comprehensive medical information, 'playing the system', following instructions, self-diagnosis, and awareness of recurrence

Source: Feinstein (1993)

been a key factor in determining the nature and focus of health education and promotion activity.

Other observers would argue that the divisions represented here are false or misleading. In part this is because the table focuses, as many such analyses do, on the individual rather than on the wider society. Thus smoking is a life-span factor, attributed here to behavioural causation. This appears to imply individual behaviour. We could, of course, consider at this point the behaviour of the tobacco company that profits from the sale of cigarettes. Many aspects of individual behaviour need to be analysed and debated in the context of a discussion of the role of the state and the big multinational companies, as well as the media, in defining the boundaries of, and shaping, individual behaviour.

If we consider the materialistic factors listed in Table 9.1, more questions arise. We can see that they are actually a mixed list, in the sense that some of the factors may relate to the economic status of the individual (e.g. housing and overcrowding; ability to pay for health care) whereas others may relate to the economic status of the state (e.g. sanitation, environmental hazards). The extent to which different factors are a matter of individual liability will relate to the extent of privatisation within a particular economy.

Then there is a confusion as to where the dividing line really comes between 'materialistic' and 'behavioural'. Let us consider diet. A poor person may know what foods are good to eat, but may not be able to afford them, or may be prevented from buying the most nutritious foods by virtue of being unable to afford to travel to the best shops. Likewise if we think about risk taking, a moment's thought tells us that workers who depend on a wage for support of their family, and who have little chance of employment other than the job they currently do, are likely to suffer risks due to occupational hazards rather than complain and risk losing the job. Yet here, occupational hazards are seen as materialistic factors. The distinction between materialist and behavioural becomes hard to uphold.

Feinstein (1993: 305) does not himself suggest that his table, though helpful in explaining many of the ongoing debates, is wholly adequate. He suggests that many of the studies of variables fail because they do not model the interactions of different variables (1993: 310). A positive approach to this type of problem was proposed by Packard et al. (1989). These authors note the polarisation between studies which focus on health behaviour, community dynamics and household decision-making, for example – micro level decisions – and those which focus on international politics, national investment in health care, and other macro level processes, as they call them. They suggest that the two need to be linked by 'interdisciplinary study of the impact of ownership, power and the technosocial details of livelihood systems on human welfare'. Thus, they suggest, 'For instance, the imposition or removal of a subsidy on the price of a stable foodstuff, the legislation and enforcement of codes for hazardous chemicals, the setting of interest rates, and programs of agrarian reform all have an impact on health.' (p. 406)

Combinations of the above

We have looked at some length at the role of cultural and behavioural factors, because these often are favoured in considering strategies for health improvement. It is tempting to seek to change the health behaviour of individuals; this kind of intervention is not politically contentious in the way that challenging the behaviour of a multinational company, for instance, might be. As we have just seen, however, behaviour happens in a social and political context. There are many complex connections between public policy and the actions of individuals. The framework proposed by Packard et al. attempts to bring to bear a political economy approach to these questions, and this is helpful in analysing the issues, and useful in its reminder that we need to understand the historical context in which social change happens.

Murray and Chen's challenging analysis (1993) also calls us to look at mortality – and thereby health trends – over a long time scale. In particular they discuss the apparent puzzle that, despite major economic setbacks in many low-income countries in the 1980s, child mortality rates continued on a downwards trend. In considering possible explanations for this, they too propose that the processes determining health status are complex and long-term, and they suggest that we need to think in terms of a nation's 'health stocks'. These are the range of assets which a society might have in relation to health. Physical assets include health care infrastructure, as well as other infrastructure such as schools and water supply. Social assets include things like the existence of a social security system, political stability, and participation in a civil society. They suggest that long-term health and mortality trends need to be seen, not in terms of this year's health campaign or last year's epidemic, but in terms of the way in which the colonial legacy may have left some countries with little to equip them to contribute to health, or perhaps the way in which cumulative post-independence investment in society may be driving health gains today.

As the authors point out, these challenging ideas are highly speculative. Yet the arguments make sense, and need to be given due consideration since they have important consequences for health policy. If governments, and others involved in funding health care such as aid agencies, were to take this approach seriously, they would need to forget short-term plans for single disease campaigns, and focus rather on long-term improvements in health stocks. Achievement would not be equated, as is so often the case, with achievement of task-oriented, short-term activities, but with significant investment in infrastructure and in the capacity of the health system.

In summary

Ill-health and deprivation

- Policy approaches to ill-health associated with deprivation can focus on the ill-health or the underlying deprivation, and may involve services or activities for the whole population, or be targeted to the needy.

Defining poverty

- Poverty must be seen as deprivation, and this does not only refer to lack of food, but more broadly to basic needs essential for survival.
- It is acknowledged that this set of needs is not fixed or absolute, but in practice a matter of debate and political decision making.
- The definition of poverty which is arrived at in a particular society may take account of a range of factors, including living conditions, commodity prices, judgements about acceptable living standards, as well as the degree of inequality in that society.
- Deprivation may be considered in terms of food, or a broader definition of basic needs; alternatively it may be considered necessary to look at people's assets and potential for creating wealth, and/or the extent to which they possess entitlements.

Wealth and poverty as determinants of health

- There is generally broad agreement that there is a relationship between socioeconomic status and health status, although the nature of that link is debated.
- Over the twentieth century there have been consistent improvements in mortality rates, and it is of interest to consider what factors have been of importance in this respect.
- Groups of people with lower incomes certainly have high mortality rates. The reasons for this may be complex.
- Mortality rate differences between social classes have been observed in

the UK and deduced in the USA and, where evidence exists, in other countries.

• Even when there have been absolute decreases in mortality rates, class differences persist.

• Societies which are relatively egalitarian enjoy lower mortality and higher life expectancies than do societies with the same income but with greater inequalities between individuals.

• There is a major debate as to whether modern health care interventions have had any significant impact on mortality rates.

• Much recent work on health improvement focuses on the importance of cultural and behavioural change. However it is noted that health behaviour often depends more on material and social determinants than on cultural ones.

• The recently proposed notion of 'health stocks' may be valuable in interpreting long-term health and mortality trends, and in assessing the future potential for gains.

Notes

1. Sen himself recognises that the entitlements model has limitations; for example, it focuses on legitimate rights to food, and in a society where law and order breaks down it would be difficult to analyse entitlements in any meaningful way. Furthermore the model, as Sen has developed it, does focus wholly on food and starvation; and de Waal (1990) has pointed out the limitations of this approach. Other authors argue that the approach has the potential to be adapted to consider not just food but a wider range of benefits, including health care (Turshen, 1989).

2. The approach used by Turshen in her study of the 'political ecology' of disease in Tanzania (1984) is of interest as a broad-ranging look at health and society.

3. This seems to be the consensus view, despite the fact that international mortality data often has to rely on estimates and even 'guesstimates' based on whatever statistical source appears most reliable, even if perhaps outdated. Murray (1987) gives a critical review of the way such data is collected, and its shortcomings.

4. For the work of McKeown and colleagues, see McKeown (1976), McKeown and Brown (1955), McKeown and Record (1962) and McKeown, Record and Turner (1975).

5. Bronfman (1992).

6. See Murray and Chen (1993).

7. See for example, Unger and Killingsworth (1986).

8. The orthodoxy concerning female literacy maintains that provision of education for females makes them better mothers, or better at attending to the health of their children; this conclusion is reached on the basis of multivariate analyses which generally demonstrate a positive statistical relationship between female education and infant mortality or child health indicators. It should however be noted that one rare study attempted to disaggregate infant mortality data on the basis of social sector, (Bronfman, 1992). For the Mexican data analysed, mothers' education within particular social class groups did not produce an improvement in the level of infant mortality.

10

Equity

What is equity?

In the course of the discussion on poverty, we referred to the notion of equity or social justice. At this point we should look a little more closely at what is meant by equity, and the way in which looking at equity can help us to look at welfare.

The concept of equity is related to that of fairness. Although the words are similar, equity should not be confused with equality. To illustrate this, imagine that you have a loaf of bread; you are asked to take the loaf with you into the nearest shop in your neighbourhood and to distribute the loaf to whoever is in the shop at the time. First, you are asked to distribute the loaf according to the principle of equality, so you count the number of people in the shop, and give them each the same number of slices of bread. Second, you are asked to distribute the bread according to the principle of equity. This means that you are asked to find some way of sharing the bread which is just. On this occasion you cannot simply divide the bread mathematically. You will have to find some criterion for deciding who gets the most. You may decide to go into the shop and ask everyone whether or not they are hungry, and then give most to the hungry. Alternatively you may decide to judge on appearances, and give the most to those who look poor. Of course, if you happen to know all the people, you may actually know who is poor! On the other hand you may feel that you need more sophisticated means tests in order to decide on what is a fair distribution. Aiming for equality, the loaf was divided equally, regardless of the possible inequalities in hunger, nutritional status or wealth between those present. Aiming for equity, the loaf would be divided on the basis of unequal shares for unequal people.

Equity and social welfare

The extent to which welfare measures are based on an attempt to achieve equity, is a central theme of social welfare studies, and one which is often pursued with the aim of giving people more equal status and resources by an unequal distribution of benefits. Yet as Le Grand (1982) has said:

> The strategy of equality has failed. It failed primarily because it implicitly accepted the ideology of inequality. Any alternative strategy has to have as an essential part an attack on that ideology; otherwise it too will fail.

What Le Grand describes as the 'ideology of inequality' refers to a notion of individual responsibility for welfare. Although concern for justice has always been at the centre of the dynamics of Western society, at least as dominant and important, and arguably more so in recent years, has been the notion of individual freedom of choice. Those following the 'ideology of inequality' position may well opt, in the division of the loaf, for equal slices for everyone on the basis that all should have a chance to share any benefits, but that the rich should not be asked to take responsibility for the poor. *Redistributive* policies would not be on the agenda. Taxation systems based on the ideology of inequality make everyone pay the same tax, irrespective of what people can afford or earn. The African colonial hut taxes or poll taxes worked in this way, as did the UK poll tax of the Thatcher government.

Freedom of choice is seen as a notion to be counterpoised against equity, because pursuit of equity implies redistribution of wealth in society. To parody the concern, if I choose to work hard and thus earn a lot of money, is it then fair that some of that must be redistributed to others who have less? As Le Grand suggests, this comes down to a question of whether we think that distribution is an outcome of individual choices – his own position being that distribution cannot be seen in this way, as it is empirically verifiable that for most people their degree of wealth or poverty was in no sense a matter of their choosing. This latter argument might be accepted by the apologists of the ideology of inequality, but while acknowledging that the distribution of wealth in society is unfair, they will then argue that to improve equity is in itself too costly in terms of personal liberty. Personal liberty, it is said, is of intrinsic value, and also is valued because it supposedly promotes diversity, whereas equity would stifle diversity and promote cultural drabness.

Of course, personal liberty is fine for those who can opt for various fascinating careers, who have leisure time and disposable income. For those who work from morning to night and still cannot earn enough to support their families, who are lucky if their children have the chance to learn the basics of reading and writing, what meaning can it have? For these people, only the promotion of equity can open up any hope of contributing to society and culture.

The two counterpoising strands – equality and justice, and individual freedom – become mixed in varying proportions to produce a whole spectrum of ideas and attitudes within the field of welfare. In some countries, it is accepted that equality should be an *aim* of social services. In others, policies actually aim at attaining minimum standards for all, not equality as such, and while for some that will be considered as a desirable end in itself, in others even minimum standards will only be considered an aim if that is necessary to promote a more efficient economy. The World Health Organization's (WHO's) Health For All strategy, as it was elaborated in the documents of the Alma Ata declaration on Primary Health Care (World Health Organization, 1978) and the Health for All

Series (World Health Organization, 1981) contains all of these elements,[1] as might be expected in documents which required the approval of all WHO member states.

A further important distinction in the way we think about welfare relates to the view of the function of welfare. For some, welfare is only ever used to 'mop up' the worst of society's problems. Money spent on welfare is, then, pure consumption; if money must be spent to provide a minimum of humanitarian relief, then it is spent reluctantly, keeping costs to a minimum. This has been termed the 'residual welfare' approach. Its opposite is the 'institutional redistributive approach', which sees expenditure on welfare as an investment in society. Here, efforts to create a greater equality in distribution of wealth and resources in society is seen as the basis for giving everyone the chance to thrive and to be productive. Money spent on welfare is not seen as money lost irretrievably, but as capital expenditure towards a more vigorous society and economy. It goes without saying that these basically different approaches produce radically different welfare systems.

We shall look in more detail at the ways in which equity might be developed as a principle in relation to health services. At this point, however, it might also be useful to ask whether social welfare in general has, or has had, any redistributive effect. MacPherson and Midgley (1987) write:

> There is a good deal of evidence to show that social policies in the Third World do not serve a 'first line' function, redistribute resources on the basis of need or cater for the whole population. Access to social welfare is highly unequal, and because social policies have been copied from the industrial countries, they are largely inappropriate to local conditions.

In other third world social sectors just as in health, patterns of distribution of services reflect a colonial legacy, having been established to serve local representatives of the colonial regime and their employees in the first instance, not the population at large. This has tended to perpetuate privilege, which is often enjoyed by the upper and middle classes of today. For new services which have developed, the middle classes are likely to be the main consumers. This has been demonstrated repeatedly; for example Jones (1990) argues that third world housing schemes are time after time too expensive for the poor; MacPherson (1982) shows how social services have an urban bias, with schemes such as day care for children serving almost exclusively the needs of white-collar workers, and Stock (1988) argues that environmental sanitation campaigns in Nigeria have tended to benefit the rich, not the poor as might have been expected.

Equity in health care

Inequalities in health affect people's health status, and also their ability to use and gain access to health services. If we decided to aim for greater equity in health care in order to improve this situation, where would we start?

Let us first contrast two extreme approaches. A simple approach would be to say that each citizen has the right to a certain amount of health care; each is given their share of 'health care credits' for each year and may spend these as they wish. This approach, put into practice literally in this way, would of course be absurd, offering health care to many fit and healthy individuals with no need for care, and leaving others short of the care needed to cure their complex ailments. However, one should not dismiss this idea as totally unrealistic; it is the approach that best fits for those who subscribe to the 'ideology of inequality', and although it has not been proposed as a recipe for health care, conservative politicians in the UK have certainly seen this kind of approach as a realistic proposition in the field of education. The opposite approach would be to say that all citizens have a right to health for all. As we have seen, the determinants of ill-health are broad-based, and to seriously strive for health for all would imply attempting to eliminate social inequality. Thus, health for all must be a goal of society at large, and can only come on to the agenda when equity is built into all aspects of our lives. Health services alone are unlikely to be able to do this.

Even if it is not possible for health services alone to achieve equal health status for all, it is certainly possible for health services to pursue policies aimed at using most resources for those who most need them – in other words, redistributive policies. Let us look at the practical approaches possible in order to do this, recognising that problems are encountered in trying to construct an approach to defining need, as well as in attempting to find a fair way of sharing out resources. 'Need' is difficult to define, since people's conception of their material status is subjective, and depends on their standard of comparison. Furthermore, power is unequally distributed in society, and the least powerful have the greatest difficulty in articulating their needs and in getting anyone to listen. This argues against the alternative solution of allowing people themselves to make demands, rather than attempting to define need. Certainly, a framework is needed within which people can have their say about what health care should offer. However this needs to be within the framework of a resource allocation mechanism.

Two basic approaches to creating a resource allocation mechanism for health services are possible. One is to start from a medical definition of need in terms of prevalence of particular diseases. However, practically it is difficult to translate different levels and combinations of disease prevalence into an index of overall need and deprivation. Attempting to assess overall need from a summation of specific needs also has problems. We only know the specific needs of people who make them known to us, and we don't know the needs, for example, of those who do not come to the health service. Furthermore, not all needs for health services can – or should – be such that we can define them as illness. No existing attempts to measure the burden of ill-health manage to encompass needs for care and comforting, nursing, or the kinds of measure which enable the disabled to lead an independent existence. Even more significantly, such attempts, in focusing on ill-health, tend to encourage us to forget that health care involves positive measures for health, through public health work and health promotion activity.

What is the alternative? If we accept that ill-health is generally linked to deprivation, then a way forward is to estimate need on the basis of overall disadvantage. One of the few attempts to do this at the level of national planning is to be seen in the approach which Zimbabwe adopted after national independence (Segall, 1983). Here, resource allocation started from a broad analysis of the social groups in the country, and it was decided that the important distinctions to be made were between the well-to-do urban dwellers, the poor urban dwellers, and the rural poor. Infant mortality rates for these three groups were known to be in the ratio of 2 : 7 : 10. This was enough information to enable decisions to be made about which health service districts should be most favoured in plans for development. Of course, as well as the infant mortality rate, the planners could use other measures such as under-five mortality rate, mean income per capita, or less direct measures such as literacy. Any of these measures should show the same relativities between social groups.

Use of such approaches can help us decide who needs to be most favoured in resource allocation, but a strategic approach is needed, in thinking how to implement a policy which, in bringing increased benefits to some, is almost certain to bring decreased benefits to others. Even those who subscribe to the 'institutional redistributive approach' described above, recognising that the long-term strategy makes sense, may balk at loss of personal benefits *now*. The Zimbabwe approach was thoughtful in this respect (Segall, 1983). In order to implement the decision to favour certain health districts, a long-term strategy was developed. Least-favoured districts would not *lose* any income; they simply would grow at an exceedingly slow rate. Most-favoured districts would grow at a much faster rate, in order to reach the required differential over a period of years.[2]

Supposing that we find a way of redirecting health resources so that more expenditure goes to the needy, have we resolved the problems of equity? While having taken a major step, other problems do remain. Mooney (1983), among others,[3] has suggested that it is important to consider whether the allocation is planned in terms of *expenditure*, or in terms of *inputs*, or in terms of *access*. Up to now, we have been talking solely in terms of expenditure. However, this may be inadequate if, for example, money buys different amounts of things in different parts of the country. Commonly met examples include differentials between capital cities, where certain costs, such as construction costs, may be high, and else-where. Equally common are high health service costs associated with remote areas, where merely transporting necessary supplies makes all activity more expensive. It could be that resource allocation should not be considered in units of money but in inputs; the attempt would be to ensure that region A and region B had equally good supplies of medicines, even if the cost of supplying the two regions was considerably different.

Aiming for equity in terms of inputs does not remove all the problems for the disadvantaged. We have only taken into account *health service costs*, but in any use made of health services there is also a *cost to the patient*. For example, a patient who lives a long way from the health centre is disadvantaged in terms of access because the cost to that patient is greater, in transport bills or time, whenever they wish to use the health service. To restore equity here, it is necessary to consider providing transport, or sending the health workers out on visits. In other words, we need to aim for equality of *access*. Access is a complex issue. People's access to health services depends on geography, as in the above example; however it also depends on a complex range of other factors. For example, a literate population may be said to have better access to health services than an illiterate one, for we know, empirically, that literate people do make use of services offered. We also know that ethnic minority groups may find themselves unable to make full use of the health care services offered, either because they are unable to communicate with the health workers or because they find the health workers unsympathetic to them. To develop equal access for all, we need to focus on the needs of different social groups, thinking not only of overall levels of deprivation, but also of class, gender, ethnic origin, geography, age and other specific parameters which stand out as important in particular communities, or which the communities themselves raise as important. To overcome problems of access, we need to work with people so as to jointly overcome *all* the barriers which prevent potentially equal utilisation of health services.[4]

Can equity be efficient?

The previous section has shown that if we are serious about giving every-one the opportunity to make use of health services, we need to make quite complex arrangements. Clearly, these arrangements are not without cost, and this introduces one more dilemma which is to be tackled if health policies are to be pro-equity. The dilemma, according to authors such as Mooney (1983), is that the more we work for equity, the greater is the risk that we will have to lose a degree of efficiency in the way health services are offered. For example, suppose that the distribution of health facilities is planned according to a criterion that no person should have to travel for more than two hours to reach a health centre. If this is to be fulfilled even in areas of extremely sparse population, we shall find ourselves providing health centres for a handful of people at great expense. Analogous examples follow from dealing with other problems of access. However, is this a case of decreased efficiency? An efficient approach is one that minimises the cost of doing something. If the health service decides to bear the cost of bringing health care to the patient, instead of the patient bearing high costs to get to the health service, that is not in itself a less efficient approach. If the health service decides on a high-cost means of bringing the service to the patient, that *is* an inefficient approach. What is important is to clearly establish goals, and then to find the most efficient way to fulfil these.

Targeting has been described by Frances Stewart (see section III.3, prepared by Stewart, in Cornia, 1984a) as 'a powerful way of increasing the efficiency of social expenditure'. In recent years, with renewed consciousness that poor countries, and in particular their governments, have few resources to spread over potentially enormous numbers of people, there has been great interest in shifting policies from those which would spread resources very thinly, to those which target available resources at the most needy. A concern to protect the very poorest people from the worst effects of structural adjustment reinforced this, and finally the trend towards privatisation in many health services has created an urgent need to ensure that the poor are not totally neglected. Targeting sounds efficient, and attractive. Let us examine how it works in practice.

The account which is mentioned above provides an excellent review of the pros and cons of targeting. Attempts to define a target population, who will be the sole beneficiaries of a certain type of action or subsidy, hinge on being able to define this group clearly and to find a way of ensuring that the right people receive the benefit. Stewart's discussion focuses on food benefits, which is a good example to use in discussion of the way targeting works. The most important considerations are listed below (points 1–3 being derived from Stewart's account).

1. Defining the target group. To decide who needs extra food, one might look at household income or at anthropometric data. The latter might be easier than the former, and also more difficult to falsify. With both measures, there is a problem that it is hard to decide on a *cut-off point*. A fine line will have to be trodden between a scheme which feeds too many people, and so becomes too costly, and one which misses people – particularly if they are extremely malnourished.

2. Choosing a type of targeting. Stewart mentions several possible approaches to targeting for food programmes, all of which could be used for other health programmes: they include targeting by *income* (the example of a Sri Lankan food stamp scheme for the poor is mentioned); by *needs* as determined by health workers; by *geography*, e.g. operating a ration scheme or a subsidy scheme in a deprived area; by *age*, e.g. food schemes for under-fives; by *employment* in workplace schemes (school-based schemes would work the same way) and by *season*, operating schemes when food is most scarce.

3. Deciding which targeting approach is most appropriate. The best targeting schemes are very simple to operate, and are relatively unambiguous

in the definition of the targeted group. A good scheme might be one which ensured basic food was supplied each year in the appropriate season, to a village known to have recurrent food shortages at this time. Such a scheme would not depend on an arbitrary cut-off point such as a 'poverty line'; the whole village would get help. Thus the information required to operate the scheme would be small. Stewart quotes the example of subsidised food shops in Brazil; these sell cheap basic food to all, and the targeting is achieved simply by siting the shops in extremely poor areas. No means test has to be applied when people use the shop, so the scheme is extremely simple to operate. A scheme of this sort scores as a good targeting scheme because it too requires little information. Both these schemes also have the advantage that they are, once started, not *discretionary* (see pp. 97–98 above). Health workers or shop assistants have no decisions to make about who gets what. This reduces the possibility of corruption and mishandling of the scheme, and helps to keep down administrative costs.

4.   It is, of course, necessary to examine the social costs of a scheme. Some food schemes could, for example, be detrimental if they reduced the incentive for local food production. Others might be detrimental if they altered the taste preferences of the local population – as has happened in parts of Asia in recent years.

5.   One area which is often neglected is the question of who makes decisions about targeting. The very term 'targeting' implies doing something to someone – and that is just what normally happens; top-down decisions are made about who should get what.

6.   We noted in Chapter 5 that indicators can become confused with goals, thus affecting the way policies actually work. There is potential for this to happen in targeting. Targeting, if not thought through, can actually be most inequitable. Let us consider the example of the *headcount index*.[5] This measures the number of the poor as a proportion of the population. One common way of measuring poverty is to calculate how many people live below the poverty line; that is below an income figure considered to be just adequate to provide an average household with its basic needs. The total number of poor is the number who at any one time fall below that line, even though some of these will have income only just short of the official poverty line, and others will be almost totally destitute.

When it comes to alleviating poverty, it takes a large effort to help the desperately poor to improve their situation. It takes much less effort to bring up to the poverty line those who are only just below it. In determining policies to combat poverty, those policies which are likely to have an effect on the latter group, the 'slightly poor' as opposed to the 'very poor', will be easier and cheaper to implement. If we focus on the slightly poor, it is possible to bring improvements to many people, making a dramatic improvement to the headcount index. Politicians may well find such policies irresistible, even if it means that the lot of the desperately poor remains unchanged.

In summary

What is equity?

- The notion of equity is related to that of fairness or justice.
- In policy terms, one school of thought equates equity with offering equal goods, resources and opportunities to all individuals, regardless of need; individuals can then exercise freedom of choice as to how things are used.
- The opposite view is that, to achieve equity, goods resources and opportunities must be shared unequally because people start from unequal positions.

Equity and social welfare

- In some countries, equality is seen as an aim of social services; in others, the aim is to achieve at least minimum standards for all.
- In a similar way, there are, in different countries, different approaches to welfare. Some see welfare as a last resort approach to mopping up the worst and most intractable problems of society. Others see welfare as an important investment towards a developing and productive society.
- In many ex-colonial counties, welfare systems have a built-in bias in favour of the better-off, a legacy from the days when the colonial rulers were the better-off.

Equity in health care

- One approach to achieving equity in health care would be to offer equal shares of health care to everyone, regardless of what people need.
- The alternative approach is to aim for distributing health care in such a way that all members of society have the opportunity to end up equally healthy.
- In practice, health care, however distributed, cannot correct for all the influences which determine people's ill-health; however, we can aim for policies which are redistributive.
- Attempts to define resource allocation mechanisms in health services in terms of medical need are practically difficult and unlikely to allow for the development of services supportive of good health.
- Health need might be estimated on the broad basis of social disadvantage.
- Any approach to resource allocation which is redistributive must be phased in strategically, over time.
- Resource allocation may be based on considerations of equality of expenditure, of inputs, or of access. These will have different results, and thus different implications for policy.

Can equity be efficient?

- Some authors argue that equity can only be gained at the expense of efficiency.

- Others would say that this contention depends upon the way in which health service efficiency is defined; i.e. in relation to what goals.
- It is frequently argued today that targeting provides a means of maximising the efficiency of social expenditure and safeguarding equity by aiming resources selectively at the most needy.
- To achieve this, targeting must aim at a clearly definable group and be implemented through a simple, practicable scheme.
- It is important to minimise the amount of discretion which health workers need to exercise in implementing a targeted approach.
- It is important to minimise the cost of running a target scheme.
- Targeting often goes with a 'top-down' approach to resource allocation.
- Without due care, targeting schemes have the potential to create greater inequity rather than reduce inequity.

Notes

1. For example, the WHO (1981) document *Global Strategy for Health for All by the Year 2000* stresses the need to reduce the existing gross inequalities in health status, and sees an equitable distribution of health resources as fundamental to that strategy (p. 34); at other points it refers to the need for at least a minimum standard of health so that all might be able to work and participate in social life (p. 15).

Successive World Health Assemblies have stressed the need for equity, e.g. resolutions WHA 39/1986/REC/1,4 section 5(2): 'to maintain high-level political commitment to social equity and leadership for the further implementation of national strategies, including the reduction of socioeconomic and related health disparities among people, thus fulfilling a fundamental requisite for the achievement of health for all', and WHA/42/1989/REC 1,2 section 1(1): 'to maintain the political commitment to reduce the inequities among different population groups'.

2. This was the plan for Zimbabwean health care in the period 1981–84. The firmness of political intention is to be seen in the fact that between 1980 and 1982 the Ministry of Health almost doubled its actual expenditure in real terms (Homans, 1989), with real growth of the 1981–82 budget of 47 per cent. It is a sad reflection on the problems which developing countries face, however, that the 1982–83 fiscal year saw a real decrease in expenditure of 9.1 per cent, due to economic recession and stabilisation measures. The most carefully developed strategies to guide the direction of growth are thus wrecked.

3. Mooney offers a slightly larger range of categories for discussion than is given here. An interesting practical exploration of different approaches to resources allocation is that of Waddington and Newell (1987), based on their work in Fiji. A useful bibliography covering the field of inequalities and equity in health is given by Pereira (1990).

4. Mooney (1983) distinguishes the aim of equality of access from the aim of equality of utilisation. This distinction can be made on the basis that, even when we have gone to great lengths to provide equal access, there may be a lack of demand, which is itself a feature of deprivation. He suggests that demand may be particularly low among the multiply deprived, and that in order to improve utilisation one would need to aim special funds at multiply deprived areas. It seems to me that this is not conceptually different from the range of problems discussed under the term 'access', and this book refers only to problems of access, to cover all aspects of giving people the chance of utilisation.

5. This measure is well described, and discussed in comparison with other measures of poverty, in the 1990 World Development Report (World Bank, 1990).

11

Development

Views of development

How do our ideas about poverty and equity relate to the various ways in which people think about socioeconomic development? This question is of great importance, because international trends in health policy have tended to mirror international trends in development thinking. A short account cannot be comprehensive; the aim here is to review some main themes that have run through contemporary approaches to development, in a way that provides a framework for discussion of health policy, and an appreciation of related social welfare measures.

First, what do we mean by 'development'?[1] Development is a bit like the concept of health; it is much easier to say what it is not, than to say what it is. Presumably, for most people, the goal of development is improvement of the human lot, towards a state of global well-being. It is quite easy to make such a vague statement, but then how do we assess whether we have achieved such well-being, or even whether we are moving slowly in the right direction? Many indicators of development are used, including measures of health, mortality, poverty and hunger; all of these are related to our well-being. Most common of all indicators for development are measures of economic growth, such as growth of the gross national product (GNP). However, we should not see development as represented by mere increases in per capita income in national statistics. Why not? The answer concerns the fact that income does not always say much about what people can buy; average income tells us little about the extremes of wealth and poverty which may be experienced within a country. While no one would deny that national income is of importance, different views of development would lead to people wanting to consider quite different features of society. For some, the issue is whether all people have shoes on their feet; for others, whether the country has modern industrial development. For some, development must allow everyone to have access to modern telecommunications, a parliamentary vote, and the chance to buy the latest products of the multinational corporations. For others, the important thing may be that rural communities have roads, that people have a say in local developments, and that there is a sense that the nation has a degree of self-determination. The way in which people come to such views is strongly related to the ways in which they see human progress, poverty and equity.

Many of the important debates about development today focus on two questions. Put crudely, these are (1) for the various human populations in the world, are things getting better or worse? and (2) what can we do to make things better? The first of these questions is viewed in two ways, which for some analysts overlap. Some see development from an *environmental perspective*, while others start from a *socioeconomic perspective* and ask whether people's material lot is improving, or likely to improve, over time.

Are things getting better or worse? An environmental perspective

Consideration of the global environment may seem remote from health policy. However, the close interrelationship between our concerns for development as it relates to people's needs, and ecological sustainability is increasingly becoming recognised. In the words of the World Health Organization's Commission on Health and the Environment,

> Health depends on our ability to understand and manage the interaction between human activities and the physical and biological environment. We have the knowledge for this but have failed to act on it, although we have the resources to meet current and future needs sustainably. (WHO, Commission on Health and the Environment, 1992: 409)

Environmentalists today are sharply divided over the prognosis for the health of the global environment and the health of the human race. Briefly, environmental analysts can be characterised as the 'boomsters' and the 'doomsters'. The former group believe that sustainable development is possible, in the sense that a way forward can be found for human progress. To the boomsters, although human activity exhausts resources of minerals and energy, causes pollution, global warming and a hole in the ozone layer, science is ingenious and will always find a way to manipulate the environment, reining in its forces to ensure novel solutions to these problems, and the survival of the human race. By contrast the doomsters believe that we are fast creating problems far beyond the capacity of science and that as a race we must change our ways or perish. For many of these issues, the boomsters are able to argue that the verdict of irreversible damage is unproven – the snag being that in the case of dramatic climatic change or atmospheric change, undeniable proof would come far too late to take any action.

Some environmentalists would argue that the whole of the history of mankind can be seen as a struggle to provide food against the pressure of growing populations, from the earliest development of agriculture onwards; today's problems are then viewed as just another step towards the biological limits for the planet. It is sobering to note the observation of Grigg (1991) that the largest class of refugees in the world – surpassing the numbers made homeless by any military or political situation – are environmental refugees, made homeless and bereft of a livelihood as a result of deterioration of agricultural land caused by unsustainable methods; at the time Grigg was writing these numbered 10 million.

Boomsters point to the success of the Green Revolution, in which the scientific development of new seed strains has led to much increased food production, particularly in parts of Asia; surely technical solutions such as these can help us out of all our problems? Some doomsters argue that such gains are short term and that comprehensive control of the global environment is a scientific impossibility. Others believe that science provides great potential for development, but suggest that the positive effects of this are limited by social context. In many places the Green Revolution has allowed those who can afford to invest in the high-technology, expensive seeds, and the fertiliser and pesticides which are needed to grow them, to become wealthy at the expense of poorer peasants. Many of these tried the new seeds, but lost out because, obliged to give a high proportion of their crop to the landlord as rent, they were unable to make enough profit to pay for next year's seeds and inputs – and then often were obliged to borrow at high interest rates. In much of tropical Asia, such processes have caused the displacement of large sections of the labour force from farming altogether, contributing greatly to the migration of families to the overcrowded cities. The Green Revolution at once shows us the potential and the limitations of technical progress.

Are things getting better or worse? A socioeconomic perspective

The consideration of global environmental aspects of development leads us surely towards consideration of socioeconomic development. Here too there are the equivalent of boomsters and doomsters; there are those who believe that, whatever local setbacks may occur, an almost unstoppable tide of progress brings with it human betterment, and that it is only a matter of time before 'development' reaches all countries. In this case, the technological fix is 'modernisation'. The pessimists argue that things are not getting better; that for many countries of the world the process labelled as 'development' is better labelled as 'underdevelopment' because it involves processes which necessitate the transfer of wealth from poor countries to richer ones, and an inbuilt tendency for this transfer to continue to be unidirectional. The last few decades of development effort have brought about little visible improvement in the position of the world's poor. At the same time, even within the poorer countries, the wealth may not be shared to the benefit of all.

Although for some analysts greater equality is both a goal and a prerequisite of development, for others human progress goes, for better or for worse, hand in hand with increasing inequality. The rich prose of Marshall Sahlin's book *Stone Age Economics* provides a vivid illustration:

> One third to one half of humanity are said to go to bed hungry every night. In the Old Stone Age the fraction must have been much smaller. *This* is the era of hunger unprecedented. Now, in the time of the greatest technical power,

starvation is an institution. Reverse another venerable formula: the amount of hunger increases relatively and absolutely with the evolution of culture.

This paradox is my whole point. Hunters and gatherers have by force of circumstances an objectively low standard of living. But taken as their *objective*, and given their adequate means of production, all the people's material wants can be easily satisfied. The evolution of the economy has known, then, two contradictory movements: enriching but at the same time impoverishing, appropriating in relation to nature but expropriating in relation to man. (1974: 36–37)

Sahlins goes on to develop the notion that the technological sophistication which some of us enjoy today is one side of the picture; this allows some people to live in comfort, and puts men on the moon: the other side of the picture sees people starving. These two things are, in Sahlins's view, necessarily concomitant; to Sahlins, poverty is the 'invention of civilisation'.

To Sahlins this is a sober assessment, and a pessimistic one which leaves us bound to question the notion of 'development' itself. For him, as for proponents of theories of *dependency and underdevelopment*, including many Marxist critics, the very notion of human progress must be questioned in a world where the gaps between rich and poor seem to become ever wider. Within dependency theory, the historical processes which made Europe rich are seen to be the same processes which took wealth away from Asia, Central/South America and Africa. Colonialism rooted such processes firmly in the world economy. That which today increases the well-being of the North, increases the misery and indebtedness of the South.

Whatever the shortcomings of using income measures to look at the detailed picture of development, the overall picture is dramatic. In 1991, 85 per cent of the world's people gained only 21 per cent of the total global income. The average GNP per capita in the rich countries of the world was $20,570; 20 times the average income in the poor and middle-income countries together.[2] This is not of course, a totally static picture. Two sets of data together illustrate vividly what is happening. First we might consider relative rate of growth of the developed countries. Dore (1992) suggests that in 1890 Europe was twice as wealthy per capita as India or China. By 1940, she argues, it was 40 times richer, and by 1990, 70 times richer. We might also consider information from the *World Development Report 1990*, which compares income and population for different regions as a proportion of that for the whole developing world, for 1960–65 and 1988–89. Over that time, East Asia increased its total income about sixfold while experiencing a population increase of about 40 per cent. Sub-Saharan Africa meanwhile only increased its income by a factor of two, while its population more than doubled. Thus there is change within the developing world, but the dominance of the richest countries continues. However one evaluates the efforts of the international and other agencies concerned with development over the last thirty years, the problem has not gone away.

What can we do to make things better?

Dependency theorists, then, may be seen as the 'doomsters' in terms of the socioeconomic analysis of development. They are frequently unfairly criticised for not producing concrete proposals for action. This approach does not lend itself to the logical development of any easy solutions, but it seems a little unfair to complain about this, given that the case of dependency theorists is based on a view that the problems of the South are inbuilt into the structure of the relationship of those countries with those of the North. Such a diagnosis *cannot* provide any easy solutions. Theories of underdevelopment lead generally to a belief that development can be possible only through processes which allow genuine change in the existing economic relationships between countries, and in the structure of the economy within them; somehow real production of wealth is needed for development, and aid alone will not achieve this. Those subscribing to this approach may feel that their logic leads them to argue that most development aid is a waste of money. Others would adopt a less extreme approach, and say that development aid cannot get to the roots of the problem, but nevertheless can hopefully alleviate some human misery here and now, or help to create conditions in which people can more effectively work to transform things within the countries concerned.

The solutions which others advocate derive from a variety of different political viewpoints, and are best seen in relation to differing views of equity. In order to throw light on the activities of international organisations and development agencies, it is helpful to consider the ways in which these views have shifted over the last thirty years or so.

Modernisation theory

First, however, let us distinguish between those theories which tend to go with the view that equity is not a crucial factor in development, and those which think it is. Modernisation theory does not ascribe a central role to equity as a factor on the path to development. The evolution of global society is seen in itself as a path from primitive to modern and from poverty to plenty. Traditional societies are seen as simple, conservative, based on family values and agricultural communities using traditional techniques. Advanced societies are considered as innovative, with high levels of investment and growth. Modernisation theorists understand development in terms of helping societies to achieve this. The work of the economist Rostow typifies the approach; he argues that in order to reach the form of a 'developed' or 'mass consumption' society, a country must reach the stage of 'critical take-off', where enough national income is going into investment in production to ensure that gains can be consolidated and further built upon, success breeding success. However, success depends not only on investment; other conditions include the existence of entrepreneurial skills, competitiveness and ambition. These are seen as the cultural assets which have enabled the achievement of greater material wealth in the North than in the South, and they are believed to be integral to modern society and to the development process. If these conditions can be achieved at least in the big towns, then the countryside will follow on behind. As a result, modernisation theorists have advocated that the way forward for the South is to mimic the social, cultural and legal character-istics of societies of the North, following the North in its approach to such diverse aspects of life as schooling, family life, legal systems, and development of two-party democracies. Within health care, the logical application of modernisation theory is to create, in the major centres of population, high-technology centres for medical treatment, along with every opportunity for up-and-coming young doctors to be trained in the latest advances in medicine. No matter that the rural areas had no nurses and no anti-malarials; this would change over time.

Modernisation theory lost its popularity and to some extent its credibility when it became clear that massive investment did not of necessity provide the key to economic growth. It is mentioned here because, as Hardiman and Midgley (1982) have pointed out, this type of approach has by no means vanished from the scene, but is constantly resurfacing both in academic circles (some aspects of monetarism fit well into this approach), and in development planning and aid circles. It is well if one can recognise such an approach and assess its validity.

Welfare and redistribution approaches to development

A range of approaches to development, including perhaps most notably the basic needs approach which is mentioned below, focus on welfare aspects of development, and the need to consider issues of inequality in society. These approaches tend not to accord such a central role to economic growth, and indeed may argue that economic growth alone, serving only to increase inequalities in society, may have a detrimental effect on the well-being of most people. For the eradication of mass poverty, economic growth alone is inadequate, and a comprehensive range of economic and social policies is needed. Growth needs to be firmly rooted in community development, and real advances will come from bottom-up planning where people can take responsibility for their own way forward. It is argued that such an approach is not based merely on altruism, but also on sound economic reasoning, in that there cannot be healthy growth of a society if wealth is concentrated in the hands of a few people, the rest unable to function as producers or consumers.

International agencies have fluctuated both in their support for an approach of this kind over recent years, and in their interpretation of it.

Changing views about development

Whereas Sahlins sees *poverty* as the invention of civilisation, others might be said to see *wealth* as the motive force of civilisation. The reasoning which creates this position goes as follows: development depends crucially on the concentration of enough capital to enable significant investment in productive enterprises, that is, in industry and in large-scale agriculture. Therefore some within society must be allowed to accumulate wealth, if necessary at the expense of others. The growth that follows will not initially reduce poverty, but over time the income of the poorest can be expected to rise, even if inequalities increase further. On this basis, redistribution would be damaging for economic growth, because the rich would be able to save less.[3]

In the 1960s development was seen as virtually synonymous with growth, and growth-promoting policies were the order of the day. The poor would find salvation in the 'trickledown effect' which would eventually improve even their living standards (if less than, and later than, those of the rich). By the 1970s, however, it was becoming obvious that little if any such trickling was happening; indeed there was a clear problem that third world development was stunted by the lack of home markets for goods produced.

This was the context in which a discernible shift in thinking about development took place within the international agencies; a shift from the view of development as being essentially about economic growth to one of development as a multi-faceted process; from seeing the poor as the also-rans of society to thinking of people as human capital, to be invested in through education, through health and nutrition programmes; through, in short, a basic needs policy. In the philosophy of the basic needs approach to development, the focus is on production at all levels of society; small-scale village level production is to be encouraged alongside large-scale industry. Investment in social welfare, and such redistributive policies, can lead to growth. This theory enjoyed great popularity in the late 1970s, in an atmosphere where the example of China's great success stood as a remarkable living testimony to such an approach, and in a relatively thriving world economy. It was in this context that the International Labour Organization espoused the basic needs approach, and the World Health Organization was able to convince and inspire with the primary health care approach. The basic needs approach was developed in the mid-1970s by such authors as Paul Streeten (for example Streeten, 1977); however, it is fair to say that by the end of the decade the enthusiasm of the international development agencies was already considerably cooled. No theoretical contribution had emerged to spell the death of basic needs; a policy that looked all right in boom was to be quickly condemned in recession.

The 1970s had been a period in which interest rates were so low that in the words of the World Bank, it was 'almost impossible to owe too much' (World Bank, 1984: 22). Simultaneously, the large surpluses of oil-exporting countries increased the lending capacity of commercial banks.

The heavy commercial debt that resulted in a number of developing countries was a new feature of underdevelopment. In the recession of 1980–83, the debt burden proved almost intolerable. The swing in development policy was dramatic. Basic needs would have to await the more pressing issues of economic recovery and – most importantly to the international financial agencies – debt repayment. By 1984 the key words were 'economic adjustment' or 'structural adjustment' – both referring to policies aimed at the highest possible growth rates.

Throughout the 1980s, developing countries were required to negotiate austerity measures – adjustment packages – which had to meet the approval of the World Bank and related agencies if the country concerned was to be deemed aid-worthy at all. The packages had a depressingly uniform appearance from one country to the next: the measures had to reduce external borrowing, cut public spending, reduce internal consumption and switch output of production into exports, rather than goods for the home market. *The World Development Report 1984* recognised that this was a drastic approach:

> Cuts in public spending have often been achieved by reducing or eliminating subsidies – not only for parastatals [state-owned or supported enterprises] but also for food, education and health. . . . a decline in spending on education and health detracts from building human capital. . . . These effects may indeed outlast the resolution of the current debt problems.

The message of the early 1980s was that growth must again take preference over equity; however bad things got, the poor must wait. The irony of this period is that, as MacPherson (1982) has pointed out with reference to child welfare provision in Tanzania, it was precisely where a country had built a broad base of welfare and service provision that the effects of recession hit hardest.

By the mid-1980s it was apparent that adjustment policies were hitting the poor so hard as to cause widespread concern both within specific countries and internationally. By 1987, James Grant, Executive Director of UNICEF, was publicly appealing for 'More sensitive national and international economic policies', arguing that these 'could avoid much of the suffering and human damage – yet so far, only limited action has been taken to protect the incomes and nutrition of the poor, and investment in social services' (see the foreword in Cornia et al., 1987).

The *World Economic Survey 1990* (United Nations, 1990) states that 'For many developing countries, the 1980s have been a decade lost for development.' It comments on the substantially weakened position of developing countries in international trade and finance, and the resulting net flow of resources from the developing to the developed countries. Although a few of the larger developing countries, notably China, India and Pakistan, achieved over 20 per cent increases in per capita income in the 1980s, about two-thirds of all developing countries experienced a decrease in per capita income, which in two out of five countries exceeded 20 per cent.

Regarding equity, the situation was even worse than might be guessed from this. Where per capita income declined, the proportion of absolute poor in the total population increased. Real wages fell: in Nigeria in the 1980s for example, by 60 per cent. The spending capacity of the poor was dramatically reduced by increased food staple prices, abolition of subsidies, and charges for health and education. Underconsumption of food and malnutrition grew in urban areas of Africa and Latin America, in the latter often despite adequate food supply. Rural incomes generally fell less than urban ones, but often savings became worth much less, and much-valued remittances from urban-based relatives decreased or stopped. In Africa, there were indications from Nigeria and Ghana that people in real desperation were migrating back from the towns to the countryside. In Latin America, rural–urban inequality remained very great; real wages dropped in agriculture, and many jobs were lost with the introduction of new technologies (United Nations, 1990).

Thus by 1990 we find that there is a renewed call for equity to be re-established as a development goal:

> The eradication of poverty and hunger, greater equity in income distribution and the development of human resources remain major challenges everywhere. Economic and social progress requires that growth be broadly based, offering equal opportunities to all people, both women and men, to participate fully in economic, social and political activities. . . . A primary objective must be to respond to the needs of and maximise the potential of all members of society. Health, nutrition, housing, population policies and other social services are a key to both improving individual welfare and successful development. (United Nations, 1990: 9)

Some sort of consensus had emerged internationally, that something must be done about those countries and population groups which were worst off.

Globalisation

In order to put the events described in the foregoing account into perspective, it is necessary to examine the major changes to the world economic system which have been taking place. To do so, the term 'globalisation' has crept into everyday vocabulary. It refers to the notion that, increasingly, all countries of the world are interdependent. This is not a new way of looking at things, and not entirely a new phenomenon. Throughout this century, and even earlier, countries of the world have been interlinked by colonialism, and then by the internationalisation of capital. Countries of the developing world are linked through the activities of big business firms: the multinational corporations.

The oil price increases of the 1970s, which led to economic problems in developing countries, led also to similar problems in the West. Structural adjustment was not restricted to the developing countries; a radical shake-up of the economy occurred in the rich countries too. The overall result has been a far greater degree of interdependence within the whole global system of economic interrelationships. Under the discipline of structural adjustment, trade liberalisation has meant a lack of protection for some of the weaker partners. For example, African exporters of primary products, and countries struggling to allow domestic manufacturing to get off the ground, now have to battle against international competition. The GATT (General Agreement on Tariffs and Trade) agreement has more recently supported and extended such policies. The whole thrust of structural adjustment has been against measures to support 'national development' and for measures intended to draw countries closer into the global economic system. In some African countries the results are extreme. Nabudere (1995) points out that in Africa, IMF credit and short-term debt rose from US\$ 82 billion in 1982 to US\$200 billion in 1993.

The total debt of the developing world has now reached US\$ 1.9 trillion. It is not however only the developing world which lives with debt today. Public debt for the combined OECD countries stands at over US\$ 13 trillion. Chossudovsky (1995) has suggested that debts and their collection dominate the global economy today, putting much monetary policy in the hands of private banking. This results in macroeconomic reform in developing countries and OECD countries alike. The process of regulation via debt collection is inimical to needs of individual states to promote economic activity and create employment.

Privatisation: a global trend

It was in the context of these radical changes that, all over the world, the 1980s and 1990s saw a shift in attitudes regarding the role of the state in development. Prior to this time there was a universal assumption that the state had an important role to play in economic affairs. It became recognised, and indeed part of accepted wisdom, that markets frequently fail to work efficiently, necessitating state intervention. In the 1950s and 1960s, even the most dedicated supporter of private enterprise expansion saw state support for development, through economic planning, strategic investments and infrastructural development, as essential. Such support was built into strategies for development, in particular, industrialisation, and was encouraged by aid agencies. For a variety of reasons too complex to debate here, the results were seen as disappointing; this has produced a reaction against state intervention in development. It is not really clear, however, that the disappointing results are related to a central role for the state – or that all the results were disappointing. As we noted above, even some of those countries held up as examples of the success of development have stories of private sector success based on very high levels of state intervention. South Korea and Taiwan for instance are seen as successful free-market economies, yet in both countries, establishment of a robust economic base has involved high levels of state support.

One might debate what caused the trend away from state intervention.

Some argue that observers were attracted by the rapid growth of Asian economies where many governments had adopted neo-liberal policies[4] – though some of these did so in the context of continuing state support. There is a strong case for seeing the economic imperative as the most basic underlying rationale; the whole structural adjustment process has been linked with a decreasing role for national governments and an increasing role for financial institutions. Yet the prevailing neo-liberal political beliefs of more recent years coexist most comfortably with such trends.

In such a prevailing political climate one would expect concern that, especially in developing countries, the public sector was inefficient and performing poorly. A belief developed that, in many developing countries in particular, the public sectors were over-extended.[5] Furthermore, it was now perceived that government policies may not always reflect the views of the whole population, and by corollary, that private sector activity might allow people's preferences as consumers to be more easily met. These points are discussed in more detail in Chapter 13. Here, we should note that the change of heart had a more obvious link with the demands of structural adjustment than with any new evidence about the role of the state.

Sector reform

It was in the context of structural adjustment, and the shift away from ideas of development centred on the state, that sector reform became a central part of the agenda of the international financial institutions. Reform programmes have been seen as part of structural adjustment packages, and indeed such packages have tended to demand reforms, from economic changes such as trade liberalisation to changes in the political system, and changes designed to reduce the role of the state. A widespread form of sectoral reform has been decentralisation.[6] This reform is concerned with the transfer of authority from central government to more peripheral agencies. As Frenk and González-Block (1992) point out, different approaches to decentralisation in different political contexts can have widely different implications. Some people see decentralisation as a reform which widens political representation. Others see this through neo-liberal spectacles, which view the best means of representing individual interests as being through the private market.

There has been extensive criticism of the technocratic approaches which have been employed in pushing reforms. Walt and Gilson (1994) refer to the prevalent tendency to ignore local politics, failing to recognise, for instance, that in Africa public enterprises have been an important source of reward and patronage (see also the discussion of the work of Shivji in Chapter 8, p. 96). Health sector reform tends to be described in such a technocratic way. For the purpose of providing a definition which covers all efforts at reform, without prejudging the intention or rationale, Frenk and

González-Block (1992) offer: 'Changes produced out of explicit intention on the part of governments or political groups to transform, for the better, the health sector.' When we encounter such definitions, it is important to bear in mind the context in which the need for reform came to be perceived. Reform is about improving management, and achieving better health care – in themselves laudable aims. However, the words must have a more specific content, for those who have attempted to organise health services have surely always striven to organise them well. Reform is about improving management in specific ways – through improving efficiency, which is believed to be achievable through increasing competition; through containing costs; through seeing a role for government not in delivering health care beyond the most basic, but of regulating its delivery by others.

The World Bank, in the *1993 World Development Report*, spells out the need for reform in terms of the need to deal with misallocation, inequity, inefficiency and exploding costs. It argues that the state has an important role to play in this, but in part this role is seen as one of promoting the private sector. We shall return to this discussion in Chapter 13.

In summary

Views of development

- Socioeconomic development is a complex notion based on the belief that we can work towards a global goal of improvement of human well-being.
- Indicators for development include measures of economic growth, of industrial development, measures of health and of nutritional status, of modernisation, and of equity.

Are things getting better or worse?

- Some would question whether there is a general trend towards enhanced human well-being.
- Questions may be raised from an environmental perspective, where there is a debate about our capacity to avert disaster.
- Further questions are asked from a socioeconomic perspective, where there is doubt that increasing technological capacity achieves more than an ever-greater capacity for inequality in society.

What can we do to make things better?

- Views of the way forward for society derive from differing political viewpoints and are best seen in relation to differing views of equity.

Modernisation theory

- Modernisation theory is now largely discredited but the notion of modernisation lives on in many approaches to aid and development.
- Modernisation theory does not see equity as an important factor on the

path to development; in fact it could be argued that it sees inequity as a precondition of development.

Welfare and distribution approaches to development

- Welfare and distribution approaches to development accord a central role to equity.
- International agencies have fluctuated in their support for such approaches.

Changing views about development

- In recent years, the goal of growth with equity has been espoused by agencies such as the World Bank.
- In practice this is being interpreted as meaning that targeting approaches must be used wherever possible.

Globalisation

- Major changes have been taking place in the world economic system, which have increased the interdependence of national economies and worked to the disadvantage of developing countries.

Privatisation: a global trend

- In the 1950s and 1960s, state support for development through economic planning, strategic investments and infrastructural development was seen as essential. The 1980s and 1990s saw a shift in attitudes to the role of the state in development, with the state seen as much less central.
- Sector reform has become a central part of the agenda of the international financial institutions.
- Reform programmes can be seen as part of structural adjustment packages, which may include demands for reforms.
- Reform is about improving management in particular ways, such as by improving efficiency, which is believed to be achievable by increasing competition.

Notes

1. A useful account is that of Seers (1979) which has stood the test of time in the way that it scrutinises the relationship between the concept of development and that of economic growth; development and poverty; development, inequality and redistribution.

2. *Investing in Health: World Development Report* (World Bank, 1993).

3. Of course, there is no logical necessity to have a group of privileged and wealthy members of society in order for capital accumulation to be possible. The state could equally create an efficient accumulation process through taxation and related mechanisms. Indeed, there is every reason to be doubtful about the value of the wealthy as the principal tool for development. Too often the surplus income of the wealthy goes on expensive consumer items, bought abroad or imported at the expense of valuable foreign exchange. Too often, the

limited industrial development sponsored by the rich results in production of luxury goods, far beyond the means of ordinary people.

4. See Walt and Gilson (1994).

5. This terminology comes from the World Bank's 'Berg Report' (1981).

6. See Collins (1994) for a useful discussion of the forms of decentralisation and its implications.

12

Aid and the Health Sector

Aid within global relationships

In Chapter 11 we considered how structural adjustment processes have
been instrumental in bringing the developing countries into an ever closer
relationship with the richer countries. Part of that relationship, of course,
is realised through the aid process, whereby resources are channelled to
the poorer countries in the form of loans and grants. In the 1960s,
development was seen as a matter of economic growth above all else and
the health sector received little aid. Today, however, health improvement
is regarded as an integral part of development.

The aid relationship is a two-way process: aid would not happen if there
were not tangible potential benefits for donors as well as recipients.
Donors generally describe their motivation in terms of wanting to help,
wanting to secure friends and influence, and wanting to secure commercial
opportunities. Donors include international (multilateral) agencies such as
the World Bank and the World Health Organization, bilateral agencies
and non-governmental organisations (NGOs) of all kinds. Funds from
bilateral agencies are channelled direct, through multilateral agencies and
also through NGOs. With the resources come conditions and demands that
things be done in certain ways, and many feel that the aid process has a
disproportionate effect on health policy; Justice (1987) for example,
suggests that 'He who pays the piper calls the tune.'

Foreign aid is a significant proportion of the total resources available in
many ministries of health of the South. In many debt-burdened economies
aid has become an essential part of the scene. Figure 12.1 shows aid flows
as a percentage of total health expenditure by world region, in 1990. The
impression given by these figures is that only in Africa are the aid flows
significant. Of course, even quite modest amounts of aid look significant
for Africa because of the limited resources otherwise available there. Table
12.1 focuses on the three world regions which figure mainly as aid
recipients. It shows, for each region, the five countries for which the
proportion of total health expenditure coming from aid is highest. For such
countries, the aid process is likely to play a dominant role in the health
sector. Of course, it is possible that in some countries where aid
contributes only modestly to total health resources, the process nevertheless exercises a disproportionate influence. This could be because there is
pressure from central government to respond to conditions being imposed
on the health sector as part of the deal in a wider aid package, because the

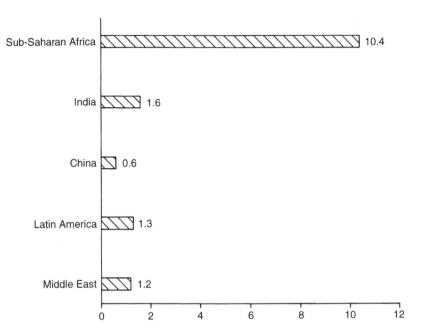

Figure 12.1   *Aid flows as a percentage of total health expenditure, 1990 (World Bank, 1993)*

Table 12.1   *Aid flows to selected countries as a percentage of total health expenditure*

Region	Country	External assistance as a proportion of total health expenditure
Africa	Burkina Faso	72.3
	São Tomé and Principe	54.2
	Mozambique	53.3
	Cape Verde	53.7
	Gambia	51.0
Other Asian	Samoa	39.7
(not India or China)	Bhutan	28.5
	Nepal	25.4
	Vanuatu	22.8
	Lao PDR	21.9
Latin America	Guyana	44.2
	Nicaragua	20.6
	Bolivia	20.5
	Haiti	19.0
	El Salvador	14.7

Source: Michaud and Murray (1994). The data refer to 1990.

health sector leadership views the relationship with donors as, for one reason or another, valuable to them, or because the nature of the aid given has itself a distorting effect on the whole sector.

Features of the aid process

It will be evident from the discussion of structural adjustment that this creates demands which shape the whole way in which governments act, and the extent to which they continue to see provision of health care as a public responsibility. The increased awareness of the role of the health sector in development goes paradoxically with calls for privatisation and a shift in the role of the state from provider to regulator of services. Aid grants and loans come with conditions attached which tend to relate to implementation of health sector reform, including such features as user charges. Conditionality has also tended to feature in recent years in the form of a basic requirement for respect of human rights, respect for the rule of law and for basic conditions for democracy. This trend can be seen both as a humanitarian one on the part of donors, and as part and parcel of the globalisation process; these are the conditions necessary for participants in exchanges within the global economy. There are times, however, when donor foreign and economic interests extend beyond their own definitions of aid-worthy (i.e. democratic) countries, creating conflict and debate.[1]

Aid is shaped not only by conditions of this kind, but also by the nature of the aid process itself. All too often in the past, aid agencies have offered aid in forms which seemed both useful to the recipient and convenient to themselves. Box 12.1 provides an illustration of some of the problems that can arise. African countries have a high proportion of health expenditure covered by aid, compared to elsewhere (Table 12.1). However, the problems listed here will sound familiar to many. It should be stressed that many of the problems here are acute problems for the aid agencies themselves; there seems to be almost no way around the problem of salaries, for example. Participants in the aid process are learning all the time, though honest appraisals such as that quoted in Box 12.1 are few and far between, at least in published form.[2] Some of the mistakes of the past have been studied, and practice changed in some agencies; others, however, perhaps latecomers to the scene, persist with practices into which problems are almost inbuilt.[3]

One such lesson from the past concerns the acceptance of large, expensive capital projects financed from outside. A good example, in health sector terms, is that of hospital construction. Two decades ago, many aid agencies subscribed to the view that hospitals were needed as a priority in many third world countries, and that to offer to provide such a large item, representing not only a major investment but also one that is expensive in foreign exchange, was an approach to health sector aid which made good sense. In addition the donor would have the satisfaction of

Box 12.1   Impact of Aid on the National Health Service in Mozambique (*From a longer description, given in Cliff, 1993*)

'Aid has been necessary to sustain the National Health Service (NHS). . . . The larger donors will use their power to influence policy. . . . Ironically, donors are advising the MOH about the necessity of good planning and management, although simultaneously making both tasks more difficult. The presence of so many donors has added an enormous administrative workload to an already struggling Ministry of Health (MOH). Many officials now spend most of their working hours entertaining visiting delegations, meeting donors, and preparing project documents.

Financial planning is almost impossible, as the MOH does not know the true extent of donor contributions. Most project aid is short-term, preventing long-term planning. The MOH has also lost control of financial administration, as donors now procure and provide many goods and services. Few are willing to transfer funds and give management responsibility to the MOH. The already weak accounting department has to produce accounts for a multitude of projects, often with different systems.

The tying of aid for imports has seriously weakened the policy of standardising equipment. Some aid actually costs the MOH money. Still too frequently, the MOH has to pay customs, storage, and transport costs for unwanted material that donors have sent without prior warning. . . .

Projects are often unsustainable, as the MOH has to finance the recurrent costs of activities set up by the project after the donor leaves. With dependence has come lack of dependability. A change of government or policy sometimes causes cancellation of funds. . . .

Donor fashions are constantly changing, especially as many seek quick technical fixes. . . . To raise more funds, donors have to keep on inventing new ideas. Already, support for vertical programmes is waning, as the programmes are unsustainable without continued massive donor support. These changes in fashion lead in turn to discontinuous non-cumulative changes in the MOH and damage institutional and capacity building.

Foreign technical assistance has also been important. . . . In 1989, the MOH estimated that donors spent 11.6 million dollars to fund around 500 expatriate health workers. The MOH payroll for around 16,000 workers was 8.8 million dollars. . . . The heavy dependence on foreign technical assistance has had many disadvantages. For example, doctors come from many different schools; they are sometimes unwilling to use Mozambican treatment norms or adhere to essential drug lists.

Box 12.1 *continued*

Expatriates are usually on short contracts and expect to achieve a lot quickly. They sometimes get impatient with their counterpart, who necessarily has a longer term perspective and cannot work fulltime because of a low salary. . . . Many agencies are helping to keep health personnel at their jobs by providing perks, such as cars, out-of-country work trips and *per diems* for seminars. These perks, however, often divert health officials from their main task of running the NHS. They are also often used to peddle influence. Low salaries have also led to a brain drain from the MOH to donor organisations.'

disbursing a large amount of aid at one time, without a lot of work to do so. At that point, donors and recipients alike failed to see that there was a catch: a hospital is expensive to build, but it is also expensive to run. Aid agencies were happy to provide *capital* costs, but much less enthusiastic about supporting *recurrent* costs, which of course are endless, so long as the hospital operates. Hospitals as aid projects went out of fashion, as primary health care came in, and as aid agencies recognised that projects with such high recurrent cost implications were bound to threaten the stability of at least the hospital, but possibly also of the health sector as a whole. Yet some aid agencies (Japan being one important example in recent years), working on low budgets for their own operating costs, continue to be attracted towards the large capital project.

Another persistent problem with aid, as Cliff (1993) mentions, stems from the commercial interests of the donor countries. It is quite common for donors to see aid projects as an entry to markets for the donor country's private companies, and often a condition attached to projects is that any goods which need to be bought from outside must be ordered from the donor country. This has led to well-known problems whereby a Ministry of Health ends up with a range of vehicles from six different countries, at once testing the maintenance skills of its mechanics to the utmost and creating major problems by trying, with an almost nonexistent budget for the purpose, to maintain a stock of spare parts for all the different models. The resulting situation, with hardly any transport in working order at any one time, is well known. Such policies actually damage sustainability of existing services.

A third problem which has received attention in the literature over a considerable time, is that of the nature of the *aid project* itself.[4] Donors need to resource clearly defined projects, because aid administrators must be able to explain to their own political bosses, and from time to time to a wider public, on what money has been spent. They also need to say how it has been spent, with what efficiency, and to what end. They must be able to evaluate the project and say whether it has had the desired effect. If the resources go simply as a contribution to a larger programme, aid administrators have the problem that there is no way of judging the effectiveness of the aid effort. Furthermore, projects have a limited life; no aid agency wants to make an open-ended commitment to a particular use of funds, both because it wants to be able to choose to back new activities, and more importantly, because there is general agreement that aid should help to initiate activity which will become locally sustainable. Unfortunately, in the past these very characteristics of aid projects have impeded sustainability. Projects have been kept separate from other health pro-gramme activity so that budgets and inputs can be reserved for the project; this has meant that the project activity always has special staff, often has its own vehicles and quite frequently is better resourced than other activities. The consequences are that the project activity never becomes a normal part of duties within the appropriate health service section, and when the project stops, all the activity lapses. Indeed, a project which has enjoyed resources others do not have may well have become the object of envy and resentment; many will be pleased to see it stop. It is just such characteristics which have proved problematic in Mozambique.

Sustainability

All these problems are referred to today in debates about sustainability. This rather clumsy term has become a talking point among aid agencies of late, who have come to realise that the successful utilisation of aid does not begin with the start of a project and finish at the end of the project's time span. Various definitions of sustainability are offered in the literature; one which is carefully worded, and provides a useful focus on the recipient, is that of the International Development Centre:[5]

> the ability of a system to produce outputs that are sufficiently well valued by beneficiaries (users of the goods and services produced) and stakeholders (actors other than the users with an interest in what the system does) so that enough inputs are provided to continue performance leading to long-term benefits and impacts.

This thoughtful definition recognises that there is more to sustainability than merely finding the financial resources for health care activities after the donor has gone – a mistake sometimes made by others. Here there is acknowledgement that if aid projects are to be sustained, they must become part of the *local* picture, no longer just something which someone else wanted to give.

Real success can only be judged when we look again, perhaps after a few years, and attempt to see whether the activities initiated are able to continue and to prosper, after the foreign support has finished. Although aid agencies have shown concern for this issue, it has been tackled largely from the aid agency's viewpoint – what can the *agency* do to reduce the problem? Few accounts ask: what can the *recipient* do to reduce the problem? In exploring the way to do this, we should note the work of Bossert (1990), who conducted a study of the sustainability of a number of US-government-funded health projects in Central America and Africa. Some of Bossert's main conclusions are summarised in Box 12.2 and provide a useful checklist of considerations for both donors and recipients.

What more can the aid recipient do to improve sustainability? Probably the answer is for the recipient agencies to develop an aid strategy of their own. If projects can be designed within an ongoing programme of activity, and specified according to local needs and wants before any discussion with individual aid agencies can start, there is some hope that the resulting projects will be relevant; the aid can be phased in a way that is appropriate to the local 'absorptive capacity' (in other words, it will be possible to use the offered resources well within a reasonable time scale). Development of a local strategy means that projects will be wanted projects, and not merely taken on by passive acceptance of an 'off-the-peg' design related to the aid agency's latest preoccupations. Despite the concerns voiced above in relation to projects, some authors (such as Foltz, 1994) feel that where there is not a high institutional capacity, project assistance may work as well as non-project assistance.

Policy makers must play a central part in the elaboration of the local strategy, taking into account broader strategic development as the framework for it. As Okuonzi and Macrae (1995) have argued in the Ugandan context, it is of great importance that local actors feel they own policies, and that there is room for proper debate. These authors suggest that sustainable programmes will result only when there is adequate local capacity for policy analysis and research, and for subsequent policy development. There are undoubtedly countries where policies are still accepted unquestioningly in exchange for hard currency aid. However, aid agencies are themselves becoming concerned about the need for local ownership of policy changes, and will increasingly be unwilling to be involved with totally passive partners.

We do need to be concerned about what policies aid agencies bring with them: while recognising that aid does not come from a monolithic global consortium, there are certainly trends which may be favoured at one point in time by many agencies. Beyond questions of capital versus recurrent aid, tied expenditure and the limitations of project activity, there lurks a broader question which will undoubtedly provide the focus for much debate in the near future. Whether or not the management changes are working, however one analyses health sector reform, it is clear that international agencies are seeing the reforms as the key to dealing with the crises of expanding demand for health care which were discussed in Chapter 2. In that discussion we referred to the notion of 'essential health packages'.[6] A national health package is meant to be what a government decides it can afford as a minimum package of public health services and medical care, on the criteria of what is most appropriate for the local major

Box 12.2   Conditions for Sustainability of Health Aid Projects
(Source: Bossert, 1990)

1. The perceived effectiveness of a project or aid activity is important. If the local people (including both beneficiaries and stakeholders) don't like a project, or see no evidence of achievement of objectives, they are unlikely to support the continuation of the activity.
2. During the life of a project, some financial responsibility must be taken locally, and ideally this should increase gradually until there is total local support for the project.
3. The projects which are least sustainable are those which relate to vertical activities such as family planning, malaria control or nutrition planning; these will not necessarily replicate themselves later. Projects which focus on infra-structural developments such as building of clinics or train-ing of health workers, are the most sustainable, particularly if the effort goes into supporting what may be a *replicating output* such as a construction agency or a training school.
4. Projects work best when there is participation of nationals in the design of the project. This both allows local priorities to be voiced, and also creates a sense of ownership of the project activity.
5. Good projects usually have a training component which allows any technical know-how essential to the project activity to be passed on. Additionally, the negotiating pro-cess should be mutually respectful, avoiding any sense that projects are being imposed from outside.
6. Vertical projects are not well sustained. In addition to the points made above concerning favoured resourcing for some projects, vertical projects lose out in the long term because there is not a network of administrators with a long-term interest in keeping the project going. Vertical programs are more likely to create institutional jealousies and the expan-sionary ambitions of bureaucrats in other programs may well sign the death-warrant of a vertical program the minute the donor has gone.
7. Project sustainability seems to be dependent upon the social and political environment within which the project is imple-mented. If there is a general lack of infrastructure and resources, there may be little hope of supporting the simplest activity.

health problems, and what is cost-effective. In other words, governments will limit their responsibility for dealing with the demand for health care, to provision of those services they define as essential and to attempting to regulate the nature of the further provision offered by private companies.

Governments will have to adopt some kind of line on resource allocation, for no government will be able to meet the potential demands made for medical care in the twenty-first century. But we need to note the dangers of too simplistic a formula, worked out as a global recipe. It is easy to see how aid agencies will find just such an idea – the latest 'magic bullet' – easy to peddle, regardless of specific national conditions. If we push for such solutions as the essential health package it would be easy to slip quickly into a situation where the rich get the care they want and the poor get very little indeed – far less than a comprehensive service. Last, a problem with any solution propounded from outside, whether by an aid agency or other experts, is that it is easy to forget that the people who above all should have a say are the local communities. Slick top-down recipes leave no room for local communities to work through the issues and priorities of real concern to them. If essential national health packages become the latest magic bullet, we may find that 'aid' is of little help to its recipients. Whether the resulting health care would constitute a sustainable system is questionable.

In summary

Aid within global relationships

- The aid relationship is a two-way process; aid would not happen if there were not tangible potential benefits for donors as well as recipients.
- Foreign aid is significant as a proportion of the total resources available in many ministries of health.

Features of the aid process

- Acceptance of foreign aid brings with it the problems of conditionality.
- Conditionality attached to aid today tends to relate to implementation of health sector reform, including such features as user charges.
- Conditionality has also tended to focus recently on a requirement for human rights and democracy.
- Other problems with aid include those related to the receipt of large capital funds with no provision for support for the recurrent cost implications of these; conditionality related to commercial donor interests, and sustainability.

Sustainability

- Sustainability may be defined as 'the ability of a system to produce outputs that are sufficiently well valued by beneficiaries and stake-

holders so that enough inputs are provided to continue performance leading to long-term benefits and impacts'.
- Sustainable aid projects must become integrated into the local health care picture.
- In the past, and still occasionally today, aid agencies have created unsustainable projects by favouring those which incur high capital expenditure, without consideration of recurrent cost implications.
- Problems also arise out of donor insistence as to what goods may be bought with their aid funds.
- Some authors argue that projects are, by their very nature, unsustainable.
- Bossert (1990) has, from his empirical studies, produced some conclusions about the features of sustainable projects, which are summarised above.
- To develop sustainable activities, it is crucial that recipient agencies develop their own aid strategy, into which outside offers of projects can be slotted if appropriate.

Notes

1. See for example Waller (1994), who describes the debates which arose in Germany (as elsewhere in the Western world) when development cooperation with China was stopped following the Tiananmen Square massacres. A strong lobby argued that economic reforms should be continued, because these would lead to improvement in the human rights situation in the long term – and that if Germany missed the business opportunity, someone else would seize it!

2. See Garner (1995) and Stockmann (1993).

3. Bollini and Reich (1994) give an interesting analysis of the Italian aid programme, describing its shortcomings in terms of diplomatic objectives taking priority over developmental ones, as well as lack in the programme itself of both technical expertise and managerial skills.

4. The debate concerning the positive and negative impacts of the aid project as a form of assistance is exemplified by Rondinelli (1983) and Honadle and Rosengard (1983).

5. Quoted in White (1992).

6. 'Essential national health packages' are proposed by, for example, Bobadilla et al. (1994).

13

Privatisation within the Health Sector

Privatisation: a global trend

The last two decades have seen major changes in the overall approach to health care delivery around the world, and to the assumptions upon which service development is based. In 1978, the constituent nations of the World Health Organization gathered together in Alma Ata in the then Soviet Union, and agreed the text of the Alma Ata Declaration on primary health care, a document that has been the touchstone for international health strategies ever since. The Alma Ata Declaration (WHO, 1978: Section V) states: 'Governments have a responsibility for the health of their people which can be fulfilled only by the provision of adequate health and social measures.' At the time such provision was viewed as the direct duty of governments themselves, in the interest of social justice and economic development. Today some of those governments would say they had a duty to ensure some basic health care, and this should, as far as possible, be provided by agencies other than government. Whereas the literature concerning optimal approaches to health care delivery was once based on the assumption that we must look to governments for effective health care, now the assumptions are overturned: responsibility for provision should be removed from over-centralised governments, and other health care providers encouraged. This section will consider the implications of these policy shifts, but first let us examine their origins.

Privatisation has become an important part of the political agenda in many countries. We must consider how this trend has come about, what people are seeking, and whether privatisation is the force for progress that it is generally assumed to be. Before doing so, it is probably worth reminding ourselves of the context in which we speak. Figure 13.1 demonstrates the extreme variations that exist in the contribution which the private sector makes to health care, variations that exist in all regions of the world. There are regional differences in the private sector figures, particularly in the health care scene in Asian countries, but as Figure 13.1 indicates, there is also a lot of intra-regional variation. Excluding established market economies and formerly socialist economies, the 1993 *World Development Report* gives data or estimates for the size of the private and public sectors in 79 countries in 1990. In 24 of these, the private sector was already larger than the public sector (as a share of gross domestic product). In many countries, health care operates in something close to a free market situation already.

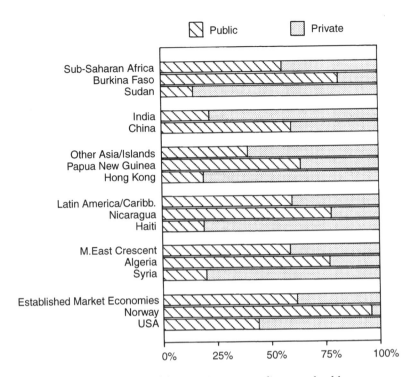

Figure 13.1   *Proportion of public to private expenditure on health care, selected regions and countries (World Bank, 1993)*

We noted in Chapter 11 that there has been a loss of confidence in state-supported enterprise as a basis for development, at least in part because the public sector in developing countries has come to be seen as over-extended – in other words, it is supposedly too big and too inefficient. In reaction, the private sector is seen as the way to provide care beyond that which governments can afford – sophisticated surgery in some cases; basic health care in others. We also saw in Chapter 11 how a market environment is now seen as a prerequisite to modern, effective services, not merely in health but generally. Central to this idea is the belief that when services are offered in line with the demands of the market place, consumers can express their wishes and services should become more responsive to real needs. Furthermore, when different providers are competing, each will attempt to cut costs and the net result will be efficiency savings, passed on to whoever bears the costs.

Such beliefs fit in with a much wider trend, towards neo-liberal political views. This means that we should be cautious about accepting what has crept in as common wisdom, when it may be that we are simply being swept along on the tide of shifting global politics. The international agencies have certainly espoused privatisation. In the 1980s, IMF-supported structural adjustment programmes usually contained policy recommendations related to privatisation measures. Sometimes these were for privatisation in the sense of change of ownership or increased competition; sometimes for sectoral reform activity in a broader sense. Observers have commented that:

> the espousal of the privatisation objective in many less developed countries has been for reasons of expediency as much as from ideological conviction. . . . The irony of the international agencies advocating the dismantling of the publicly owned institutions that they themselves created in the 1960s, has not gone unnoticed.[1]

It may well be that the extent to which privatisation and sectoral reform activity in developing countries has occurred is a measure of what governments perceive as the minimum movement towards a market environment needed to secure a continued inflow of foreign assistance.

Is there really evidence that the public sector is over-extended, or are we dealing simply with a fashion here? Alternatively, as some observers have suggested, do governments go for privatisation as a quick way to improve their financial position? Is it that creation of a market environment, in the sense of creating room for competition within health services, will improve equity, efficiency and quality of services, all of which are claims being made? Not everyone would accept these claims, and we need to evaluate them. We shall first consider the anti-public-sector elements of the debate, and then scrutinise the potential role of a market environment in health care.

Is there a case against the public sector?

Is the public sector too big?

We actually know very little about the total role of state sector activity in most developing countries. There is certainly a *perception* that it is big, and has weaknesses. Documents such as the World Bank's 1981 'Berg Report' have suggested that the public sector in developing countries is 'over-extended' – trying to do more than available resources and organisational capacity will allow. However, this assertion has never been substantiated, and we do not even know very much about the size of public enterprises, and the total role of state-sector activity in developing country economies.[2]

Selling off state enterprises has been seen as an attractive way of producing funds for government, not only in developing countries but also in industrialised countries. It is quite possible that for some governments in the Western world, it is convenient to suggest that the public sector should be slimmed down. On the other hand, such divestment has uncertain results in countries where the capital market is small. Furthermore, there is not likely to be unqualified political support for such activity. There will be all sorts of groups who benefit from the status quo. Public enterprises can be very important as a source of reward and patronage.[3] Others point out that there will also be opposition to divestment in the not uncommon situation where one ethnic group is likely to benefit over another, and where foreign capital is likely to benefit more than local interests.[4]

Is the public sector inefficient?

There has been concern about inefficiency and poor performance within the public sector. It is claimed that public enterprises become overly bureaucratic, and that there is little incentive on the part of employees to seek to improve efficiency. Indeed it is argued that public employees are likely to be preoccupied with rent seeking – that is, with trying to maximise their own gains from government resources, rather than trying to maximise public benefits. It is also argued that if public enterprises had to behave like private firms, they would behave more efficiently – that is, do the same job for less resources.

This claim has been made in recent years the world over. Because it is made so often, people come to believe it, but there is little firm evidence to support this. There is a real problem in comparing public enterprises and/ or government departments with private enterprises. This is because efficiency can only be assessed in relation to stated goals. In private business these goals are clear. They are to maximise profits and/or economic growth. In the public sector, however, these goals are not so clear. It may not be important for a government department to make a profit, provided it performs functions defined as essential for the community or for another department. Thus, a government may decide that transport subsidies will help the whole economy, so transport will be allowed to be an unprofitable sector. In the case of health care, people argue that support is needed because good health is essential to development (World Bank, 1993).

On the basis of such arguments, one could propose that the health sector should if necessary carry activities supported as a public good, *despite* their low profitability and apparent inefficiency in conventional economic terms. For example, we noted in Chapter 10 that the effort to ensure reasonable geographical access to health services for all citizens, even those in remote areas, would conflict with goals of efficiency. In the same way, health services may be regarded as 'inefficient' if a great deal of effort and resources are needed in order to ensure that marginal groups and minority ethnic groups have fair access to health care. It may well be 'inefficient' to offer care to old people for chronic conditions which can only be alleviated, not cured. It may well be 'inefficient' to keep people in hospital after an operation because we know that there is no one at home to care for them. Yet people may feel that such coverage is important in a caring, decent society. The stated goals of the health service must recognise these needs, and *then* set about providing for them as efficiently as possible.

It is essential to recognise, then, that efficiency must be measured in relevant terms. If our concerns are social concerns, an efficient system is one that produces well-being at the lowest cost to society. If our concerns are to make profits out of health care, an efficient system will be one that produces well-being at low cost to the health service – quite probably by increasing costs elsewhere in the system, whether to the community or to social services. With a mixed public/private system, there is a great danger that the private providers will gravitate towards the services where it is easy to make a quick profit, leaving the public sector carrying the inherently unprofitable activities, and once again, being dubbed 'inefficient'.

What is the market environment for health care?

We have seen that selling off services is one obvious approach to privatisation, but not necessarily a popular one. When people refer to privatisation in the health sector, they are usually talking about providing a market environment in a more general sense. A market environment is an environment in which there is outright private provision of services, or one in which there is ample opportunity for a competitive atmosphere. This can be created by a variety of arrangements, such as private management contracts, creation of internal markets, encouragement of private/public sector competition, contracting out of specialist services. Box 13.1 summarises some of the main forms in which a market environment has been cultivated in health service provision.

A market environment can also be cultivated in relation to *finance*. Publicly financed services are paid for out of taxation. Privately financed services are paid for by a range of mechanisms such as user charges, health insurance policies, and health maintenance organisations. Services financed in any of these ways can be provided by government or by private agencies. Box 13.2 summarises some of the main ways in which health services are privately financed.

Of course, publicly financed services are actually paid for by the people, and it is pertinent to ask why health services should not be paid for out of the taxes and revenues collected by the government from ordinary citizens. The argument which is sometimes advanced in developing countries is that public finance is too small a fund to rely on in a situation where taxation only reaches that minority of the population who are in formal employment, and/or who buy consumer goods. Some proponents of private financing argue that multiple financing mechanisms can be cultivated, provided that the state ensures that provision is nevertheless equitable.[5] Whether this is possible remains to be tested.

Many governments are shifting to a belief that they must somehow shed responsibility for at least the more expensive – and least essential – forms of curative care. This is because it is believed that, with rising population sizes and the inexorable expansion of technology, medical care demands will escalate far beyond the scope of the spending power of health services. Such a conclusion may seem logical, though some would argue that there are so many practical problems associated with this approach as to make it impossible to implement. Either the poor become deprived of access to

Box 13.1   Approaches to Privatisation in Health Service Provision

Privatisation measures allow health service provision to be offered, in part or in whole, by a range of non-governmental providers. Some of these may be commercial (for-profit) organisations; others may be not-for-profit organisations. Examples of the latter would include charities, community organisations, consumer cooperatives and health maintenance organisations

(a) Change in ownership   This is denationalisation or divestiture. In less developed countries, there are limited markets for equity sales. Parts of the health service have rarely been sold off.

(b) Liberalisation or deregulation   This does not involve the transfer of any assets from the state to the private sector. It means that activities which the state has organised may now be undertaken by private agencies. Liberalisation means that government agencies must give up these activities or compete with the private sector. Possible liberalisation measures include:

1. Arrangements which encourage the private sector to compete, e.g., allowing doctors to practise privately out of hours, allowing doctors to use public facilities for private practice, allowing subsidy through the use of public facilities or through tax reforms.
2. Deregulation of activities related to the health service, e.g. retail pharmacies, supply of family planning devices, water supply.
3. UK-style trust arrangements to encourage competition within the state-supported health sector.

(c) Government support for private provision

1. Contracts from public agencies. Contracting out of services is becoming popular in many countries and situations. Contracted-out services are those which a government agency tenders to private sector firms and agencies. Common examples in the UK and in some developing countries include contracting out of laundry, catering, security and cleaning services. Specialist clinical services e.g. radiography or laboratory services can also be contracted out.

Box 13.1 *continued*

2. Management contracts. Occasionally, state owned facilities may be managed privately through management contracts. For example, the National University Hospital of Singapore is 100% government owned but has an 'autonomous' management. It has also been known for a government agency to contract out an entire service; this would be a monopoly franchise arrangement. Governments may also invite other agencies to tender for the award of a 'turnkey contract' for the construction and setting into operation of an entire hospital.

3. Vouchers. Each citizen is offered an equal number of vouchers to be used as they would like, so each person would have access to equal amounts of health care, paid for by the state but provided by any recognised provider. A sophisticated version of the voucher system is the capitation system whereby the state makes capitation payments to a health facility on behalf of each person who chooses to use it.

expensive treatments, or else complex, and not necessarily equitable or workable, means tests must be attempted.

However, many governments would feel politically unable to completely deny responsibility for health care. People are used to some form of state provision of medical services, and to withdraw such provision would be an act of provocation which many governments would prefer not to risk. In this context, the 'essential package of health service' idea which was discussed in Chapter 12 comes into play. All manner of claims are now made for a partially privatised system. We are led to expect increased democracy and community participation, freedom of choice, equity and efficiency. These are extravagant claims, but if they can be substantiated, then we must revise all the old ideas and presuppositions about the best ways to achieve the primary health care approach. We must therefore examine them with care.

Does a market environment enhance democracy and community participation?

It is sometimes argued that an interventionist state may be *too* powerful, and thus anti-democratic. Some advocates of the market environment see dangers in a monolithic state health care system which can be manipulated to serve the needs of the ruling group.

These same people believe that the existence of private health care increases people's freedom by fostering their freedom to choose. Theoretically, if there is a range of different health care providers, people can 'shop

Box 13.2   Approaches to Privatisation in Health Care Financing

User charges

Patients pay directly for medical care, for drugs, or for both. It is often argued that making people pay something towards health care will deter them from over-using the services for minor ailments. Both arguments and evidence can however be given for the opposite view – that user charges constitute a barrier to treatment which is really needed.* It is also easy to forget that collection of charges creates its own administrative costs.

Community financing

Some authors would describe user charges as a form of community financing, but others reserve this term for schemes which involve some sort of pre-payment; communities may contribute to the capital for a revolving drug fund, or create an informal health insurance fund so that individuals do not have to find the money when they are sick. The term may usefully be reserved for systems which operate at the level of local communities, and within which any proceeds are retained by the health sector and managed at local level.[†]

Private health insurance

Private health insurance schemes have received a lot of attention as a means of financing health care; however, insurance schemes are expensive to run, partly because there are sales costs for policies, and also because health services tend to push charges up if they feel the burden will not accrue to individual patients. As private insurance schemes make no allowance for the subscriber's income, the fees are high for poorer people.

Charitable organisations

Some health care may be offered through such bodies as religious charities. However, such health care while subsidised is rarely offered without some sort of charge to individuals, and charges in some charitable institutions such as mission hospitals can be quite high.

* Abel-Smith gives a succinct and useful summary of this debate.
[†] See McPake et al. (1993).

around' for the best deal. In reality, the choice may be minimal. In many countries people can only afford care through insurance schemes, and the insurance companies may dictate where care can be received. In the UK the creation of health service hospital trusts has led to limited enhancement of consumer choice.[6] World-wide, apparent freedom of choice is totally meaningless to those who have no way of paying for care.

It has also been argued that the private market provides a neat mechanism for increasing responsiveness to local communities. The idea is that, whereas a centralised state service would have to deal with two-way information flows through a complex information system, private sector decisions are automatically decentralised to local actors, and it is possible to maximise the use of information at the points where crucial decisions are made. Furthermore, consumer preference is demonstrated by the simple mechanism of people voting with their feet. This is probably quite effective, if everyone has the opportunity to be a consumer, and provided that all expressions of need can be voiced in terms of supply and demand. But we must doubt whether such a mechanism can cope with the needs of those who can't afford care. It is particularly hard to see how it can cope with community, rather than individual, needs.

If we believe that fostering a free health care market will allow greater consumer preference, we need to consider whether what people get is worth having. Research has shown that consumers are not always good judges of the technical quality of health services,[7] and sometimes may use criteria of choice which work perversely against them, such as preferring expensive services.[8] Though in some countries formal consumer representation is growing, for example on hospital boards,[9] the level of consumer organisation in most developing countries is weak compared to that in the West. People may on occasion be given a say, but may have very little recourse to litigation or even back-up from consumer groups if things go wrong.

Some would argue that a decentralised state system will offer the benefits without these drawbacks. Such a system might for example improve access for the poor, while allowing scope for local responsiveness to communities. Yet there is need for caution in analysing what decentralisation means. One approach to decentralisation has been to assume a reduction in central government responsibility for funding health services. In this view, getting communities to pay for their own health care directly, rather than through taxation or any such mechanism, is to be equated with community participation[10] – yet such an approach does not guarantee the public any greater say in policies or services. Decentralisation may be supported in order to allow for the creation of local arrangements such as contracting out of services, with bids handled locally.[11] This is not always a satisfactory process, and can lead to outcomes which some would regard as highly undesirable, such as reduced remuneration for those performing essential services, and difficulty in ensuring that work such as cleaning comes up to standard.

Does a market environment increase equity?

Proponents of outright privatisation in health care would argue that privatisation brings real benefit to all consumers by allowing the production of lower-priced goods; if a free market is allowed to operate, competition will force prices down. It is dubious whether this always works. It is also dubious whether such benefits of competition could ever be equally distributed. Private for-profit medical practice will always flourish best in those areas where the market is robust and profitable: in the rich areas, and particularly the rich urban areas. In some countries there have been efforts to control the location of private practices.[12] It is uncertain whether these arguments apply within the medical field. The phenomenon of supplier-induced demand is real and probably of great importance;[13] in other words, the private practitioner can claim that expensive – and profitable – surgical intervention is necessary where a cheaper treatment might have sufficed.

If the state has in the past subsidised medicine, privatisation will be to the detriment of poorer sections of the population. There is quite a strong lobby of people these days who argue that health care is only valued by ordinary people if they have to pay; that if they don't have to pay, they will abuse the services offered. This lobby tends to argue that people will always manage to find money from somewhere. Against this, there are others who argue that money might or might not be found depending on the power and prestige of who is sick; it seems that there is evidence that imposition of user charges on health care has a particularly negative effect on children's health care.[14] Sometimes people only manage to pay by spending money on health care which had been put aside for other household purposes such as food and education, and even sell assets to pay, thereby setting off down a path of permanent impoverishment.[15] It has even been argued recently that the expenditure the poor are likely to make on health care is actually bad for their health,[16] insofar as it distracts people from spending money on more basic requirements such as food.

These considerations bring us back to the pros and cons of targeting, which was discussed at length in Chapter 10. If targeting becomes a matter of discretion for either health workers or communities, the evidence is that (a) there are huge difficulties in trying to distinguish who should be favoured; (b) communities are unwilling to pick out people for exemptions and very few are likely to be granted; (c) there is a danger of corruption and favouritism.[17]

Does a market environment increase efficiency?

We have already noted that public enterprises have been said to be inefficient: they serve a large number of goals beyond mere profit making and therefore do not perform well when assessed in a one-dimensional way. Health care facilities interested in profit will shy away from work with communities; they will be reluctant to get involved in the unprofitable activities of health promotion and prevention. Private hospitals sometimes appear to be efficient and cost-effective because they avoid difficult cases which would be complex and expensive to treat, leaving these to the 'inefficient' public sector. At other times they are not even efficient in business terms.

It is claimed that competition creates neutral, non-political procedures which exclude the ineffective adoption of the latest technology for its own sake. There is some evidence from the USA that where a third party is involved in paying for health care, for example through insurance schemes, this may be so. However, where there is no third party, competition can all too easily lead to adoption of new technologies as trendy gimmicks, devices to increase profits. We noted above that physician-induced demand is an important phenomenon. If profits are linked to the sale of drugs through the health service or individual practitioner, this too is a source of over-spending.

Though contracting out may be introduced to increase efficiency, it may in fact have the effect of *decreasing* efficiency, for example if the newly contracted-out services are located at a geographical distance from the main service. Decreased efficiency will also result from contracting out if the transaction costs involved in the process – the administrative costs connected with negotiation, information and accounting systems – become too high. Worries about efficiency have also been expressed in relation to health maintenance organisations,[18] for which both the administrative costs and the requisite initial start-up size may be a concern.

It is often argued that the public sector environment is less productive than the private sector environment. The arguments are that public sector officers suffer from too much political interference, from lack of adequate autonomy to be creative and innovative, and from lack of motivation to improve productivity. Undoubtedly, some of these charges may be important, but there is no conclusive proof that the private sector produces better health services.

Does a market environment improve the services on offer?

It is argued that cultivation of a market environment will have a positive effect on the standards of health care and the concern for quality in health care organisations. It is uncertain whether this is true, and it is not always easy to know what standards apply in the private or public sectors. Competition is said to stimulate quality awareness. However, in the private sector we have other worries: pursuit of high profit margins may well lead to neglect of quality of care and even of safety.

The degree to which quality of health care is in any sense controlled is highly variable, and regulatory systems are often notably lacking in developing countries. In some countries there is not even a clear system for registration of medical practitioners. This can mean that some practitioners operate, unlicensed, outside the mainstream system: this is often the case for complementary or traditional practitioners. In countries where there is a clear system of registration at least for Western-trained practitioners, there may nevertheless be a lack of systematic updating of records, which leads to great confusion about who is practising. It has been suggested that parastatal bodies and professional organisations could do a lot more to regulate not only registration, but also standards of care and fee levels.[19] Regulation of the amounts spent on investment in new and expensive technologies is also a neglected area. However, the cost of regulatory systems must also be counted before such ideas are embraced too enthusiastically.

Some authors consider that privately financed services tend to be of better quality than publicly financed services; it is suggested that if fees can be retained by a health facility and used to improve services, then quality of care will improve, creating improved utilisation rates and initiating a cycle of constant improvement. It is also suggested that competition will eliminate poor quality services. Against this there is considerable evidence from a number of countries of the inadequacy of much private sector medical care, and the lack of any attempt to control quality in the private sector.[20] It is all too easy to beguile the public with better 'hotel' facilities or a charming bedside manner, or lack of queues. This does not equal better care.[21]

A further concern is that privately provided health services will tend to focus on the provision of the kinds of health care which are most profitable. Many authors agree that private services are unlikely to enthusiastically offer preventive and promotive care, while being perhaps over-enthusiastic about fairly routine but highly profitable surgery. On the other side, governments keen to join the privatisation bandwagon may assign to the private sector responsibilities which will be fulfilled only partially. Study of the privatisation of fertility control in Brazil has provided a recent example of just such problems; poor women are left accumulating the ill effects of unwanted pregnancies and illegal abortions.[22]

Finally, it is important to acknowledge a broad concern which has been expressed: that the mere existence of a private medical sector will have negative effects on the state health sector.[23] This concern is based upon the fact that the private sector attracts more resources at the expense of the public sector. Private beds in public hospitals are often subsidised by the state; private medical insurance policies attract subsidies and tax relief. At the same time, medical practitioners are attracted away from state health services by the higher earnings to be had in private medicine.

In summary

Privatisation: a global trend

- Privatisation has become an important part of the political agenda in many countries.
- It is increasingly supposed that a market environment is a prerequisite to modern, effective services, not merely in health but generally.
- Extreme variations exist in the contribution which the private sector makes to health care in different regions of the world. In many countries, health care operates in something close to a free market situation already.
- The public sector is sometimes seen as a poor basis for development. It is said to be 'over-extended'.
- The private sector is advocated as an alternative.
- This belief fits in with the wider trend towards neo-liberal political views.
- Some governments may espouse privatisation under pressure from international agencies.

Is there a case against the public sector?

- Some say it is too big but in fact not much is known about the total size of public sector activity in most developing countries.
- Divestment is not likely to be a quick route to political popularity by reduction of government budget deficits.
- It is claimed that the public sector is inefficient.
- There is a real problem in comparing public enterprises and/or government departments with private enterprises.
- The government health sector may carry out activities supported as a public good, *despite* their low profitability and apparent inefficiency in conventional economic terms.
- With a mixed public/private system, there is a great danger that the private providers will gravitate towards the services where it is easy to make a quick profit, leaving the public sector carrying the inherently unprofitable activities and, once again, being dubbed 'inefficient'.

What is a 'market environment' for health care?

- A market environment is an environment in which there is outright private provision of services, or else one in which there is ample opportunity for a competitive atmosphere.
- This can be created by a variety of arrangements, such as private management contracts, creation of internal markets, encouragement of private/public sector competition, contracting out of specialist services.
- A market environment can also be cultivated in relation to *finance*.
- Privately financed services are paid for by a range of mechanisms such

as user charges, health insurance policies, and health maintenance organisations.
- The claims made for a partially privatised system are that it will bring increased democracy and community participation, freedom of choice, equity and efficiency.

Does a market environment enhance democracy and community participation?

- Private health care supposedly increases people's freedom by fostering their freedom to choose.
- In reality this choice is nonexistent for those who cannot afford to pay.
- It has also been argued that the private market provides a neat mechanism for increasing responsiveness to local communities.
- This only works if everyone can afford to be a consumer, and it is unlikely to work at all in relation to community rather than individual needs.
- The level of consumer organisation in most developing countries is weak compared to that in the West.
- A decentralised state system may offer benefits without these drawbacks.

Does a market environment increase equity?

- Proponents of outright privatisation in health care would argue that privatisation brings real benefit to all consumers by allowing the production of lower-priced goods.
- It is both doubtful whether this works, and also whether the benefits of competition can be equally distributed.
- It is argued that health care is only valued by ordinary people if they have to pay.
- However, considerable evidence indicates that people are becoming impoverished by having to pay for health care, even to the detriment of their health.

Does a market environment increase efficiency?

- Private hospitals sometimes appear to be efficient and cost-effective because they avoid difficult cases which would be complex and expensive to treat, leaving these to the 'inefficient' public sector.
- Unregulated competition can all too easily lead to adoption of new technologies as trendy gimmicks, devices to increase profits.
- Though contracting out may be introduced to increase efficiency, it may in fact have the effect of *decreasing* efficiency.
- For health maintenance organisations, both the administrative costs and the requisite initial start-up size may be a concern.

Does a market environment improve the services on offer?

- The degree to which quality of health care is in any sense controlled is highly variable, and regulatory systems are often lacking in developing countries.
- There are claims that the standard of private services will be better than that of public ones.
- However, there is considerable evidence of the inadequacy of much private care.
- A further concern is that privately provided health services will tend to focus on the provision of the kinds of health care which are most profitable.
- A broad concern has been expressed, that the mere existence of a private medical sector will have negative effects on the state health sector.

Notes

1. Cook and Kirkpatrick (1988: 30).
2. Cook and Kirkpatrick (1988) query the evidence for the assertion that the public sector is too big, or 'over-extended', as some authors claim (pp. 9–10). Commander and Killick (1988) have indicated the paucity of information on the actual size of the public sector in developing countries.
3. Walt and Gilson (1994) discuss this point, alluding to the work of Herbst (1990).
4. See Commander and Killick (1988).
5. See Frenk and González-Block (1992).
6. That is, as far as we know. As Hunter (1994) has pointed out, the absence of evaluation of the UK NHS reforms has been a major deficiency and is especially worrying because the UK example is much-quoted as a precedent. He also queries whether the UK reforms are actually understood by the public – let alone seen as enhanced choice.
7. See Bennett et al. (1994).
8. See for example McPake et al. (1993: 1385).
9. See Bennett et al. (1994) for some examples.
10. In Mali for instance there is today a non-profit making private health care sector which is termed the 'community sector' (see Balique et al., 1993). Although the community does have some say in the kind of services which exist, they also have to pay for these.
11. McPake and Banda (1994: 28). These authors do however point out that there are many practical problems in achieving any performance gains through contracting out in really remote areas with poor infrastructure. They also indicate the need for a considerable level of local skills, e.g. in negotiating and drafting contracts, which are required for such a process to work effectively at lower health service organisational levels.
12. Bennett et al. (1994) cite the example of Tanzania, where there are planning restrictions on the establishment of new private practitioners willing to set up practices in rural areas. Bennett (1992) mentions further examples of the latter practice in Mexico and in Malaysia.
13. See Rice and Labelle (1989) for an interesting recent discussion of this subject. McGreevey (1988) provides a useful discussion of the Brazilian case, and Barros et al. (1986) have offered a case-study of the way in which physician-induced demand works in relation to Caesarian sections in southern Brazil.
14. See Gertler and van der Gaag (1990).
15. See Abel-Smith (1994) and McPake et al. (1993).
16. See Werner (1995: 147–148). He quotes a mother involved in a health project in the

Philippines, commenting on how she and her neighbours have cut down on medical care expenditure: ' "But now when our children have coughs or colds or diarrhoea we give them home-made medicines", explained one mother. "That leaves more money for food (and for medical help when really needed). So our children are fatter and get sick less often. We save even more on health expenses. So we can feed our children still better! And now they die less often!" "You know what we're saying!" exclaimed one mother. "We're saying it was what we were spending on health care that was killing our babies!" '

17. See Abel-Smith (1994) and McPake et al. (1993).

18. Tollman et al. (1990).

19. Contracting out of specific health services is sometimes seen as an effective and relatively simple way of bringing market forces fruitfully into the health sector. Contracting out can be highly successful. However, there are pitfalls, in that competition for contracts may be inadequate in resulting in good prices for the services, and also in that the setting up of a system, and making decisions as to which services to contract out, can be very time-consuming. Considerable expertise is required before contracting becomes routine and risk-free.

20. See for a discussion of these issues Abel-Smith (1994).

21. See Giffin (1994).

22. See Bennett et al. (1994).

23. See Segall (1983).

PART V

CAN THE STUDY OF HEALTH POLICY IMPROVE THE PROCESS?

14

Developing Health Policy

The way ahead

This book has attempted to provide a guide for the study of health policy, particularly for those with an active role or potentially active role in the policy arena. Part II discussed the way in which policy studies might be conducted, and relevant information gathered. Part III introduced some concepts which are basic to all policy analysis. Part IV looked at some of the policy areas on which the big debates of today are focused. In this short final section, we ask how all this might help in furthering applied studies with real practical applications. To do this, we shall focus on two questions. The first is, does reference to the concepts and debates discussed give us insights into the value of the primary health care approach today? Does this then help us to see the way forward in practical efforts to implement primary health care (PHC)? Some of the issues discussed have been, as indicated, part of the policy environment in which most managers work, rather than part of the system which they are able to help to shape. Nevertheless, if we can see clearly the trends and their policy implications, we can work more clear-sightedly for specific goals. The second question concerns the extent to which policy studies can be translated into practice.

Developing policies for health for all

Debates about health care policies in the 1970s and for a considerable proportion of the 1980s were dominated by discussion of the PHC approach. Today the buzz-words 'health sector reform' dominate the agenda. Has PHC fallen by the wayside? Has the struggle for 'Health for All by the Year 2000' been dropped – or is the consensus that health sector reform actually replaces PHC as a strategy, working still to that end? Some authors feel that health sector reform does not oust PHC as a goal but rather gives us a means of improving strategies for PHC.[1] The suggestion is that PHC needs to be developed by means of a more proactive, strategic approach than has been the case in the past, restructuring the whole health system towards the goal of population-based care.

To be fair to many earlier commentators on PHC, the call for a radical restructuring of health care is not new. What is new is that health sector reform is seen as the means by which this restructuring can be achieved. Health sector reform is to some observers an open-ended concept; to others it comes with certain assumptions about the specific types of reform necessary. This is to be expected in view of the way in which health care has moved up the political agenda in recent years.[2] The whole health care policy debate has become less consensual and more conflictual.[3] PHC debates have always been played out in the context of debates about equity, and those who recognised the full implications of this have always argued that the PHC debate is about the structure and form of the whole health system,[4] not just about what has been described (Green, 1991) as primitive health care for the poor. However, in earlier debates the context of the state as the health care provider was taken for granted by most analysts. Now this one constant factor is pulled away, many of the assumptions about PHC must be re-examined. If it is possible to use the health reform process constructively, then PHC may still be the way forward to world health.

Frenk and González-Block (1992) are optimistic on this score. Analysing the situation in a number of Latin American countries, and considering the need to break out of the present cycle of social inequality, they propose four major strategies to guide the next stage of health sector reforms: (1) universality (2) redistribution (3) integration and plurality and (4) quality and efficiency. In the context of the debates reviewed in this book, let us briefly examine these important areas.

Universality refers to two concerns: health service coverage, and access to health services. In most countries, particularly developing countries, improvements in both coverage and access are sorely needed. The political pressures towards universality are probably strong in many situations. This is because the pressure comes from several quarters: from the public with its ever-growing awareness of the potential of health care for them, and demand for it; from the health care business interests where these emerge; from the health professionals who seek to enlarge the stage on which they perform. The political debate is about who pays. We have not looked in detail at issues of access to health care; there is an agenda for policy study here for the health services manager. In most countries today there are problems of differential access to health care on the basis of gender, class, ethnicity and other factors such as religion. Political support for working towards universality by removing these differentials is not always forthcoming.

Redistribution gets closer to many of the debates with which this book has been concerned. Everyone is happy about paying lip-service to equity if we can be content with throwing (targeted) crumbs to the poor. However, it is easy to ignore the practical problems of so doing; we have seen the difficulties of leaving to the discretion of health workers, judgements about who is poor. Even more importantly, the rich are happy until the results of any real redistribution begin to bite. It may well be that health care business interests would at first welcome any redistributive moves if these have the long-term potential for opening up the size of markets – but it must be remembered that these interests may conflict with more personal ones for the rich, and/or with elite-group or class interests. Health systems reform may be the key to rationalisation. It has been suggested that in the USA, the insurance corporations have already, in the role of corporate rationalisers, achieved more to reform the health care system than the Clinton proposals were able to bring about. One has to ask however, whether public provision is being marginalised in the health sector reform process, and whether short-term redistributive gains might not be achieved at the expense of long-term assurance that such gains will be perpetuated.

The medical profession is, in the estimation of some observers, fighting a last-ditch battle in favour of curative, high cost medicine – and is still 'among the world's most effective interest groups'.[5] One major problem for publicly provided health services is that as the private sector grows, the public sector competes unfavourably for professionals. In Zimbabwe, of the 496 doctors produced by the University of Zimbabwe from 1980 to 1988, only 14 per cent remained in government service in 1988,[6] the rest lured away by high salaries. In many developing countries today, there is practically a crisis as professional salaries decrease in relation to earlier years, and to comparable professionals elsewhere. Furthermore, health service career structures have remained remarkably undeveloped, and people lack any sense of career direction or incentive to perform well; this increases general dissatisfaction. Health sector reform may be able to achieve something in this regard.

Trends which favour private medicine endanger redistribution. They also threaten the strategies of *integration and plurality*. Integration refers to the characteristics of a health system which ensures even-handedness in provision of, and arrangements for access to, services – even perhaps while recognising a plurality of financing systems.[7] Integrated services should ensure that referral systems receive priority attention in developing a system where people get the help they need, not merely what is on the doorstep. Integration here is also taken to refer to what others have called a multisectoral approach to PHC – the necessary links with other sectors whose activities affect health, such as housing, education, agriculture, environmental protection; even defence. Historically, the medical profession has not embraced a social or environmental model of health with open arms. Yet biomedicine has enlarged its boundaries in recent years;

doctors now do accept that disease causation operates at levels beyond germ theory. A summation of the index entries of the *Lancet* for two years in the 1970s, the 1980s and the 1990s reveals an interesting trend. Over the 20-year period, references to 'environment/al' increased from virtually none to 78 in 1992–93; 'health and climate change' and 'global warming' became established as index categories by the 1990s. On a broader social front, modern entries have included 'poverty', 'violence', 'war' and 'women'. Biomedicine is capable of opening its frontiers, although private for-profit medicine has problems in so doing.

The capacity for adaptability on the part of medicine and the medical profession may stand the profession in good stead in terms of self-preservation through health sector reform. As we have seen, there is the danger that professionalism may lose out to business efficiency on the new health policy agendas. Yet the signs are, in the UK for example, that clinicians will rise, phoenix-like, as 'clinician-mangers', some of them at least more powerful than before.

Our last category is *quality and efficiency*. These are natural partners for the private businesslike approach which often accompanies health sector reform. We considered the problems of defining efficiency in Chapter 13. Quality is of course seen as desirable, but there is reason for concern about the extent to which resources should be directed at monitoring quality. This can be expensive, adding to the cost of services in the same way as tendering, contracting out and other market-related activities. The mention of quality does bring us to thoughts of acceptability and appropriateness of care. In turn this leads us to one area which did not figure on the above list of strategic considerations – that of community participation.

Community participation has been regarded as a vital plank in PHC strategy, and it is important to know whether this element will survive health sector reform. Concern for quality may well work in the interest of users of health services, but does not necessarily involve any participation. We saw in Chapter 12 that aid conditionality can work against community involvement in health care, and in Chapter 10 the way in which targeting can also create a top-down approach to planning. Green (1991) comments that communities become involved in health care when called upon to pay for it; as he puts it: 'more burden imposing than burden sharing'.

Perhaps this will be the crunch issue for PHC as we near and pass the year 2000. If Armstrong's optimistic view was right,[8] the imperative of modern health care necessitates the active involvement not only of patients but of communities. However, it is possible to envisage quite active lay involvement in treatments and services, while a role for the same people in decisions about resource allocation and priorities is denied. Community participation is not yet squeezed out of the picture, but there is a real challenge to managers here. Can management take this challenge seriously? Is it possible to envisage reform of health structures so as to make them truly responsive to local communities? Can staff be trained to listen rather than order people, to foster confidence in people rather intimidated by professionals, to say what they really want? Can we develop priority-setting processes which are actually capable of taking community views seriously?

There is a considerable agenda of issues which face the health service manager, and which demand study at a local level. Strategies can be developed which make health sector reform work for PHC – if we can appraise the possibilities and consider the policy implications of alternative courses of action.

Evidence-based policy making

We noted earlier that health care policy debates have become more conflictual in nature. One element of this conflict is about the epidemiological picture – and the implications for resource allocation decisions which derive from knowledge of the population-based picture of disease, chronic illness and disability.[9] In recent years, 'evidence based medicine' has come to be seen as the clinical arm of health sector reform.[10] Undoubtedly knowledge of the epidemiological picture is of great importance as a basis for some aspects of health policy. However other elements of conflict are as important – finance, reform and so on, and the kinds of solutions we might seek are to be found in the sphere of policy and management.[11] In this context, there is increased need for policy studies.[12]

There is recognition of what is frequently a wide gap between research/study findings, and practice.[13] A wide range of explanations are offered for this. These include the suggestion that the pressure of everyday considerations in the health care setting may squeeze out any hope of study, research and thinking.[14] Another claim is that governments frequently undervalue efforts to inform policy. But it is also suggested that this picture has changed somewhat in the USA, where the emphasis on health care as a business has led to a demand for certain types of information relevant to managerial control and competition.[15] In such an environment, it is argued, the research into practice environment is more supportive. Another point, of course, is that policy development depends on factors beyond the research base; these include the legal environment, the level of commitment of officials to change, and the level of support for change from other stakeholders.[16]

Yet there is hope; the Joint Project on Health Systems Research for Southern African Countries for example, found in its peer review that there was encouraging evidence that research findings were being implemented.[17] The same review process did have a number of specific suggestions for improving implementation. It was suggested that there was a need to improve the input of policy makers in prioritising topics for research. At a practical level, health departments needed to recognise the importance of having a budget line for health research, as well as one for dissemination of findings, and as well as making provision for research training for health workers. These are highly practical points which are all too often overlooked.

Other positive suggestions for improving research utilisation are also often highly practical and to do with process. Thus Boone (1989) has suggested that researchers should *plan* dissemination and utilisation as an integral part of the research design, not expect these processes to occur automatically. Others recommend that the timeliness of policy research is most important: policy makers do not want to wait several years for a considered academic piece of work; they want to answer questions and adjust policy now.[18] For this reason, time-effective methods such as those of rapid appraisal may be the most appropriate.[19] Another important area to explore is that of the involvement of stakeholders in the research process; if those who are concerned can participate in research design and in evaluation of the results, the chances are higher that they will support research utilisation.[20]

The other important way in which the chances of research utilisation can be improved is through bringing the research even closer to the policy maker, and making it even more immediate. A particularly attractive model is the 'structured flexibility approach' proposed by Brinkerhoff and Ingle (1989). This allows managers to develop strategy, but nevertheless to follow an adaptive management approach.

Such an approach means, for managers, a constant learning process; surely that is what good management is all about. It is hoped that this book has brought together insights which can help along the way.

Notes

1. See Frenk and González-Block (1992).
2. See Chapter 1 and also Walt (1994).
3. See Green (1991), Frenk and González-Block (1992) and Walt and Gilson (1994).
4. See for example, Unger and Killingsworth (1986), Segall (1983).
5. See Green (1991).
6. See Woelk (1994).
7. We have not looked in depth at financing systems, and this is not the place to start. However, it is relevant to note here that Frenk and González-Block were writing in the context of Latin America, where in many countries historically there has been a multiplicity of sources of finance as well as of health care providers. Focusing on integration of provision while leaving financing less coordinated may be a suitable strategy there, but not necessarily elsewhere. Different financing systems certainly have very different impacts on equity.
8. See Chapter 2, p. 17 and Armstrong (1993).
9. See for example Dixon and Welch (1991), Jamison et al. (1993), Murray et al. (1994) and also the World Bank 1993 *Development Report*.
10. See Anon. (1992), Woolf (1992), Fox (1993), Davidoff et al. (1995).
11. Walt (1993) has suggested that WHO's failure to recognise the importance of economics and social sciences in informing health policy has contributed to it being sidelined in the international health policy arena.
12. See Ham et al. (1995) and Walt and Gilson (1994).
13. The gap may not be as wide as is sometimes perceived. Weiss (1977) suggests that social research may play a function in conceptualisation; in the definition of problems and in revising

the way in which policy makers see them. Knorr (1977) suggests that utilisation may be higher than is imagined, but difficult to detect, in that social science findings may lead to changes which are indirect, diffuse, difficult to localise and possibly delayed – therefore of low visibility.

14. Harrison (1994).

15. Hunter and Pollitt (1992).

16. See Dey (1990).

17. 'Peer review' (1994).

18. See for example Rylko-Bauer et al. (1989).

19. Rapid appraisal methods have not been dealt with separately here, as they do not differ fundamentally from other ways of collecting information relevant to policy making. For more information about such methods see Chambers (1986) and Scrimshaw and Hurtado (1987).

20. See Drake (1989). Drake suggests that working with stakeholders is valuable, but has its own problems in that skills of collaborative research management are essential if the research coordinator is to avoid power struggles in the advisory group!

References

Abel-Smith, B. (1994) *Introduction to Health: Policy, Planning and Financing*. Harlow, Middlesex: Longman Group.

Al-Swailem, A. (1991) 'Should opinion polls be more widely used in developing countries?', *Health Policy and Planning*, 6(2): 185–187.

Alford, R.R. (1975) *Health Care Politics*, Chicago and London: University of Chicago Press.

Anionwu, E.N. (1989) 'Running a sickle cell centre: community counselling', Chapter 14 in E.N. Anionwu, *Ethnic Factors in Health and Disease*, London: Wright.

Anionwu, E.N. (1993) 'Genetics – A philosophy of perfection?', Chapter 8 in A. Beattie, M. Gott, L. Jones and M. Siddell (eds), *Health and Wellbeing: A Reader*. Basingstoke and London: Macmillan Press/Open University.

Annandale, E. (1989) 'Proletarianisation or restratification of the medical profession? The case of obstetrics', *International Journal of Health Services*, 19(4): 611–634.

Anonymous (1992) *Journal of the American Medical Association*, 268(17): 2420–2425.

Antonowsky, A. (1993) 'The sense of coherence as a determinant of health', pp. 202–211 in A. Beattie et al. (eds), *Health and Wellbeing: A Reader*. Basingstoke and London: Macmillan Press/Open University.

Armstrong, D. (1993) 'From clinical gaze to regime of total health', in A. Beattie et al. (eds), *Health and Wellbeing: A Reader*. Basingstoke and London: Macmillan Press/Open University.

Bachrach, P. and Baratz, M.S. (1970) *Power and Poverty*. New York: Oxford University Press.

Balique, H., Lejean, Y. and Annaheim, I. (1993) 'Mali's new private sector', *World Health 46th year*, 6 (Nov.-Dec.): 18–20.

Barker, C. (1983) 'The Mozambique pharmaceutical policy', *Lancet*, 1 October: 780–782.

Barker, C. (1995) 'Research and the health service manager in the developing world', *Social Science and Medicine*, 41(12): 1655–1665.

Barker, C. and Green, A. (1996) 'Opening the debate on DALYs', *Health Policy and Planning*, II(2).

Barros, F.C., Vaughan, J.P. and Victora, C.G. (1986) 'Why so many Caesarean sections? The need for a further policy change in Brazil', *Health Policy and Planning*, 1(1): 19–29.

Beattie, A., Jones, L. and Sidell, M. (1992) *Debates and Decisions in Everyday Health: K258 Health and Wellbeing Workbook 2*. Milton Keynes: Open University Press.

Bennell, P. (1982) 'Professionalisation: The case of pharmacy in Ghana', *Social Science and Medicine*, 16: 601–607.

Bennett, S. (1992) 'Promoting the private sector: A review of developing country trends', *Health Policy and Planning*, 7(2): 97–110.

Bennett, S., Dakpallah, G., Garner, P., Gilson, L., Nittarayamohong, S. and Zwi, A. (1994) 'Carrot and stick: State mechanisms to influence private provider behaviour', *Health Policy and Planning*, 9(1): 1–14.

Bhattacharya, N., Chakraborty, P., Chattopadhyay, M. and Rudra, A. (1991) 'How do the poor survive?', *Economic and Political Weekly*, 16 February: 373–379.

Bibeau, G. (1985) 'From China to Africa: The same impossible synthesis between traditional and Western medicines', *Social Science and Medicine*, 21(8): 937–943.

Bobadilla J-L., Cowley, P., Musgrove, P. and Saxenian, H. (1994) 'Design, content and financing of an essential national package of health services', *Bulletin of the World Health Organization*, 72(4): 653–662.

Bollini, P. and Reich, M.R. (1994) 'The Italian fight against world hunger. A critical analysis of Italian aid for development in the 1980s', *Social Science and Medicine*, 39(5): 607–620.

Boone, M.S. (1989) 'A utilisation study using network analysis: Maternal and infant health policy change in Washington DC', in van Willigen et al. (1989). pp. 89–122.

Bossert, T. (1990) 'Can they get along without us? Sustainability of donor-supported health projects in Central America and Africa', *Social Science and Medicine*, 30(9): 1015–1023.

Bottomore, T., Harris, L., Keirnan, V.G. and Miliband, R. (1983) *A Dictionary of Marxist Thought*. Oxford: Blackwell.

Bridgmann, R.F. (1976) 'Foreward', in R. Kohn and K.L. White, *Health Care, An International Study*. London: Oxford University Press.

Brinkerhof, D.W. and Ingle, M.D. (1989) 'Integrating blueprint and process: A structured flexibility approach to development management', *Public Administration and Development*, 9: 487–503.

Bronfman, M. (1992) 'Infant mortality and crisis in Mexico', *International Journal of Health Services*, 22(1): 157–167.

Brown, D. (1989) 'Bureaucracy as an issue in Third World management: An African case study', *Public Administration and Development*, 9: 369–380.

Brownlee, A. (1991) *Promoting Health Systems Research as a Management Tool*, Vol. 1. Health Systems Research Training Series. Geneva: Programme on Health Systems Research and Development of the World Health Organization; Ottawa: International Development Research Centre.

Brownlee, A., Gonzales, L.D. and Pathmanathan, I. (1992) *Strategies for Involving Universities and Research Institutes in Health Systems Research*, Vol. 3, Health Systems Research Training Series. Geneva: Programme on Health Systems Research and Development of the World Health Organization; Ottawa: International Development Research Centre.

Caldwell, J., Findlay, S., Caldwell, P., Santow, G., Cosford, W., Braid, J. and Broers-Freeman, D. (eds) (1990) 'What we know about health transition: The cultural, social and behavioural determinants of health', *Health Transition*, Series 2, Vols I and II. Canberra: Australian National University.

Cameron-Blackie, G. (1993) *Complementary Therapies in the NHS: National Association of Health Authorities and Trusts Research Paper No. 10*. Birmingham: NAHAT.

Chambers, R. (1986) 'Rapid rural appraisal: Rationale and repertoire', *Public Administration and Development*, 1(2): 95–106.

Checkland P. (1989) 'Soft systems methodology', pp. 71–100 in J. Rosenhead (ed.), *Rational Analysis for a Problematic World*. Chichester, UK: John Wiley.

Chelf, C.P. (1992) *Controversial Issues in Social Welfare Policy: Government and the Pursuit of Happiness*. Newbury Park, CA: Sage Publications.

Chossudovsky, M. (1991) 'Global poverty and New World economic order', *Economic and Political Weekly*, 2 November: 2527–2537.

Chossudovsky, M. (1995) 'A truly global debt crisis', *Third World Resurgence*, 59 (July): 27–39.

Cliff, J. (1993) 'Donor dependence or donor control? The case of Mozambique', *Community Development Journal*, 28: 237–244.

Collins, C. and Barker, C. (1995) 'Health management and action research: Bringing them together for the district medical officer' *Tropical Doctor*, 25 (April): 75–79.

Collins, C. and Barker, C. (forthcoming) 'Management research and the role of the health services manager: Promoting action research'.

Collins, C.D. (1994) *An Introduction to Management and Organisation in Developing Health Systems*. Oxford: Oxford University Press.

Commander, S. and Killick, T. (1988) 'Privatisation in developing countries: A survey of the issues', in Cook and Kirkpatrick (1988).

Commission on Health Research for Development (1990) *Health Research Essential Link to Equity in Development*. New York: Oxford University Press.

Cook, P. and Kirkpatrick, C. (eds) (1988) *Privatisation in Less Developed Countries*. Brighton, Sussex: Wheatsheaf Books.

Cornia, G.A. (1984a) 'Social policy-making: Restructuring, targeting, efficiency', pp. 165–182 in Jolly and Cornia (1984).

Cornia, G.A. (1984b) 'A survey of cross-sectional and time-series literature on factors affecting child welfare', pp. 17–32, in Jolly and Cornia (1984).

Cornia, G.A., Jolly, R. and Stewart, F. (1987) *Adjustment with a Human Face*. Oxford: Clarendon Press.

Crenson, M.A. (1971) *The Un-politics of Air Pollution: A Study of Non-decision Making in the Cities*. Baltimore: Johns Hopkins University Press.

Cunningham, Sir C. (1963) 'Policy and practice', *Public Administration*, 41: 229–237.

Davidoff, F., Case, K. and Fried, P.W. (1995) 'Evidence-based medicine: Why all the fuss?', *Annals of Internal Medicine*, 122(9): 727.

De Waal, A. (1990) 'A reassessment of entitlement theory in the light of the recent famines in Africa', *Development and Change*, 21: 469–490.

Dey I. (1990) 'The failure of success and the success of failure: The Youth Polytechnic Programme in Kenya', *Public Administration and Development*, 10: 179–198.

Dixon J. and Welch H.G. (1991) 'Priority setting: Lessons from Oregon', *Lancet*, 337 (13 April): 891–894.

Dore, E. (1992) 'Debt and ecological disaster in Latin America', *Race and Class*, 34(1): 75–87.

Drake, H.M. (1989) 'Using stakeholders in the research process: A case study in human services', pp. 237–256 in van Willigen et al. (1989).

Dwivedi, O.P. and Nef, J. (1982) 'Crisis and continuities in development theory and administration: First and Third World perspectives', *Public Administration and Development*, 2: 59–77.

Easton D. (1972) 'A systems analysis of political life', in J. Beishon and G. Peters (eds) *Systems Behaviour*. London: Harper & Row/Open University Press.

Engelkes, E. (1990) 'Process evaluation in a Colombian primary health care programme', *Health Policy and Planning*, 5(4): 327–335.

Feierman, S. (1984) 'The social origins of health and healing in Africa'. Conference paper commissioned by the ACLS/SSRC Joint Committee on African Studies for presentation at the 27th annual meeting of the African Studies Association, 25–28 October, Los Angeles.

Feierman, S. (1986) 'Popular control over the institutions of health: A historical study', Chapter 10 in Last and Chavunduka (1986).

Feinstein, J.S. (1993) 'The relationship between socioeconomic status and health: A review of the literature', *The Milbank Quarterly* 71(2): 279–322.

Foltz, A-M. (1994) 'Donor funding for health reform in Africa: Is non-project assistance the right prescription?', *Health Policy and Planning* 9(4): 371–384.

Foster, G.M. (1987) 'World Health Organization behavioural science research: Problems and prospects', *Social Science and Medicine*, 24(9): 709–717.

Foucault, M. (1986) 'The subject and power: An afterword', pp. 208–226 in H.L. Dreyfus and P. Rabinow (eds), *Michel Fouault: Beyond Structuralism and Hermeneutics*. Brighton: Harvester Press.

Fowlie, M. and Berkeley, J. (1987) 'Quality of life – a review of the literature', *Family Practice*, 4(3): 226.

Fox G.N. (1993) 'Evidence-based medicine: A new paradigm for the patient', *Journal of the American Medical Association*, 269 (10) 10 March: 1254.

Frenk, J. (1994) 'Dimensions of health system reform', *Health Policy*, 27: 19–34.

Frenk, J. and González-Block, M.A. (1992) 'Primary care and reform of health systems: A framework for the analysis of Latin American experiences', *Health Services Management Research*, 5(1): 32–43.

Friedson, E. (1986) 'The medical profession in transition', pp. 63–97 in L. Aiken and S. Mechanic (eds), *Applications of Social Science to Clinical Medicine and Health Policy*. New Brunswick, NJ: Rutgers University Press.

Garner, P. (1995) 'Is aid to developing countries hitting the spot?', *British Medical Journal*, 311 (8 July): 72–73.

Gertler, P. and van der Gaag, J. (1990) *The Willingness to Pay for Medical Care: Evidence from Two Developing Countries*. Baltimore, MD and London: Johns Hopkins University Press for the World Bank.

Giffin, K. (1994) 'Women's health and the privatisation of fertility control in Brazil', *Social Science and Medicine*, 39(3): 355–360.

Gordon, I., Lewis, J. and Young, K. (1993) 'Perspectives on policy analysis' pp. 5–9 in M. Hill (ed.), *The Policy Process: A Reader*. Hemel Hempstead, UK: Harvester Wheatsheaf.

Gramsci, A. (1971) *Selections from the Prison Notebooks* [1929–35] ed. Q. Hoare and G. Nowell Smith. London: Lawrence & Wishart.

Green, A. (1992) *An Introduction to Health Planning in Developing Countries*. Oxford: Oxford University Press.

Green, A. and Barker, C. (1988) 'Priority setting and economic appraisal: Whose priorities – the community or the economist?', *Social Science and Medicine*, 26(9): 919–930.

Green, R.H. (1991) 'Politics, power and poverty: Health for all in 2000 in the third world?', *Social Science and Medicine*, 32(7): 745–755.

Grigg, D. (1991) 'World agriculture: Productivity and sustainability', Chapter 2 in P. Sarre (ed.), *Environment, Population and Development*. London: Hodder & Stoughton for the Open University.

Ham, C. (1992) *Health Policy in Britain*, 3rd edn. Basingstoke: Macmillan.

Ham, C. and Hill, M. (1984) *The Policy Process in the Modern Capitalist State*. Brighton: Wheatsheaf Books.

Ham C., Hunter D.J. and Robinson R. (1995) 'Evidence based policymaking', *British Medical Journal*, 14 January: 71–72.

Hardiman, M. and Midgley, J. (1982) *The Social Dimensions of Development: Social Policy and Planning in the Third World*. Chichester and New York: John Wiley.

Harrison, S. (1994) 'Knowledge into practice: What's the problem?', *Journal of Management in Medicine*, 8(2): 9–16.

Hegedus, A. (1983) 'Bureaucracy', pp. 57–59 in Bottomore et al. (1983)

Herbst, J. (1990) 'The structural adjustment of politics in Africa', *World Development* 18: 949–958.

Hill, M. (ed.) (1993) *The Policy Process: A Reader*. Hemel Hempstead: Harvester Wheatsheaf.

Hogwood, B. and Gunn, L., (1984) *Policy Analysis for the Real World*. Oxford: Oxford University Press.

Homans, H. (1989) 'Equity in health: Has Zimbabwe achieved its objectives?', Unpublished conference paper.

Honadle, G.H. and Rosengard, J.K. (1983) 'Putting 'projectised' development in perspective', *Public Administration and Development*, 3: 299–305.

Hudson, B. (1993) 'Michael Lipsky and street level bureaucracy: A neglected perspective', pp. 386–398 in Hill (1993).

Hunter, D.J. (1993) 'Restructuring health care systems: A paradigm shift in policy and management', Inaugural lecture, Leeds, Nuffield Institute for Health.

Hunter, D.J. (1994) 'Towards an understanding of the British NHS changes', *The Health Exchange*, June–July: 11–12.

Huntington, D. and Schuler, S.R. (1993) 'The simulated client method: Evaluating client-provider interactions in family planning clinics', *Studies in Family Planning*, 24(3) May–June: 187–193.

Jamison, D.T., Mosley, W.H., Measham, A.R. and Bobadilla, J.L. (1993) *Disease Control Priorities in Developing Countries*. New York: Oxford University Press.

Jeffery, R. (1977) 'Allopathic medicine in India: A case of deprofessionalisation?', *Social Science and Medicine*, 11: 561–573.

Jeffery, R. (1982) 'Policies towards indigenous healers in independent India', *Social Science and Medicine*, 16: 1835–1841.

Johnson, T.A. (1973) *Imperialism and the Professions: Notes on the Development of Professional Occupations in British Colonies and the New States*, Sociol. Rev. Monograph, 20.

Jones, H. (1990) *Social Welfare in Third World Development*. Basingstoke: Macmillan Education.

Justice, J. (1987) 'The bureaucratic context of international health: A social scientist's view', *Social Science and Medicine*, 25(12): 1301–1306.

Khan, M.E. and Manderson, L. (1992) 'Focus groups in tropical diseases research', *Health Policy and Planning*, 7(1): 56–66.

Kitzinger, J. (1994) 'The methodology of focus groups: The importance of interaction between research participants', *Sociology of Health and Illness*, 16(1): 103–121.

Knorr, K.D. (1977) 'Policy-makers' use of social science knowledge: Symbolic or instrumental?', pp. 165–182 in Weiss (1977).

Korten, D. (1980) 'Community organisation and rural development: A learning process approach', *Public Administration Review*, Sept./Oct.: 480–511.

Kronenfeld, J.J. (1993) *Controversial Issues in Health Care Policy*. Newbury Park, CA: Sage Publications.

Last, M. (1986) 'The professionalisation of African medicine: Ambiguities and definitions', Introduction, in Last and Chavunduka (1986).

Last, M. and Chavunduka, G.L. (eds) (1986) *The Professionalisation of African Medicine*. Manchester: Manchester University Press and the International African Institute.

Le Gales, C. and Moatti, J-P. (1990) 'Searching for consensus through multicriteria decision analysis', *International Journal of Technology Assessment in Health Care*, 6: 430–449.

Le Grand, J. (1982) *The Strategy of Equality: Redistribution and the Social Services*. London: Allen and Unwin.

Leblebici, H. (1985) 'Transactions and organisational forms: A re-analysis', *Organisational Studies*, 6(2): 97–115.

Linstone, H.A. and Turoff, M. (eds) (1975) *The Delphi Method: Techniques and Applications*. Reading, MA: Addison-Wesley.

Lukes, S. (1974) *Power: A Radical View*. London: Macmillan.

MacPherson, S. (1982) *Social Policy in the Third World*. Brighton: Wheatsheaf Books.

MacPherson, S. and Midgely, J. (1987) *Comparative Social Policy and the Third World*. Brighton: Wheatsheaf Books.

McGlynn, E.A., Kosecoff, J. and Brook, R.H. (1990) 'Format and conduct of consensus development conferences', *International Journal of Technology Assessment in Health Care*, 6: 450–469.

McGreevey, W.P. (1988) 'The high costs of medical care in Brazil', *Bulletin of the Pan American Health Organisation*, 22(2): 145–168

McKeown, T. (1976) *The Modern Rise of Population*. London: Arnold.

McKeown, T. and Brown, R.G.. (1955) 'Medical evidence related to English population changes in the eighteenth century', *Population Studies*, 9: 119–141.

McKeown, T. and Record, R.G. (1962) 'Reasons for the decline of mortality in England and Wales during the nineteenth century', *Population Studies*, 16: 94–122.

McKeown, T. Record, R.G. and Turner, R.G. (1975) 'An interpretation of the decline of mortality in England and Wales during the twentieth century', *Population Studies*, 29: 391–422.

McKinley, J. and Stoeckle, J. (1988) 'Corporatisation and the social transformation of doctoring', *International Journal of Health Services*, 18(2): 191–205.

McPake, B. and Banda, E.E.N. (1994) 'Contracting out of health services in developing countries', *Health Policy and Planning*, 9(1): 25–30.

McPake, B., Hanson, K. and Mills, A. (1993) 'Community financing of health care in Africa: An evaluation of the Bamako Initiative', *Social Science and Medicine*, 36(11): 1383–1395.

Marsh, C. (1982) *The Survey Method*. London: Allen and Unwin.

Mata, L.J. (1978) *The Children of Santa Maria Cauqué: A Prospective Field Study of Health and Growth*. Cambridge, MA: MIT Press.

Maynard-Tucker, G. (1994) 'Indigenous perceptions and quality of care of family planning services in Haiti', *Health Policy and Planning*, 9(3): 306–317.

Michaud C. and Murray C.J.L. (1994) 'External assistance to the health sector in developing countries: A detailed analysis, 1972–90', *Bulletin of the World Health Organization*, 72(4): 639–651.

Miliband, R. (1983) entry on 'State', pp. 464–468, in Bottomore et al. (1983).

Mooney, G.H. (1983) 'Equity in health care: Confronting the confusion', *Effective Health Care*, 1(4): 179–184.

Moore, M. (1990) 'The rational choice paradigm and the allocation of agricultural development resources', *Development and Change*, 21: 225–246.

Mosley, W.H. (1985) 'Will primary health care reduce infant and child mortality?', Chapter 5 in J. Vallin and A.D. Lopez (eds), *Health Policy, Social Policy and Mortality Prospects*. Liege: International Union for the Scientific Study of Population: proceedings of a seminar in Paris, 1983, Paris: Ordina Editions.

Murray, C.J.L. (1987) 'A critical review of international mortality data', *Social Science and Medicine*, 25(7): 773–781.

Murray, C.J.L. and Chen, L.C. (1993) 'In search of a contemporary theory for understanding mortality change', *Social Science and Medicine*, 36 (2): 142–155.

Murray C.J.L., Kreuser, J. and Whang, W. (1994) 'Cost-effectiveness analysis and policy choices: Investing in health systems', *Bulletin of the World Health Organization*, 72(4): 663–674.

Nabudere, D.W. (1995) 'The impact of globalisation on Africa', *Development and Co-operation*, 4 (July–Aug.): 4–5.

Okuonzi, S.A. and Macrae, J. (1995) 'Whose policy is it anyway? International and national influences on health policy development in Uganda', *Health Policy and Planning*, 10(2): 122–132.

Oranga, H.M. and Nordberg, E. (1993) 'The Delphi panel method for generating health information', *Health Policy and Planning*, 8(4): 405–412.

Packard, R. and Epstein, P. (1991) 'Epidemiologists, social scientists, and the structure of medical research on AIDS in Africa', *Social Science and Medicine*, 33(7): 771–794.

Packard, R.M., Wisner, B. and Bossert, T. (1989) 'Introduction', *Social Science and Medicine*, 28(5): 405–414.

Pathmanathan, I. (1992) *Managing Health Systems Research*, Vol. 4, Health Systems Research Training Series. Geneva: Programme on Health Systems Research and Development of the World Health Organization; Ottawa: International Development Research Centre.

Pathmanathan, I. and Nik-Safiah, N.I (1991) *Training of Trainers for Health Systems Research*, Vol. 5, Health Systems Research Training Series. Geneva: Programme on Health Systems Research and Development of the World Health Organization; Ottawa: International Development Research Centre.

Patton, M.Q. (1990) *Qualitative Evaluation and Research Methods*, (2nd edn). Newbury Park, CA: Sage Publications.

'Peer review of the joint project on health systems research for Southern African countries, June 1993' (1994) *Health Systems Research Newsletter*, February: 6–8.

Pereira, J. (1990) 'The economics of inequality in health: A bibiography', *Social Science and Medicine*, 31(3): 413–420.

Petras, J. (1989) 'Class politics, state power and legitimacy', *Economic and Political Weekly*, 26 August: 1955–1958.

Preston, S.H. (1975) 'The changing relation between mortality and level of economic development', *Population Studies*, 29: 231–248.

Preston, S.H. and Haines, M.R. (1991) 'Response to comments on Fatal Years', *Health Transition Review*, 1(2): 240–244.

Ratcliffe, J.W. and Gonzalez-del-Valle, A. (1988) 'Rigor in health-related research: Toward an expanded conceptualisation', *International Journal of Health Services*, 18(3): 361–392.

Rice, T.H. and Labelle, R.J. (1989) 'Do physicians induce demand for medical services?', *Journal of Health Politics, Policy and Law*, 14(3): 587–600.

Rifkin, S.B., Muller, F. and Bichmann, W. (1988) 'Primary health care: On measuring participation', *Social Science and Medicine*, 26(9): 931–940.

Rondinelli, D.A. (1983) 'Projects as instruments of development administration: A qualified defence and suggestions for improvement', *Public Administration and Development*, 3: 307–327.

Rondinelli, D.A. (1993) *Development Projects as Policy Experiments: An Adaptive Approach to Development Administration*. London and New York: Routledge.

Rosenhead, J. (1989) *Rational Analysis for a Problematic World*. Chichester: Wiley.

Rostow, W.W. (1963) *The Economics of Take-off into Sustained Growth*. London: Macmillan.

Royal College of Physicians of London (1989) *Prenatal Diagnosis and Genetic Screening: Community and Service Implications*. London: Royal College of Physicians of London.

Rylko-Bauer, B., van Willigen, J. and McElroy, A. (1989) 'Strategies for increasing the use of anthropological research in the policy process: A cross-disciplinary analysis' pp. 1–26 in van Willigen et al. (1989).

Sahlins, M. (1974) *Stone Age Economics*. London: Tavistock Publications.

Schrettenbrunner, A. and Harpham, T. (1993) 'A different approach to evaluating PHC projects in developing countries: How acceptable is it to aid agencies?', *Health Policy and Planning*, 8(2): 128–135.

Scrimshaw, S. and Hurtado, E. (1987) *Rapid Assessment Procedures for Nutrition and Primary Health Care: Anthropological Approaches to Improving Program Effectiveness (RAP)*. Los Angeles: UCLA Latin American Center Publications.

Seers, D. (1979) 'The meaning of development, with a postscript', pp. 9–30 in D. Lehmann (ed.), *Development Theory: Four Critical Studies*. Bournemouth: Cass.

Segall, M. (1983) 'Planning and politics of resource allocation for primary health care: Promotion of meaningful national policy', *Social Science and Medicine*, 17(24): 1947–60.

Sen, A. (1981) *Poverty and Famines: An Essay on Entitlement and Deprivation*. Oxford: Oxford University Press.

Shivji, I.G. (1978) *Class Struggles in Tanzania*. London: Heinemann.

Staniland, M. (1985) *What is Political Economy? A Study of Social Theory and Underdevelopment*. New Haven and London: Yale University Press.

Stevenson, A.C. and Davison, B.C.C. (1976) *Genetic Counselling*. London: Heinemann.

Stock, R. (1986) '"Disease and development" or the "the underdevelopment of health": A critical review of geographical perspectives on African health problems', *Social Science and Medicine*, 23(7): 689–700.

Stock, R. (1988) 'Environmental sanitation in Nigeria', *Review of African Political Economy*, 42: 19–31.

Stockmann, R. (1993) 'The long term impact of development aid', *Development and Cooperation*, 5: 21–2.

Streeten, P. (1977) 'The distinctive features of a basic needs approach to development', *International Development Review*, 19: 2–12.

Szreter, S. (1988) 'The importance of social intervention in Britain's mortality decline c. 1850–1914: A re-interpretation of the role of public health', *Social History of Medicine* 1(1): 1–37.

Thunhurst, C. (1985) ' The analysis of small area statistics and planning for health', *The Statistician*, 34: 96–106.

Thunhurst, C. (1992) 'Operational research: A role in strengthening community participation?', *Journal of Management in Medicine*, 6(4): 56–71.

Tollman, S., Schopper, D. and Torres, A. (1990) 'Health maintenance organisations in developing countries: What can we expect?', *Health Policy and Planning*, 5(2): 149–160.

Townsend, P. (1979) *Poverty in the United Kingdom*. Harmondsworth: Penguin.

Townsend, P., Davidson N. and Whitehead M. (1988) *Inequalities in Health (The Black Report)*. Harmondsworth: Penguin.

Trostle, J. (1992) 'Research capacity building in international health: Definitions, evaluation and strategies for success', *Social Science and Medicine*, 35(11): 1321–1324.

Tullock, G. (1993) 'The economic theory of bureaucracy', pp. 110–120 in Hill (1993).

Turshen, M. (1984) *The Political Ecology of Disease in Tanzania*. New Brunswick, NJ: Rutgers University Press.

Turshen, M. (1989) *The Politics of Public Health*. New Brunswick, NJ: Rutgers University Press.

Ugalde, A. (1979) 'The role of the medical profession in public health policy making: The case of Columbia', *Social Science and Medicine*, 13c: 109–119.

Ugalde, A. (1980) 'Physician's control of the health sector: Professional values and economic interests. Findings from the Honduran health system', *Social Science and Medicine*, 14A: 435–444.

Unger, J-P. and Killingsworth, J.R. (1986) 'Selective primary health care: A critical review of methods and results', *Social Science and Medicine*, 22(10): 1001–1013.

United Nations (1990) *World Economic Survey 1990*. New York: United Nations.

Van Dijk, J.A.G.M. (1990) 'Delphi questionnaires versus individual and group interviews. A comparison case', *Technology Forecasting and Social Change*, 37: 293–304.

Van Norren, B., Boerma, J.T. and Sempebwa, E.K.N. (1989) 'Simplifying the evaluation of primary health care programmes', *Social Science and Medicine*, 28: 1091–1097.

Varkevisser, C.M., Pathmanathan, I. and Brownlee, A. (1991) *Designing and Conducting Health Systems Research Projects*, Vol. 2, Health Systems Research Training Series. Geneva: Programme on Health Systems Research and Development of the World Health Organization; Ottawa: International Development Research Centre.

Waddington, C. and Newell, K. (1987) 'Different therefore equal: Towards equity in the health services in Fiji', *Asia Pacific Journal of Public Health*, 1(3): 24–31.

Waller, P. (1994) 'Aid and conditionality', *Development and Cooperation*, 1: 4–5.

Wallis, M. (1989) *Bureaucracy: Its Role in Third World Development*. London: Macmillan.

Walsh, J.A. and Warren, K.S. (1979) 'Selective primary health care: An interim strategy for disease control in developing countries', *New England Journal of Medicine*, 301(1B): 967–994.

Walt, G. (1993) 'WHO under stress: Implications for health policy', *Health Policy*, 24: 125–144.

Walt, G. (1994) *Health Policy: An Introduction to Process and Power*. London: Zed Books.

Walt, G. and Gilson, L. (1994) 'Reforming the health sector in developing countries: The central role of policy analysis', *Health Policy and Planning*, 9(4): 353–370

Weber, M. (1947) *The Theory of Social and Economic Organisation*, ed. and trans. T. Parsons. New York: The Free Press.

Weber, M. (1993) 'Rational-legal authority and bureaucracy', in Hill (1993).

Weiss, C.H. (1977) 'Introduction', pp. 1–22 in C.H. Weiss (ed.), *Using Social Research in Public Policy Making*. Lexington, MA: Lexington Books.

Werner, D. (1995) 'Turning health into an investment: Assaults on third world health care', *Economic and Political Weekly*, 21 January: 147–151

White, J. (1992) 'Towards sustainability in health care', *Action for Health*, 17 (Spring): 4–5.

Wise, P.H. and Pursley, D.M. (1992) 'Infant mortality as a social mirror', *New England Journal of Medicine*, 326(23): 1558–1559.

Woelk, G.B. (1994) 'Primary health care in Zimbabwe: Can it survive? An exploration of the political and historical developments affecting the implementation of PHC', *Social Science and Medicine*, 39(8): 1027–1035.

Woolf, S.H. (1992) 'Practice guidelines, a new reality in medicine. II. Methods of developing guidelines', *Archives of Internal Medicine*, 152(5): 946–952.

World Bank (1981) *Accelerated Development in Sub-Saharan Africa* (The Berg Report). Washington, DC: World Bank.

World Bank (1984) *World Development Report 1984*. New York: Oxford University Press for the World Bank.

World Bank (1990) *World Development Report 1990: Poverty*. New York: Oxford University Press for the World Bank.

World Bank (1993) *Investing in Health: World Development Report 1993*. New York: Oxford University Press.

World Health Organization (1978) Director-General of the World Health Organization and the Executive Director of the United Nations Children's Fund, *Primary Health Care*, a joint report. International Conference on Primary Health Care, Alma-Ata, USSR, 6–12 Sept. Geneva: WHO.

World Health Organization (1981) *Global Strategy for Health for All by the Year 2000*, Health for All Series, No. 3. Geneva: WHO.

World Health Organization Commission on Health and the Environment (1992) 'Health and the environment: A global challenge', *Bulletin of the World Health Organization*, 70(4): 409–413

Wortman, P.M., Vinokur, A. and Sechrest, L. (1986) 'Do consensus conferences work? A process evaluation of the NIH consensus development program', *Journal of Health Politics, Policy, and Law*, 13: 469–498.

Zalot, G.N. and Lussing, F.J. (1983) 'A process for establishing health care priorities', *Health Management Forum*, 3 (Winter): 31–44.

Zola, I.K.(1972) 'Medicine as an institution of social control', *Sociological Review*, 20(4): 487–504.

Index